Sounds from the Heart

"Kokoro is the Japanese word for heart. But it's not simply heart as the seat of the emotions; kokoro is also the seat of the intellect—the mind/heart, if you will. Thus, the Sino-Japanese character for "idea" combines the ideograph for the word "sound" with the ideograph for kokoro. So an idea is a sound from the heart."

Katherine Paterson (1990)

Sounds *from the* Heart

Learning to Listen to Girls

Maureen Barbieri

Foreword by Myra Sadker

Heinemann

Portsmouth, NH

Heinemann
A division of Reed Elsevier Inc.
361 Hanover Street
Portsmouth, NH 03801-3912

Offices and agents throughout the world

We would like to thank those who have given their permission to
include material in this book. Every effort has been made to contact
the copyright holders for permission to reprint borrowed material where
necessary. We regret any oversights that may have occurred and would
be happy to rectify them in future printings of this work.

Reprinted with permission of Margaret K. McElderry Books, an imprint of Simon
& Schuster Children's Publishing Division, from POLAROID AND OTHER POEMS
OF VIEW by Betsy Hearne. Copyright ©1991 by Betsy Hearne.

Reprinted from HEROES IN DISGUISE by Linda Pastan, with the permission of
W. W. Norton & Company, Inc. Copyright ©1991 by Linda Pastan.

continued on page 262

Barbieri, Maureen.
    Sounds from the heart: learning to listen to girls/Maureen
Barbieri.
        p.   cm.
    Includes bibliographical references.
    ISBN 0-435-08843-2 (acid-free paper)
    1.   Women—Education (Secondary)—United States.   2.   Feminism and
education—United States.   3.   Interaction analysis in education—
United States.   4.   Teacher-student relationships—United States.
    5.   English language—Study and teaching (Secondary)—United States.
    I.   Title.
LC1755. B37 1995
376' .973—dc20   94-45705
                                                            CIP

Editor: Toby Gordon
Production: Renée Le Verrier
Cover photo: Erin Blahut
Cover design: Gwen Frankfeldt

Printed in the United States of America on acid-free paper
98   97   96   95   EB   1   2   3   4   5   6

for Richie,
whose presence in my life
is its truest blessing

Contents

Foreword

"It is only recently that I've been listening to the voices of my young female students," says Maureen Barbieri, and English teacher at Laurel, and all-girl private school in Ohio. Initially Barbieri felt blocked by Laurel's quiet propriety. How could she uncover the authentic, hidden voices of "good girls," hesitant to say what they thought for fear of angering others or jeopardizing *A* grades? *Sounds from the Heart* chronicles this teacher's efforts to pierce the silence that too often envelopes schoolgirls, especially during adolescence. It also provides a blueprint for others who want to help students realize and express heartfelt ideas.

Barbieri developed a curriculum that would empower girls to read and write and also explore important questions about their lives. Using writing practice or freewriting as a springboard for more formal work, she discovered the key to opening the hearts of her students. The class wrote about boys, anger, friends, fitting in, the need for both independence and connection, and the conflict between family and career they imagined they would face as tomorrow's women. Authors such as Bette Greene, Robert Cormier, Ann Rinaldi, and Cynthia Rylant provided the literary experience that sparked passionate reaction and pushed girls to define who they are—and who they hoped to become.

The students read *My Brother Sam Is Dead* and struggled to answer the question, "Is war ever justified?" The class became a ping pong match of dissension and debate over *The Drowning of Stephen Jones* as the girls explored the power of prejudice to destroy lives. Convinced that poetry could break through the silence suffocating her "perfect girls," Barbieri filled the classroom with works by Maya Angelou, Nikki Giovanni, Emily Dickinson, Lucille Cliften, Robert Frost, and others. Through memoir and personal stories, girls considered the shape of their own lives.

As this caring teacher heard the voices of her female students, she also began to hear the silence within herself. As she faced her own reluctance to voice ideas, her knee-jerk flight from controversy, she began to change her behavior to model the independence she wanted to foster in her students. Confronting the sys-

tem, she replaced traditional grades with portfolios, a more indi-
vidualized approach to evaluation, and one less likely to upset the
personal relationship between student and teacher.

Barbieri also refused to let coeducation squelch female students. In a fascinating contrast, she shows the difference between
teaching at single-sex Laurel and teaching in a coeducational
school. In the coed class the boys openly defied her. Each day became a challenge to win them over. Before she knew it, male students had become the center of her classroom, the focus of attention, the target of instruction. In contrast, she writes, "The girls
seemed bunched together in my mind, a quiet group. . . . I didn't
know them as people, the way I knew the boys."

Barbieri's experience mirrors the research David Sadker and I
have conducted. After almost two decades of looking in classrooms, using a systematic observation instrument, we discovered
that even the most well-meaning teachers tend to focus on male
students. More likely to shout out answers, boys demand teacher
attention; but even when boys are not calling out, teachers still ask
them more questions and offer them more precise and helpful
feedback. In Failing at Fairness we show how too many girls are
missing in interaction, left on the sidelines, spectators to the educational process.

Females aslo find themselves in the margins of their textbooks.
Reading books that feature the achievements of men, girls receive
another lesson in second-class citizenship. When we ask students
to list twenty famous women from American history (not counting entertainers and athletes), few can name even five.

These harmful lessons are costly. Although girls begin school
with an academic edge, by the middle grades both their achievement and self-esteem have slipped. According to standardized
tests, girls are the only group to start school scoring ahead and
leave having fallen behind.

Although Maureen Barbieri knew the research, although she
knew the importance of listening to the voices of girls, she still fell
into the gender trap. Shocked to see the patterns of male domi-
nance that developed in coeducation, she worked with the school
administration to try an experiment: creating single-sex classrooms early in the year and later integrating the boys and girls.
She says of this experiment. ". . . I do believe . . . that we who
teach girls must be ever vigilant to their willingness, even their
preference, to avoid conflict, discord, or risk, and that such vigilance is certainly more possible in single-sex classrooms. Boys, it

seems to me, will find ways to get what they need from the system; it's the girls who are in the greatest danger of slipping away from us, quietly, unobtrusively, politely slipping away."

Sounds from the Heart is more than a reminder that we must not let this happen. It offers a way to halt the quiet erosion of female talent, a loss too often unnoticed in our nations's schools.

—Myra Sadker

Acknowledgments

When I reread Mark Twain's *The Adventures of Huckleberry Finn* recently, the closing words had new meaning for me. Huck says, "If I'd a knowed how much trouble it would be to make a book, I never would have started." Still in the midst of my own writing, I was tempted to agree with him. But there were people who kept me going.

First, always first, there is Donald Murray. I entered his class many years ago feeling frightened, clumsy, and inadequate and left believing I could be a writer. At every juncture of my adult life he has been there to urge courage, faith, and common sense. His writing is, like Don himself, wise, compassionate, and provocative; I read his books and his columns again and again, always finding exactly what I need to know. He continues to be my strongest inspiration in all my professional endeavors and in many personal ones as well. I cannot begin to thank him.

At UNH I was privileged to study with Donald Graves who showed me how to listen to children. With him I grew more and more curious, and his words, "I want to know, I want to *know*," echo in me whenever I am with students. Tom Newkirk let me argue my way into his already filled English methods course and has not stopped teaching me yet. It is Tom who has been a steadfast advocate and mentor, from his generous encouragement that I publish my writing to his kind invitation to teach in the New Hampshire Writing Program.

Jack Wilde and Jane Kearns were my own instructors in the program and both have been crucial in my development as a teacher. Jane's humor and wisdom ignited in me the desire to teach writing, and her encouragement enabled me to have faith in my students and in myself. Jack Wilde, quintessential learner, shared poetry and gentle words of advice, and his excellent work on genre studies has been a major source of guidance to me in recent years.

Tom Romano taught me how to turn adolescents on to writing, first in the pages of his book, *Clearing the Way: Working with Teenage Writers* and later, in person, by word and by example. Like

Murray, he weaves the writing, teaching, and living into a seamless whole and makes me realize there is no other way for those of us who care about what we do.

Like all teachers, I am indebted for life to Nancie Atwell whose intelligence, imagination, and grit have changed the face of classrooms everywhere. "Teachers' observations do count," she insists, "as real research." It is Nancie who elevates us, who shows us both the responsibility and the joy in teaching. As I read her books and listen to her talks, I want to know more, give more, *be* more, for my children. Nancie is the living example of what Nel Noddings calls "one-who-cares." Her work affects every single decision I make in classrooms.

Terry Moher gave countless hours to listen to my hopes, plans, and experiences, and to offer sage counsel during my early days as a teacher. Sensitive and compassionate, she understands the complexities of school life and the enormity of what we attempt to do when we foster literacy.

Leah Rhys had enough faith to bring me to Laurel School and to give me girls to teach. She is a woman of vision—Carol Gilligan came at her invitation—and of courage. I will always be profoundly grateful to her. JoAnn Deak, director of the lower school, was patient and kind during my first years in Cleveland, and I thank her for that.

Bill Johnson of University School worked with me on a memoir project and on a joint middle school literary magazine, frequently getting together after school with students. But our best talks were always over breakfast when he would share drafts of new poems or dreams of a changing curriculum and enhanced community service. His thinking permeates this text.

At Laurel, I was privileged to work with an outstanding team of teachers: Betsy Sampliner, Gene Rosaschi, Nancy Smekal, Almuth Riggs, Margaret London, Kathy Lacey, Kaye Ford, Chris Murphy, and Fred Christian. Mary Nodar, Anne Esselstyn, and Becky Chandler, my colleagues in the English department, are dynamic, creative, and devoted to students; together they have launched thousands of girls on the path to lifelong literacy.

Andrea Archer is the best thing that ever happened to Laurel. As director of the middle school she has been innovative and courageous. She respects both students and faculty in ways I have not seen elsewhere, and I will always be deeply grateful for her leadership. Without her, my last year at Laurel—the heart of this book—would have been quite different indeed.

Marilyn Kent and Susan Barkett, two members of the Laurel-Harvard research affiliates, spent hours sharing white papers and explaining Gilligan's work-in-progress to me. Both women remain committed to girls' learning and well-being, and their insights informed my thinking immeasurably.

Mary Krogness, consummate middle school teacher, lover of books, poems, and words, welcomed me to Cleveland with warmth and enthusiasm. In spite of the heavy demands on her schedule, she found time to meet with me, to listen to emerging thoughts, and to read early drafts of this text. Her specific response gave me the much-needed assurance that I could pursue this project.

Michael Steinberg, professor at University of Michigan, is another avid writer who took an early interest in this book and responded to several chapters with care and insight. Jo Woodyard, guidance counselor at the Spartanburg Day School, also read many chapters with an open mind and a magnanimous spirit.

Karen Smith, associate director of NCTE, middle school teacher for more than twenty years, keeps her heart in the classroom. Her incredible generosity has given me professional opportunities I had never dreamed of, and I am grateful. Thanks also to Susan Stires for hours of good late-night talk about kids, books, and life; she is a rare friend.

Ruth Hubbard read the prospectus and opening chapters of *Sounds*. Without her gracious endorsement there would never have been a book. Her enthusiasm for the project enabled me to pursue it with determination. I treasure her eloquent response to the manuscript and I will always be profoundly grateful to her for all she has done.

Two other people came to my rescue when my computer disk was erased and I was sorely tempted to abandon this book altogether. John Hall worked wonders on the defective disk and salvaged important chunks of information. This is not the first time he has been there for me, and I have come to look upon him as a miracle worker. Susan Frazier, the most thoughtful, thorough, and organized person I know, typed my printed manuscript onto new disks and taught me enough about my computer to give me faith that I could continue writing. Sincere thanks to both of them.

The whole idea for this book came from Toby Gordon, and she has been here through every phase of its development, assuring me that, yes, my students did have stories to tell. Toby has a commitment to girls and to their teachers that is unequaled anywhere. Never did I leave a meeting or end a phone call with Toby feeling less than invigorated, renewed, and eager to write more. This is her book as much as anyone's.

No one's friendship means more to me personally or professionally than Linda Rief's. Her contributions to American education are staggering, and I learn from her constantly. But more than that, Linda makes time, no matter where she is, to listen to my concerns and to offer insight and encouragement. She works harder and cares more than anyone I have ever known, both on her own writing and in the service of her students and colleagues, honoring all teachers by her example. Linda was the first to express her support for this book, and I would never have attempted it without her faith in its viability.

My daughter Erin, a voracious reader from her earliest days, has helped me in innumerable ways. She was eager to listen to my classroom anecdotes and to offer her own insight on why the girls were doing what they did. As she pursues her interest in women's studies, she leads me in surprising directions and urges me to broaden my perspective. It was Erin who introduced me to Naomi Wolf, Carol Tavris, and Susan Faludi; Erin who challenged many of my assumptions as I began to write; Erin who read drafts of chapters and asked hard questions. A painter and a human rights activist, she is helping me see the world differently. This book would not have come to be without her influence.

Nor would it have been written without my husband's steadfast belief in its significance. Throughout our marriage he has understood—even respected—my need to come back to New England each summer, as well as my obsession with writing and my passion for teaching. Eager to be a part of whatever I do, he cooks me meals, listens to my incessant stories, and soothes my recurring panic. His integrity, his strength, and his kindness have shown me what a real marriage can be. He is the type of husband I would wish for my daughter and my students, although there will never be another like Richie anywhere. To him I offer heartfelt thanks, not only for the book, but for the continuing adventure that is our life together.

Finally, I want to thank the gutsy girls of Laurel's classes of '95, '96, and '97, and Spartanburg Day School's class of '99 who taught me more than any book could ever convey. You have reminded me of an essential truth: Teaching must embody loving, or we are all wasting our time. Yours are the voices of the future, and hearing them, I am filled with hope.

1

Introduction:
Learning to Listen

———

My friend has a voice
wild with roses and thorn.
I've hidden in thickets
of her song, surrounded
by their scent, sight, sting.

—Betsy Hearne, *"Listening"*

IT IS only recently that I've been listening to the voices of my young female students, chagrined as I am to admit it. I thought I'd always listened. But the fact is, I am only lately coming to understand girls' unique ways of developing, of learning, and of being in the world. As a former girl myself, it should have been obvious to me, but I think we women forget as we mature. We know that we are capable, equal to any challenge. We welcome competition; we begin to think in terms of hierarchy, of win-lose. We wear sweatshirts that say, "The best man for the job is a woman," and we're proud that old barriers in the workplace are coming down. Equal in ability on any scale we choose, we eschew the suggestion that we are "different" in any sense. "Some women fear, with justification, that any observation of gender differences will be heard as implying that it is women who are different," writes Deborah Tannen, "different from the standard, which is whatever men are. The male is seen as normative, the female as departing from the norm. And it is only a short step—maybe an inevitable one—from 'different' to 'worse.'" (1990, p. 15)

We women strive for independence, feel embarrassed when we behave "emotionally," and make every effort to assert ourselves with reason and logic, just the way men do. But, Tannen says, "Pretending that women and men are the same hurts women, because the ways they are treated are based on the norms for men." (1990, p. 16) We are different, we have always been different, and no matter what we gain in terms of equal opportunity, we will always have a view of life that is profoundly female, profoundly our own. Thank God. Ironically, it was my husband's work that led me to this new, age-old, awareness.

Moving

The news that we'd be moving from New Hampshire, where I was immersed in a teaching job I loved, to Ohio, a faraway place inhabited by strangers, shocked me and filled me with horror. How could I leave my students, my colleagues, my work? How could I leave the University of New Hampshire where I had such a strong network of support and friendship, where each summer and each new semester brought graduate courses in poetry, fiction, research, and more? Would teachers in Ohio value the things I valued? Would I be given the freedom and autonomy there that I enjoyed in New Hampshire? Would I even find a classroom of my own?

Being a good wife and a reasonable person, I put on a brave face and packed up the family to accommodate my husband's job. I sent out fifty résumés in hopes of finding work in a middle school and received one return phone call. Leah Rhys of Laurel School had no teaching positions available but wanted to meet me anyway. When could I come in? I had heard of Laurel School. Harvard psychologist Carol Gilligan, author of *In A Different Voice* (1982), was conducting research there on girls' psychological development. I made an appointment.

September found me at Laurel, not in a middle school classroom where I longed to be, but in the lower school library reading picture books to preschoolers and organizing mixed-grade authors' circles for kindergartners through fourth graders. To my amazement, the days flew by. I fell in love with these eager young children as we discovered together the magic of Eric Carle, Jerry Pinkney, Molly Bang, Chris Van Allsburg, Cynthia Rylant, Arnold Adoff, and dozens of other authors and illustrators I'd missed in middle school.

The Girls

By January I was teaching one section of seventh grade English, in addition to the library job, and beginning to realize that life had not ended with my leaving New Hampshire. At first I missed my boys. . . . The classroom seemed out of kilter somehow, too quiet, too orderly; it was like waiting for the other shoe to fall. I also had qualms about being in a private school. How did it fit with my belief in equal education for all children? In New Hampshire I had been happiest working with reluctant readers and writers, students who fought the idea that literacy held anything for them. Nothing was more exciting than hearing one of them say, "This is the first book I've read all the way through, and I really loved it." or "Mrs. B., wait 'til you read what I wrote. I never knew I could do it!"

What was I doing now at Laurel School, this bastion of tradition, with these young women of privilege? What did they need from me? But as I came to know the girls better, I realized I had a new and different challenge on my hands. Many of my students had been at Laurel since preschool—lifers, they were called—and had grown into high achievers, eager to please both parents and teachers with their academic performance. To these girls school seemed a huge, complex system of figuring out what to do and what to give in order to achieve the prize of prizes—high honors.

Most of them loved books. And they were all quite willing to write. "How long should it be?" "When is it due?" "Do you take off for spelling?" seemed their biggest concerns. My own concept of writing—shaped over the years through studying with Donald Murray, Tom Newkirk, Jane Kearns, and Donald Graves—involved finding, not merely reiterating, ideas. My students wanted to know what I was looking for in their work. How could they do well in my class? How could they get A's? I wanted them to make discoveries, surprise themselves, come up with their own purposes for writing. How could I help them see that making the honor roll ought to be a by-product of engagement in literacy, not its goal? How could reading and writing become integral to their lives when all they cared about was the grade at the end of the trimester? We seemed at an impasse.

Writing and reading conferences (Murray, 1985; Calkins, 1986; Atwell, 1987), the heart of my curriculum in New Hampshire, were much more difficult at Laurel. As I waited for young writers to speak to me, asking them what they heard in their own writing, what they thought of the novels or poems they were reading, I watched eyes glaze over and brows furrow as they tried to determine the "right answers." Were they so programmed to please everyone around them that they had forgotten how to think for themselves? So it seemed.

As I struggled over the next year to make real writing and real response to literature come alive in the classroom, Carol Gilligan and her associates continued their research on how girls change as they grow up. Faculty members were invited to read "white papers," works-in-progress, and to attend monthly discussion groups to keep abreast of the data. The researchers found that, while primary grade girls are clear about their feelings and belief systems, older girls become less so. Relationships are always significant to females, according to Gilligan, but the notion of an ideal relationship, one free of conflict and discord, becomes a major goal for girls approaching adolescence. They become willing to sacrifice their authentic opinions and feelings in the interest of finding such relationships. They strive to become "perfect" or "ideal" girls and often lose their awareness of what is authentic in their friendships and in themselves. They become less willing to speak up, particularly when their opinions do not conform to others'. Many avoid conflict at all costs. Gilligan and her associates term this phenomenon "silencing" or "going underground."

"Each will struggle with a central relational quandary: how to stay with herself and be with others, how to keep her voice in connection with her inner psychic world of thoughts and feelings and also to bring her voice into her relationship with other people," note Brown and Gilligan. (1992, p. 184)

Many teachers scoffed at these ideas. Wasn't this a normal part of maturing, becoming socialized? Who among us can say exactly what we think all the time? Shouldn't girls become more sensitive to the feelings of others as they grow up? We were, some teachers insisted, oversaturated with talk of "gender issues." Others, already overwhelmed with the demands of a rigorous curriculum—after all, Laurel is a college prep school—chose not to involve themselves with the research. No effort was made by the faculty to explore Gilligan's findings and their implications on the Laurel curriculum. Perhaps that would come once the research was completed.

But I was already curious. I began to read Gilligan's other work and was intrigued with her ideas. I became aware of other research being done in this field by the American Association of University Women and by others. Myra and David Sadker, in a research project sponsored by the American Association of University Women, found a serious decline in self-esteem among girls as they go through school, along with increases in episodes of depression. (1990) I read Deborah Tannen's books on conversational differences in men and women; depicting women as being more comfortable with a "rapport" type of talk. (1990) What might all this mean to my students? Were they experiencing these phenomena as seventh graders? I knew that their peer relationships were crucial to them, but wasn't that true of all adolescents? Were girls really so different? I thought back to my years in Exeter, New Hampshire, where I'd taught boys and girls. What had I seen? Why hadn't I read Gilligan earlier?

If I thought in terms of gender at all back then, my concern had been for the boys. How could I get them to love poetry? How could I find more contemporary novels to hold their attention? And what about writing? Were they doing enough reflecting? Were they stretching themselves? When I look back, I realize I expected the girls to read and write; I expected the boys to need my extra attention and encouragement. As I read some of the student journals I've saved from those years, I am filled with remorse. My girls were calling out to me from their own "underground." There were issues on their minds, turmoil in their lives, and questions in their hearts that I had been unwilling or unable to hear.

"The women in this book are so fradgil," Heather had written as she read *A Day No Pigs Would Die* by Robert Newton Peck. "That doesn't make sense to me because they are literate and the men are not. The women are treated as inferior and *I dont like it.*"

I wrote back to Heather, agreeing with her that literacy ought to mean power. But I did not make time in class for us to discuss her observation or, more importantly, her anger. She perceived an injustice in the way the female characters were treated, and I missed an opportunity for rich exploration of gender stereotyping and role-modeling. Would other girls have seen what Heather saw? What would they have thought of Peck's intentions? Would they have challenged the assumption that these women's lives are necessarily circumscribed? I will never know.

Cindy read *The Color Purple* by Alice Walker and wrote in her log: "I don't understand Celie. She acts as if she has no say. Mrs. B. says we all have a say, but Celie docsn't act like it. Why does she let herself be treated this way?"

In my response, I wrote, "Celie has grown up in a rural area and is very poor. She has not been taught to stand up for herself . . . I don't want to ruin the story for you. Keep loving your book and Celie."

I backed away from Cindy's dismay and attempted to smooth it over with a glib explanation for Celie's behavior. But what Cindy really wondered was, did she herself have a voice in her own life? Would she be able to fight for herself in ways that Celie could not? In retrospect I see so clearly that Cindy had a gender issue on her mind. All of us could have benefited from frank and extended conversation of her fears and her irritation. Again, I had missed an opportunity for something meaningful and real. I do not know what my students would have said about Celie or about women's rights to fight oppression in their homes, nor do they know what I thought. In responding to their reading logs, I looked at each child as an individual reader and writer. I believed they were individuals more than they were boys or girls. I did them a disservice.

It was my love of writing that drew me to teaching. The two are so similar, both full of frustration, surprise, challenge, delight, and mystery. I keep teaching for the same reason I keep writing; I never quite get it right. But I want to. I want to do it better. I want my teaching and my students' learning to be meaningful and real, and for me this has always meant knowing my students as people, valuing their unique strengths, their separate obsessions, their idiosyncratic ways of constructing knowledge.

But at Laurel I began to wonder, is this enough? Or is Carol Gilligan right in her assertion that girls are different; that they need particular, informed understanding, special but more honest nurturing from their female teachers, lest their voices get lost in the chaos of conforming to unreal expectations in a world that does not value intimacy. She writes, "Girls at this time have been observed to lose their vitality, their resilience, their immunity to depression, their sense of themselves and their character." (1992, p. 2) The more I read the researchers' work, the more I came to see and hear many of their theories embodied in my classroom at Laurel.

Voice

Voice is an important focal point for Gilligan and for me. We talk about voice in writing and have trouble defining it. "It is the imprint of the person on the piece," says Graves. "You know it when you hear it," says Murray. "I want you to help these girls find their voices," Leah Rhys told me when she put me into the seventh grade classroom. Did she know what an enormous challenge it would be? But such a worthy goal: work that is real and meaningful, personal and political. For as long as I've been teaching, I've believed that the only valid goal of education is to improve the quality of life. I teach writing and reading because these things give my own life meaning, and meaning is what I want for my students. How does what I know as a female fit in? Is it relevant at all? Reading Gilligan, I seem to think it is. But are there silences in my own life? When did they begin? What do they mean?

"What do you think?" is a scary question for a girl at Laurel School, as it is for many women in today's American culture. What will be the consequences of speaking out? How sincere is the person asking the question? Why does she want to know? If I say something she doesn't agree with, will she be angry? What will be the cost to me if I do not speak out, if I hide myself? How do I know what I really think anyway? Maybe I'm wrong. . . .

I knew I wanted to conduct my own teacher research on some of the issues Gilligan was raising. As I struggled to find a clear focus, my friend Toby Gordon asked me, "How do your girls use their reading and writing to define themselves as female? How do they use literacy to define their futures?" Her interest piqued my own, and I began to look for answers to her questions in my girls' work. But, due in large part to the "silencing" that Gilligan speaks of, answers were not easy to find. Authentic writing and authentic responding to literature are risky, sometimes too risky for twelve- and thirteen-year-old girls. And thus, my quest to discover what they knew, felt, and, believed led in turn to my need to find better ways to help them look honestly at the big questions: Who am I? What does it mean to be a female? What does it mean to have a friend? What will my life be? I began to notice episodes of withdrawal, of silencing.

"Removing themselves from relationship," according to Brown and Gilligan, "these girls struggle daily with the seduction of the unattainable: to be all things to all people, to be perfect girls and model women." (1992, p. 180)

Questions

What part was I playing, inadvertently or not, in the girls' unwillingness or inability to express themselves authentically? Did I contribute to their reluctance, even their refusal, to become truly engaged in literacy? How could I be a supportive, caring, candid adult female and maintain my role as mentor, coach and, perhaps most uncomfortable of all, evaluator? How could my relationship with them provide encouragement and safety as well as enticement and challenge? My own efforts to know these girls turned out to be the most personal of my professional endeavors to date. Even as I became painfully aware of the inevitable chasm between us, I saw myself in them.

I saw struggle and resistance to societal expectations, and I labored to understand in new ways what it all meant. But I also saw the power of literacy to address any and all issues of human significance. While I now have more questions than ever, I am renewed in my conviction that writing remains our best hope of self-discovery and reading our clearest way to encounter human experience beyond our own. What Carol Gilligan and the students at Laurel School have given me is something more: the knowledge that being female matters, that as educators we have a responsibility to look at issues of gender just as carefully as we look at and value issues of culture, race, class, and kinds of intelligence. We want all our students to embrace lifelong learning and lifelong literacy, but we must have broader concerns. How do empathy and compassion and courage take root in young hearts? How will literacy make a difference to them and to the world at large? What is it all for? My girls have shown me that their being female must play a part in answering these questions.

Sounds from the Heart marks my own awakening to this realization. Katherine Paterson tells us that the Sino-Japanese character for our word "idea" is really a combination of two characters—sound and heart. (Paterson, 1989) An idea, then, becomes a sound in the heart, and, in some cases, a sound from the heart. This image grew more compelling to me the longer I worked with seventh graders at Laurel. These girls do have ideas, big ideas, that are clearly heartfelt. They are not, however, always spoken aloud. The sounds are not always heard in the classrooms or beyond. I began to hear them as I listened more carefully, more deliberately, through the amplification of Gilligan's work. I heard Kristin as she used her writing to try on moral behavior, her voice distorted in class by habitual "I don't knows" but loud and clear in her fiction. I heard Wallis's question, "What is the purpose of what we are doing?" and watched classmates flinch at her audacity. I heard Caroline respond to *The Drowning of Stephan Jones* by Bette Greene with the words, "I think Carla should be proud of her opinion, not afraid," raising the whole issue of taking risks with friends. I heard Bernice cry out, "You just don't understand," with such vehemence that I was forced to consider the possibility that she was right. And I heard Amy admit, voice shaking, "Sometimes I forget what I really think," and knew that this was precisely what Gilligan had warned us was happening to adolescent girls.

Sounds from the Heart is a collection of their stories. How did these particular girls address their existential dilemma, the conflicting tasks of becoming autonomous human beings and of remaining, as females, strongly connected to their community of others? *Sounds from the Heart* is also the story of my own struggles as a teacher who is female, a female who fears and avoids conflict, a female who cherishes real friendship among colleagues, a female who often feels woefully inadequate to the monumental task of being in the classroom every day. It marks the beginning of my fascination with girls. Or does it? If we are all embarked on our own journey of discovery in life, perhaps it is also my own female knowing I am re-examining here as well.

There are lingering questions, and I welcome them, since we teachers are engaged in the process of learning, of inquiry, and of challenging assumptions. *Sounds from the Heart* is an invitation to examine these questions, as well as others that will inevitably surface, with me. Please help me think about girls. Answers will not come easily and will vary from teacher to teacher, just as our students and our classroom situations do. But I think we need to begin somewhere. I began at Laurel, reading Carol Gilligan and Lyn Mikel Brown, and now I'm wondering:

How can we help girls discover, trust and value what they already know?

In what specific ways can we make sure each girl feels confident and safe sharing her authentic ideas, opinions, and questions in our classrooms?

Since relationships are particularly significant to girls, how can we provide opportunities for collaboration?

Recognizing that girls' ways of knowing center on connectedness, what can we do to create greater integration among the disciplines in our buildings?

Are there certain young adult books that could promote or foster discussion of particular female dilemmas? Should we be assigning such books? What does this do to the notion of individual choice? Is it wrong to use literature to raise "issues?"

How can we promote critical discussion of literature that includes dissent and even conflict? Does respect for others mean that individuals silence themselves on occasion? How much of this is appropriate?

What does writing practice (freewriting) contribute to girls' willingness to discover what they know? What do our writing assignments contribute?

How can we continue to encourage and support risk-taking in writing and in reading, while at the same time valuing writers' critical assessments of one another's work?

To what extent does our classroom management silence girls? Are we able to tolerate the unexpected? Are we able to tolerate conflict? How do we show this tolerance to the girls in our personal and professional lives?

How do our methods of evaluation contribute to girls' self-discovery and self-expression? To what extent does our evaluation system silence girls' voices?

How much interaction among boys is necessary or desirable for girls in the language arts curriculum? What do girls miss when they work apart from boys? What do they gain? To what extent does coeducation make it more difficult for girls to know what they know and tell about it? (Gloria Steinem: "Every boy should have the opportunity of going to school with girls; every girl should have the opportunity of going to school without boys." Remark at book signing in Cleveland, April 1992: Pavillion Mall)

In what ways can we recognize specific gender concerns in planning the language arts curriculum? To what extent *should* these concerns be recognized?

What role should feminism play in our curriculum? How political can we allow our classrooms to become?

What is the responsibility of the English/Language Arts teacher to foster healthy psychological development as Carol Gilligan and others have begun to define it?

How do our personal relationships with our female students affect their views of themselves as adult women? How do our experiences as women (or as men)—in and out of the classroom—affect these relationships?

Painful as it was to leave New Hampshire, I am grateful that fate brought me to Laurel School at this particular time in its history, for Laurel has changed me forever. I am grateful for friends and colleagues, male and female, who will help me ponder these questions. And I am grateful to have begun at last the process of listening for and recognizing the truest sounds from the hearts of girls.

2

Sometimes I Wish: Figuring Out What Matters Most

———

Writing is making sense of life.

—Nadine Gordimer

THE QUESTION, asked with exquisite politeness, was nonetheless curt and skeptical. "Exactly what is the purpose of writing practice?" Wallis wanted to know. Eighteen other pairs of eyes looked straight at me, waiting for justification of what I had just proposed.

The Theory

Writing practice, as developed by Natalie Goldberg, is close to what Peter Elbow and writing process advocates call freewriting. The idea is to write quickly, without censoring words, in an effort to get at what the writer really thinks, to be at the level where "energy is unobstructed by social politeness . . . to the place where you are writing what your mind actually sees and feels, not what it thinks it should see or feel." (Goldberg, 1986) It seemed to me, suspecting the girls' inclination to censor everything, not only in writing but also in conversation, to be just what we needed to pursue.

"To catapult you out of complacency," I wanted to reply. "To get you past all the 'shoulds,' all the careful, controlled thinking that you think everyone expects."

Carol Gilligan describes problems of connection for girls at this age. Longing to sustain the close relationships they have enjoyed thus far in their lives, but needing also to assert their individuality as they enter adolescence, twelve-year-old girls are often forced to make difficult, almost impossible choices: Do I please others first, or do I think of my own needs? They begin to glimpse the prohibitions and compromises that society will impose on them as adult women. "Adolescence," Gilligan says, "seems a watershed in female development, a time when girls are in danger of drowning or disappearing." (Gilligan et al, 1990, p. 10)

Could writing practice help my girls avoid either fate? While I applauded Wallis's forthrightness and welcomed her need to know why she should do whatever I asked—teachers have no right to waste students' time—I also knew that it was a need born of anxiety. Would this help her improve her writing? Would it improve her writing enough to help her make the high honor roll? Would it make her work easier once she got to upper school? Would it give her the all-important edge in applying to colleges? And she had other concerns. If she wrote without thinking, what might come out onto the page? Would she write something her teacher or her classmates saw as less than "nice," less than appropriate? Would anyone value her ideas? Shouldn't she protect herself?

"Given the heightened self-consciousness of teenagers and their intense fear of ridicule or exposure," writes Gilligan, "secondary education poses a major challenge to teachers: How to sustain among teenagers an openness to experience and a willingness to risk discovery?" (Gilligan et al, 1988, p. xxxii)

Exactly what, Wallis wondered, would the payoff be for spending time doing this kind of writing? Writing practice, as I described it, may have seemed more like play to Wallis than work; it may also have seemed more like risk.

I thought of my own experiences with freewriting, how exhilarating it has always been for me to write fast, write without considering the logic of every word, every sentence. As a child I would fill notebooks with rambling stories—back in a time when story writing was not part of anyone's curriculum—instead of doing homework at night. Then I would hide my notebooks under folded sweaters in my bureau drawer, embarrassed that I had wasted time this way. Writing felt good to me even then, felt honest and real, even though it did give me a guilty conscience. I remember the first time I was ever aware of finding a new idea during the act of writing; I was seventeen years old, a senior in high school, working on the introduction to our yearbook. Words came onto the page that I had not intended; the whole point of what I had been trying to say became clear to me, and I knew what I needed to write next. Stunned, I thought I had discovered magic.

I remember, too, my first year teaching, my determined efforts to establish the workshop atmosphere I had experienced in my courses with Donald Murray at the University of New Hampshire, an atmosphere later refined eloquently by Nancie Atwell in her book, *In the Middle: Writing, Reading, and Learning with Adolescents.* (1987) I urged my students to write freely, as fast as they could, without stopping to ponder what should come next. This way, I promised, good ideas would appear right on the page, surprising them, leading them towards topics that they could really dig their teeth into.

Whenever I proposed journal writing, someone would invariably ask, "When is this due?" Those New Hampshire students understood that freewriting, like brainstorming or mapping, was a step in the process toward creating a finished product. This was rehearsing, warming up, developing fluency. But what the students seemed to want was structure. They knew they were expected to write, but they wanted to know how much, when to turn it in, and how it would be evaluated. We discussed the necessary parameters and became, finally, writers working on a craft together. Instead of using freewriting as a daily routine, as many other teachers did, I showed students how it might help them find and develop ideas for writing.

But no two years are ever the same, and my philosophy of teaching continues to evolve as I learn more about my students' needs and about the craft of teaching itself. Like most of my colleagues, I look for ways to make school more meaningful within the present moment, not just for future reference, and always within the context of passionate literacy. Now Carol Gilligan's research was making me realize I might want to pay more attention to Laurel students' development as females, not just as adolescents. And I had a hunch these girls would need more than occasional freewriting.

Girls at Laurel have a strong sense of purpose. They want to meet expectations—their parents and teachers have high standards—because they are convinced that doing well in school will lead to admittance to "a really good college in the east," which will in turn lead to a productive and prestigious career. Many of them have been at Laurel since preschool: by seventh grade a total of almost ten years. They know the drill: Figure out what it takes to get an *A* in this class: Exactly what does this teacher want? Competition is alive and well, and making high honors is what good girls aim to achieve. It's considered cool.

During my first year at Laurel I thought, naively, that my approach to teaching reading and writing would be a welcome respite, an oasis in the midst of stress, an island of blessed relief from all the complexities and demands of other, more traditional classes. Here, I told them, we would learn to love literature; we would read it, talk about it, and create it. We were a community of writers whose purpose was to support and nurture each other in workshops and in conferences. I wanted it to be real. I wanted them to come to know themselves better through immersing themselves in reading and writing. They wanted to figure out how to get an *A* from me.

By the time I met Wallis and company I was much more hip to Laurel's culture. I understood now that assuaging their fears about performance and evaluation was a big part of my job as the year began. My goals for them may have been different from the ones they had for themselves—I was not concerned with preparing them for upper school or even for eighth grade; I was determined instead to help them see that reading and writing could profoundly change their lives—but I believed I could convince them that our intentions were not mutually exclusive. Becoming an effective writer, whether for self-fulfillment or for greater ease in climbing the academic ladder, is certainly of vital interest to everyone.

The Reality

But why writing practice? I had explained our curriculum for the year. We would write every day on topics of our own choosing, and yes, I would write with them. We would share drafts in progress, responding in a variety of ways. We would compile portfolios which would include examples of effective work as well as pieces that had personal significance to us. Even more than my New Hampshire students, these girls wanted the bottom line: "How many pieces of writing?" "When are final drafts due?" "How will they be graded?" All the typical questions smart, "good girls" have every right to ask.

They had done a fair amount of writing in years past and had learned by now that every teacher has her own idiosyncracies. I was not comfortable setting down hard and fast guidelines, but I knew these would provide the security students so desperately need. I wanted to be flexible; they wanted to know the requirements. We attempted to reach a consensus. Three final drafts per trimester seemed a good minimum to them, although I knew that for many girls this would not be enough. More important than finished products, I insisted, was the daily habit of writing. I expected them to learn something about themselves as readers and writers and, even more importantly, as human beings. Furthermore, I wanted them to be able to articulate their insights on a regular basis.

Natalie Goldberg (1986) had intrigued me with her concept of writing practice. More than a way to set the stage for other writing, she insists, it can become a way of looking at one's life. Her rules are simple:

Keep your hand moving.
Don't cross out.

Don't worry about spelling, punctuation, grammar.
Lose control.
Don't think.
Don't get logical.
Go for the jugular.

I wrote these on chart paper and hung them in my room.
"We're going to try this," I told them, "because I think it's good to
make writing a habit. The more we write, the more comfortable
we'll be with writing, and the more surprises we'll begin to find."

The next question came from Danielle: "How can you lose
control and go for the jugular at the same time? What do you
mean by, 'Don't think,' I don't get this." The resistance in the
room was palpable.

Wallis frowned. "Do we have to share?" Another tough question. If the writing is intended to reveal the writer's inner thoughts
and feelings to the writer herself, then what business does anyone
else have reading or hearing it? But, on the other hand, this was
school, and I knew that the writing no one reads is eventually de-
valued by students as a learning experience. (Indeed, students had
complained to me in the past about former teachers who never
read or responded to what they wrote in their journals. Writers
need readers.) I wanted them to learn from one another, and I
wanted to nudge and support their risk-taking in writing practice.
We would have to share some of what we wrote, but each writer
would choose specific excerpts herself. Private writing would remain private.

I understood the girls' particular reluctance. What is more
threatening to a twelve-year-old girl than letting her friends know
what she is thinking? I wanted to be sensitive to their dilemma,
but I wanted to help them find ways out of it.

"We'll try volunteering," I suggested. "If you'd rather not read
yours, that will be fine."

And so, warily, we were off. Following Goldberg's advice, I'd
occasionally suggest topics: "Write the word "Home" at the top of
the page. Now write for ten minutes. Keep that hand moving."
"Write the word "Hope." Now try "Friendship.""

Sometimes I'd read a children's book or a short story aloud.
Cynthia Rylant's *The Relatives Came* inspired memories of family
visits. *The Other Way to Listen* by Byrd Baylor brought us outdoors
to hear what we usually missed and spawned writing practice unlike any we'd done inside. James Howe's *I Wish I Were A Butterfly*

with Ed Young's stunning illustrations sparked experiments in metaphor.

Other days writing practice was left wide open: "Write for five minutes without stopping. Go as fast as you can. Don't let your inner critic get a word in." I made it clear that writing practice is an exercise intended to make them more comfortable using language, to give them ideas for possible writing projects—ways to write for real purposes and audiences. I definitely did not want to take a giant step backwards to the days when teachers assigned the same topic to the entire class. Digressing from the prompt was not only permitted but celebrated. That is what writing is all about, following ideas that come along unexpectedly, using writing to examine what matters most in our lives.

Awakening Insight

Emily: I hope that people will be accepting. I hope that when I get to be 15 I'm not as crabby as my sister. I hope that I'll be able to finish my homework in time for Blossom. I hope my Nana and Boompa will never die. I hope my mom, my dad, my sister and all my other relatives will never die. I hope Molly will stop cracking on me to make herself feel better. I hope Kristin T. will leave me alone. I hope some time people in our class will stop being cruel to "underdogs." I hope I never lose my necklace. I hope there are still crew neck shirts at Gap for Kristen. I hope I will always be friends with Kristen and Naeta. I hope that I won't have to get spacing wires in my teeth again because the band fell out. I hope for peace. I hope that Ben Hobbs will break up with his girl friend. I hope to always be friends with Sara S. Brady, Katie, Kelly and Ali and HALEY FOREVER.

Sarah: Today I started a fight with my friends. I didn't mean to, but I really wanted to know why they were excluding me from conversations. Brooke yelled at me she told me that I think everyone likes me, when I know that's not true. I know that because of something that I have done. I've alienated many people but that does not bother me because I have a lot of good friends. She also said that I thought I could turn the world with my one little pinky and that's not true either. Maybe I shouldn't have been so forward with my approach as I was, but I believe in being forward about EVERYTHING!

Maybe I shouldn't be, not if it means losing good friends like her. Then again I think maybe she overreacted. When I went to ask my friends if they were mad at me for something, she started screaming. That wasn't fair. I was being calm. Why wasn't she being calm too?

Sarah seems to be resisting the messages to censor her feelings; she is determined to say what she thinks, no matter what the consequences. It is a lonely role.

Sarah, the next day: The more I think about the fight with my friends, the more I decide that if all of them are going to back up B, then I don't really want them for friends. I don't want to be part of a clique. Why limit myself to just them? I don't want to be part of, have to depend on them for friendship. It hurts to think that B's friendship is more important to L and E and K. I have never excluded anyone including J that's why it was just so surprizing to me when she said that I had excluded her sometimes. . . . Maybe I'll form my own clique, the leftover clique. I know that by tomorrow we will have made up, but I will bring up the cliqueyness of our group. If I feel they are the cliques, then how will the average person feel?

As I read Emily's and Sarah's writing practice entries in their notebooks, Gilligan's research came thundering around my ears. Clearly they were struggling with the issues she had defined: compassion for others, tempered by a need for life to be "fair," a strong desire to be connected to others, a longing for real friendship, and an emerging need to hide real feelings. Even Sarah's comments about forming a "leftover clique" echoed Gilligan's research on this subject. "A sense of relational treachery is everywhere at this age. Divisions and cliques are visible reminders of the potential hazard of being too different, not pretty enough, not nice enough, subtle enough, smart enough." (Brown and Gilligan, 1992, p. 101)

But what was my role here? Should writing be used as therapy for the girls to work out their developmental issues? I wondered what parents and colleagues would think. There were, after all, serious expectations, high standards, time-honored traditions at Laurel School. Would people think I wasn't really teaching? But already writing practice was helping me look at my girls differently. Could this be a way for them to express their inner turmoil? Was this a function of their learning in my classroom?

A few girls continued to feel anxious. Just what did I want them to do, they wondered. "I know I'm not doing it right," became a frequent lament. As had happened from time to time in the past, it was my own writing that helped to break the ice. If no one volunteered to read aloud, I would read my own. . . .

Another year begins and this seems like a good class, feels so big, compared to last year's, and so many with the same names, Kristens and Mollys and Jennifers. Will I ever learn them all? How did I ever manage in Exeter? Terry always says it's important to know all the names fast, and she has so many more than I do, although half are boys, so that may cut down on the confusion somewhat, even if it does present other challenges. I remember when we worked with those engineers at the shipyard. She learned all their names—all men—on the first day. And then she brought them doughnuts, which helped a lot, just as she knew it would—food being very important to people—but that was still the hardest job I ever had. And I survived. Laurel is quite a different kettle of fish, that's for sure. . . . .

Are they writing? Will this be good for them? It's such a great day, should we be outdoors? They would love that, I know, but I want to get work done, real work, Marge Piercy kind of work. Danielle is frowning again, and Jenifer is erasing. We need to review the rules. . . . I want this to be fun but I also want them to learn that they already know a lot, have a lot to say and share. . . . Sharing is so scary. I remember Andy's class and how it overwhelmed me when they trashed my writing, Andy leading the charge, but everyone in the whole class agreeing that my writing was trite and full of clichés, that they were turned off by the whole thing. I wanted to die.

But I miss NH. . . . Summer goes so fast. Like life. Feels as if I ought to be here still with Neera and Anne and Lesley. . . . or even back with Amanda and Zoe and Marquettes. . . . Some people have their shoes off. Could be a good sign. . . . so much I want to do with this class, so many possibilities. What are they like underneath all the polite, perfect exteriors? What makes them angry? What gets them excited? Boys. . . . Sports. . . . Each other. . . . Time to stop.

Giggles. Shoulders relaxing. It really was okay to write about anything at all. There is no wrong way to do writing practice. And soon the hands would go up for sharing: "Can I read mine?" We didn't respond to these as pieces of writing, asking the writer how we might help her with her piece. (Murray, 1985) Instead we talked to each other as friends. "I've often thought of that too," or "I know what you mean."

Of course, in those early weeks, many girls used writing practice not to examine big issues, but to show me that they really were grateful, happy, polite young women:

> *Sara:* Seventh grade so far is wonderful. It's better than sixth grade. It seems like we get a little bit more freedom. It seems like we have to be more responsible. But I really like it. So far this year I like all the subjects and teachers. Everyone is nice. I'm getting more used to Mr. R. and his homework and map quizzes. It's not easy but I know that the skills I learn from him will help me through life. Mrs. Sampliner is very nice. She gives us a good amount of homework a night. It is challenging but not too hard.
>
> If you study and really try hard, you will probably do okay. Besides getting used to the teachers, I'm getting used to my friends. A lot of people change and I'm beginning to see who my real friends are. Some people need to grow up. I feel like some of my friends are very childish, but I think that will change soon. I hope it will because we might get to be closer friends. Seventh grade is better than sixth. . . .

Sara may have been an eternal optimist, but this entry makes me wonder whether she has gotten beyond her natural desire to censor out any and all negative thoughts or feelings. She comes close to taking an honest look at the friendship dilemma but backs quickly away, assuring herself that everything will work out and that life will be even better than it is now. If I had not heard nearly everyone in the class lamenting the homework situation, I would be more inclined to take the comments on school at face value. But the fact is, seventh graders at Laurel carry a heavy workload and feel pressured to do well. Most feel overwhelmed by expectations, and sometimes parents call to ask whether all this stress is necessary for seventh graders. Most Laurel girls are somewhat uptight about school, for one reason or another.

> *Danielle:* Why do people embarrass you when they know you'll be embarrassed? Why do people act as if other people don't have feelings? Why do people have no consideration of other people? Why do people always criticize? Why do people humiliate you when you don't like being humiliated?

Why are people so mean to you when you haven't done anything? Why do people dislike you at their first glance of you?
Why don't people give you a second chance? Why do people
forgive on big things but don't forgive you on little things?
Why do people remind you of things that are bad or things
that you don't want to be reminded of? Why can some people
brag so much when others are so modest? Why are people
prejudiced? Why do people hide when they can come out
and talk? Why are some people rude but when you're rude
they make a bigger deal out of it or why when some people
criticize themselves and you agree, do they get mad? Why
can't some people keep their mouths shut at times? Why
can't we take back words we've said or don't say words if we
know it's going to come out wrong? Why do people criticize
you but if you criticize them back they get mad and act as if
they have all the feelings? Why can't people not judge a person by what they are on the outside when they haven't yet
discovered how they are deep down inside? Why can people
not take jokes or why do people joke in an embarrassing
way?

Danielle, like most of her classmates, expresses extreme concern with what others think of her. They hate feeling embarrassed,
they seek the acceptance of their peers, and they want to be
friends forever. They are embarked on their journey towards becoming "adult good women," but they are uneasy, sensing what
they will have to give up along the way: "Which friend is a true
friend?" "What will I have to do to keep my relationship with her?
Must I bury what I really think and feel?" On the brink of womanhood, they already seem prime examples of Gilligan's assertion
that "women's sense of self and of worth is grounded in the ability
to make and maintain relationships." (1982)

When I asked them to write, "Sometimes I wish . . .," they did
not hesitate:

> *Loren:* Sometimes I wish I could lose my nervousness. It
> doesn't happen a lot, but sometimes when the spotlight's on
> me, I blank out and freeze in my tracks. Especially in math
> class. My best subject is math, and though I have the highest
> grade in my advanced algebra class, whenever it's my turn to
> say an answer or read a question, my tongue gets tied, and a
> thousand thoughts go through my head, or I just black out. In
> English even I'm afraid to read things out loud, 'cause I get
> scared that no one will like it.

Nina: Sometimes I wish I were not me. Sometimes I wish I could do things without even trying. Sometimes I wish I could trade places with people who are "perfect."

Catherine: Sometimes I wish someone knew me. Sometimes I wish there was another me, another you . . .

Rachel: Sometimes I wish people in school wouldn't start rumors about you. It hurts, but I guess all kids do this. Sometimes I wish that you didn't get fat and you didn't have to eat. If you didn't eat then you didn't starve but if you did eat tons you wouldn't get fat. Sometimes I wish I knew if there was a heaven or hell. If there is a devil and if there is a God and angels. Is there an after life?

As the girls became more and more comfortable with writing practice, I realized we had lots of other work to accomplish together in class. I suggested that they do their practice at home each night, making it what I hoped would be a lifelong habit. *"Nulla dies sine linea"*—"Never a day without a line"—is an old adage given to me by Don Murray and is one of the principles I try to adhere to faithfully, no matter what else is going on in my life. I wanted my girls to have the same solace of using writing to cope with the increasing complexities of their worlds.

Eventually, as we became involved in a variety of writing projects in our workshop class, writing practice became an option, instead of part of the mandatory routine. All writing leads to insight and discovery, and revising offers opportunities to dig deeper, to refine thinking, to follow new trains of thought. Many girls embarked on complicated pieces—writing that mattered—but they knew that when they were at an impasse or when they just wanted to fish for new material, they could turn back to writing practice. Rereading this fast writing often helped them see threads of meaning over time. (Calkins, 1991) What emerged as significant as they wrote without censoring themselves? Could this lead to other, more polished, writing? What could they do with the insights they discovered?

I had seen writing practice as synonymous to freewriting, a springboard for "real writing." It was, I was sure, the place to sow the seeds for pieces that would move writers and readers to think and feel more deeply than they had before. But could we afford to take ten minutes every day—add at least another five for sharing—to do it? It was a means to an end. Class time is so precious. We teachers want to be sure we use it well, use it to imbue our students with the joy of composing—discovering, creating, and communicating meaning; use it to engender a love of words and of the music in language; use it to instill a passion for literature—for poetry and stories and plays—that will sustain them throughout their lives; use it to foster confidence in speaking and performing drama; use it in one thousand other ways we know they will need to experience. As much as I love literature, teaching writing has always been my own priority for using class time. Writing practice should lead to the creation of writing for real purposes and audiences, I thought. It would be well worth big chunks of class time, if such pieces were the result.

But the Laurel girls helped me reconsider. Oh, good writing did spring from these writing practices, as fluency clearly improved. But, as I read their notebooks each week, it soon became evident that something else was going on. Many girls were using this opportunity to speak more honestly than I had heard them speak anywhere else. They were speaking to themselves.

> *Wallis:* It's simply not fair, I'm so sad; growing up is no fun. One moment I'm happy, then I feel as if I could cry. Sometimes I do. . . .
>
> I never had any close friends at school. Now, I have none. I could cry for hours on end . . .
>
> I don't want to be like last year. *Noooooooooooooooooooooo*!! Everyone seems mean now. Best friends are secretly enemies. I want a true friend, but one just isn't around.
>
> Why don't they mention this in health class? All they say is how exciting and wonderful growing up is. I don't know if this is weird or not.

> *Sarah:* I think that people shouldn't judge someone by their looks but by their inside. I sometimes wished everyone was blind and would only know you by your voice and your brain. If we were all blind, we wouldn't be able to judge people by their outside but then again we would probably be judged by our voices. Maybe talking to guys on the phone is a good idea, then they would have nothing to judge by except your personality. It's not that I'm a dog, but I wish I were beautiful. In my opinion, I'm o.k. pretty, but not beautiful. I wish I could go up to any guy at the dance and ask him to dance and he would snap to attention and answer, "I'd be a fool to turn you down."

Naeta: I'm a little sad. All my friends have plans tonight that don't include me. I don't know what to do about it. . . .

I have always loved writing and teaching writing because it is the best way I know to develop as a human being—this is a clear prejudice, and I admit there may be other ways to self-realization—but I see now that I had a hierarchy. I wanted my students to write pieces that would be published, widely read, and admired. Most of all admired. My unspoken goal was to have my students write the best narratives, poems, stories, and essays in the school or in any school. Reaching a large, perhaps even unknown, audience was the ultimate achievement. Being read beyond the classroom would convince my girls that they were, after all, real writers. The power of the written word was in its ability to move readers to think or to behave differently, and my girls could do it.

Their writing practice entries brought me back to earth, as I came to know again that the real magic of writing lies in what it can do for the writer. I should have remembered. How many times had I survived stress, crisis, and grief by sitting up at night writing furiously? How many times had I written my way out of confusion, anger, or despair? I should have remembered.

Sarah: Guys are trouble in ways they don't even know. They make a normally confident girl change to mush in a matter of seconds. I wonder if guys are as unsure as me, if they stare at a girl for hours just hoping she'll glance their way, if they dial a girl's number ten times and then hang up.

It was in their writing practice that my girls voiced their real fears, their anger, and their longing. Much of what they wrote in practice never left their notebook pages, and this seems to me now all right, more than all right. This seems to me a valid use of class time, of any time. I had been nervous looking at writing as therapy when the fact is, writing is therapy.

"We write because we need to write," says Don Murray, "and the act of writing rarely solves our problems, but it is a way of dealing with problems and of achieving a momentary distance from them. The act of writing about even the most painful subjects seems both necessary and therapeutic." (Murray, 1985)

Writing practice served a very real purpose, perhaps not the purpose Wallis had been seeking, but a good purpose, after all. The fact is that my students' self-esteem—so important to me—is clearly in jeopardy at this point in their lives. How much class time should we give to writing practice? Plenty. For isn't every girl's voice worth saving? Isn't seeing a problem the only way to begin to solve it? Isn't the daily practice of reflecting on one's life in an honest manner always a valuable endeavor? The writing practice we did together at Laurel may have kept many writers in touch with themselves and prevented them from either "drowning" or "disappearing." At least for the time being.

3

Listening Harder:
Echoes from the Island

———

All that non-fiction can do is answer the questions. It's fiction's business to ask them.

—Richard Hughes

THEY GATHER in clusters before and between classes, these child-women, twelve and thirteen years old. They hold whispered conversations behind locker doors, huddled around window benches: "He said what?" "Do you think he's going to call her?" "How do you know he didn't mean it?" "Are you sure?" They plan elaborate meetings for later: "You call me." "My mom said she can drive if we can get a ride home." "I can only have two people sleep over. Call me." "Chris said Joe might call tonight . . ."

The clusters shift. Who is "in" this week? Who the victim of cruel taunting?—"Do you suppose you'll always be flat-chested?"

Developmental Crossroads

Seventh grade life at an all girls' school. The innate need for relationship, for connectedness, by the time girls reach this point in their lives is so strong that they will go to almost any length to win the approval of others. Their greatest fear becomes the disapproval of the group, and so the girls make compromises, saying or doing things they don't really believe in, to ensure their continued inclusion.

Such a pressing need to connect, according to Gilligan, is both normal and necessary. Girls must, however, come to terms with the other developmental task facing them at this time—the need to assert their independence, their individuality.

The more I read and heard about the researchers' data, the more sensitive I became to what was going on in the seventh grade. How could I, as their English teacher, help the girls deal with such weighty issues? My students are writers, "using language to discover meaning in experience," (Murray, 1985) but they are female writers who have unique reasons to write and needs that are central to their development as healthy young women.

Fiction as a Vehicle

The girls' need to write became even more evident when we embarked on our study of fiction. In lieu of total free choice in writing, I decided to examine with the girls a specific genre this trimester. To my surprise, instead of preventing them from writing with authority and commitment, the genre structure seemed to enable them to become engaged with their writing in more compelling ways, giving them new lenses on their worlds, on themselves. (Murray, 1982)

I have never felt particularly comfortable teaching or writing fiction, and from time to time I wonder whether it is even necessary in the busy school year. My girls write memoir, persuasion, poetry, even essays, well, but their fiction, like my own, feels pretty flat. As I thought more and more about the power of literature, I become intrigued with the notion of really learning to write fiction with my girls.

Jack Wilde suggests that students concentrate on plausibility and a change in a character. (Graves, Hansen, Newkirk, 1985) We used these parameters when we began our fiction writing at Laurel. But before characters can change, we realized, we have to know who they are in the first place.

We followed Donald Graves' recommendation that we assume the persona of the character and let classmates conduct interviews in turn. (Graves, 1989) Each student became her character, and through the interview process, discovered minute details of that person's life, past and present. Flesh and blood characters emerged on the page, as we spent days in writing workshop making notes, doing freewriting, and sketching maps of their lives.

To say the girls were excited was an understatement . . . "I love these exercises," someone said. "Can we do more of this?" But after about a week of prewriting, many girls were eager to begin plotting their stories.

Joyce Carol Oates has said, "My writing is full of lives I might have led. A writer imagines what could have happened, not what really happened." (Murray, 1990, p. 86)

Not surprisingly, much of what the girls dreamed onto the page involved friendships, loyalty, belonging.

Connecting and Separating

Ali's Story

Ali is one of the more chipper, confident girls in the class. Vivacious and sharp-witted, she often keeps us laughing in and out of class and seems the proverbial "friend to all the world." She chose to write her first-person fiction, entitled "Winning," about two girls who enter into competition for a place on a track team.

Winning

Jaime and I both enjoyed running, although Jaime ran more for the fun of it, and I ran because I wanted to have the best time in my class for the mile run, also because I wanted to make the Hillside cross-country team. . . .

Miss Nelson chose Jaime and one other girl named Sara to do the warm-ups in gym class. Miss Nelson often chose Jaime, because she was such a great athlete. Jaime and Sara instructed us on doing jumping jacks and push-ups and sit-ups. . . .

My class really took running seriously because only one seventh grader was going to be chosen for the team. Our school had gone to States the last three years and each time was one game away from winning. . . .

Ali presents seeds of a conflict almost immediately. The first-person character seems to envy her friend Jaime, sensing that the teacher favors her. Girls at this age are sensitive to ways in which adults seem to perceive them. Their self-esteem is closely linked to the approval they receive from the adults in their lives. (Sadker and Sadker, 1994) In her story, Ali lets us realize that the narrator really wants to go to this track meet. She begins to feel annoyed that Jaime is outrunning her.

Jaime's long curly blond hair was bobbing side to side whacking me in the face. If I had had scissors at that moment, I probably would have cut it off. . . . Jaime's long perfect legs were taking large, smooth strides, while my short legs took quick short jerky strides, as I tried to keep pace with Jaime. Jaime would do a little leap every once in a while and throw me a large grin when I was about to collapse from exhaustion.

Jaime and I had been running together since the second grade when I first came to Hillside, and every year she would speed up at the end and beat me. Today I had a feeling that I could beat her and get a faster time than hers. I was so determined that today was the day I would come in first and make the cross-country team, which would surely make my parents happy.

Although we were pretty good friends, I had always taken running more seriously than Jaime. I had practiced running all summer and all spring, and out of all my classmates, even Jaime, I thought I deserved to be the best mile runner in the seventh grade. As I watched Jaime run, I noticed the breeze blowing her beautiful hair back and not a drop of sweat on her face. As I ran, my orange curls were waving in my face as I was drenched in sweat. An anger was building up inside me; I did not understand why any person could be so perfect, when I was so far away from that. Even if she was my friend, I couldn't help being mad at her.

Now we can hear the narrator's jealousy escalate. She feels that she deserves to win—it's only fair—and she resents the fact that this all out breakneck running comes so easily to Jaime. Ali's story is an honest look at real feelings—feelings of competition are healthy and normal—but as her story progresses, the plot thickens. Jaime begins to breathe heavily and decides to sit out the race.

"Are you okay," I asked, not wanting to slow my pace.

"Yes, I'm fine, I think I'm going to sit down on those bleachers," panted Jaime. "You go on running, don't worry," replied Jaime as she gave me a weak smile and turned towards the bleachers.

I hesitated, but then noticed Sara and Kim, who were pretty good runners, not far behind, so I started up my pace again. It finally occurred to me I was now in the lead and even Jaime couldn't beat me now. I had been waiting so many years for this chance, and finally I had it. I now had the chance to impress my parents.

Both of my parents had been wonderful athletes in school and all of their talents seemed to have been given to my sister Jessy. In school I would get mostly A's, hoping that would please my parents, but what they always seemed more interested in was if I had made the soccer team like Jessy, or the basketball team, or the baseball team. Every time I would say, "No," they would go into a long talk on how disappointed they were in me. If I could just make the cross-country team that would be the one sport that Jessy wasn't good at. In a way, Jessy was a lot like Jaime, almost perfect in every way.

In class we discuss the importance of slowing things down sometimes—pace is a new concept to them—and we pay attention to plausibility. (Wilde, 1985) Ali is being careful not to have the action happen too quickly here. She has her narrator flash back now to the sense of sibling rivalry she feels with her sister Jessy, the great athlete. She yearns for her parents' approval. Thinking of her parents gives this girl a burst of energy and makes her run faster. But, as she begins to think of how alike Jaime and Jessy are, she feels something else.

> Right then I remembered Jaime. This whole time running, thinking about myself, I had completely forgotten about Jaime. I started to think of how horrible I had been acting. I thought that maybe I could run faster so I could quickly finish and find out what was wrong with Jaime. All of my happiness disappeared, and I couldn't seem to run any faster.
>
> I started to remember when we had run a half-mile race on Labor Day weekend. We were about half way done when I tripped and scraped my knees and Jaime stopped to help me up. Jaime walked the rest of the race with me instead of running, when she could have easily won and gotten a trophy.
>
> Right then I could not stand the guilt of being such an untrue friend, so I cut across the field to find out what was wrong with Jaime. I almost started to turn back, thinking of what my parents would say, but at this point, I didn't care. Faster than I had ever run before, I dashed across the field. The nurse and some other classmates were crowded around her. She was lying on the ground just recovering from what the nurse said was "an asthma attack." I bent down beside her, still feeling guilty for leaving her, and she gave me a faint smile and whispered, "It's okay."

I like Ali's story for its surprises and for the immediacy of the race—all the thinking and action takes place in the context of running hard—and I admire the way the narrator cares about her friend. What is sad is that she has to give something up. Because the friendship is so crucial to her, the narrator relinquishes her chance at winning and, in the process, thrilling her parents with her achievement. When I ask Ali whether she thinks her character has made the right choice, she responds, "Yes definitely. She knows her friend is more important than winning." And when the class listens to the story, many remark that it is "plausible" and that the narrator is a "true friend," someone they admire.

Carol Gilligan urges us "to listen for the ways in which girls orchestrate themes of connection and separation and concerns about care and justice in speaking about themselves, about their relationships and about their experiences of conflict." (Gilligan et al, 1989) It seems that Ali is talking about all of this in her fiction. I can raise questions about her characters' motivation and behavior, but I must honor the fact that it is Ali's story, and that right now these are her values.

A Moral Voice Emerges

Kristin's Story

Tentative and mercurial in this class of seventh-grade girls, Kristin yearns for acceptance, connection, and inclusion. Her blond hair falls below her shoulders, and her grey-blue eyes look out eagerly from behind large glasses. Her manner is docile, amenable. But Kristin also struggles with her need to separate herself from the crowd, to assert her individuality, and to define her own principles, even if it means disagreeing with the attitudes of her friends.

"We know it's wrong to pick on someone," Laurel seventh graders often say, "but it's worth it, if it gets you in with the popular kids."

Protesting small cruelties becomes all but impossible for girls. They fear being ostracized; their not condoning the nasty remarks may ultimately lead to their being the next victims. And their strongest desire is to belong.

I listen in conference as Kristin's piece develops, encouraging her by asking questions when I feel genuinely curious—Who is Molly? What is her part in the story? Why is this such a difficult decision for Cathy to make?—and soon Kristin is bursting with pride as she reads the piece to the class.

No matter how long I work with young people, they continue to perplex, astonish, and delight me; but this is something new. Kristin has discovered, in her writing, a way to examine her own existential dilemma.

Kristin's story, "Friends Mean All the World," centers on a group of girls, a bit younger than she and her friends. Cathy, the main character, observes the popular kids taunting shy, awkward, lonely Anne. Molly, Cathy's friend, participates in this behavior and exhibits contempt for Anne.

"Hey ugly, by the wall!" It was Dan, the school bully. All faces turned to see who it was, and laughter filled the air. I stood there with my mouth open.
"How could they be so mean?" I asked myself.

> I felt for Anne, who was now kicking a rock back and forth. Soon the bell rang, signaling that it was time to go in. Molly and Beth came running up to me with broad smiles on their faces. Molly looked as though she was going to explode with the new gossip she had. I wanted to mention to her what had happened to Anne, but I didn't know how to say it."

"I didn't know how to say it" seems a predominant and nagging state of mind for Cathy, as it is for Kristin. It became clear to me that she was writing about herself. This was a story, not only of Cathy, Molly and Anne, but also—and more importantly—of Kristin, Emily, Naeta, Erica, Brady, and the other girls in this seventh-grade class.

> "Listen!" Molly grabbed my arm. "Don't feel bad for her. You're just wasting your time."
> "Ya, o.k.," I agreed reluctantly.
> That day walking home for me was different. I felt strange. What had happened to Anne that day seemed to have had an effect on me. I tried pushing out the guilty feeling. But why did I feel guilty? I had never done anything to her, or had I? Maybe all the times she was made fun of I should have protected her or at least said something in her favor. But what would the crowd say? It would be awful if they thought I liked her, and they'd start making fun of me and hating me.

Gilligan terms Cathy's response an exercise of the voice of care. (Gilligan, 1982) Cathy cannot push Anne's pain from her mind, because she knows that, in some way, she is connected to Anne. She is "seeing a world comprised of relationships rather than of people standing alone, a world that coheres through human connection rather than through a system of rules . . ." (Gilligan, 1982)

But Cathy is also concerned with other connections. She needs to sustain her membership in, her connection to, the group that tolerates, indeed encourages, the cruel behavior. It is Kristin's struggle every day.

> I felt as though maybe, if I forgot about what had happened at school and didn't dwell on it, I wouldn't feel bad anymore. . . . The next day in school, I reminded myself not to say anything to any of my friends about Anne. I really didn't want them to

think I felt sorry for her; then they would think I was like
Anne. . . . I started picking the players when I saw Anne in
her usual place by the wall. Something inside me told me to
ask her to play, but I dared not for fear of embarrassment."

Cathy, like Kristin, struggles. Her compassion for Anne is now
in direct conflict with her desire to please her friends. She knows
in her heart what is right, but she questions whether doing the
right thing will be worth the price she will pay. When Cathy articulates her concern for Anne, she is met with scorn:

"Oh, and now you're protecting her? What is wrong with
you?"

Sure enough, Cathy's friends begin to exclude her from their
games at recess, confirming her worst fears.

"I felt awful. Embarrassment and anger filled my body. I
could feel my face getting red as a beet. I wanted to run inside
and cry. Millions of thoughts started going through my mind.
Why is the crowd turning on me? I didn't do anything to
them. Just because I was nice to Anne, they were ignoring
me. But then it hit me. Why was I nice to Anne? Who cared
about her? She probably didn't even care that I had called
her. Why did I sacrifice all my friends for a squeaky-voiced
kid who didn't even care about friends?"

Here Cathy feels a strong pull back to the familiar world of
"friends." Why trade the known for the unknown? It is a dilemma
I know Kristin faces often. There are girls in our class like Anne,
isolated, shy, left out of things.

Slowly my thoughts changed as I saw Anne by the wall. She
was a sad kid who maybe didn't know how to get friends . . .
Maybe friends take time to come, and Anne didn't know how
to get friends.
    I really felt sorry for Anne right at that moment. All this
time people were mean to her, and she never had anyone
to be with, and my being mean to her only added to her
misery.
    That day I think many ridges formed in my brain, because I
learned a lot. Just that little incident at recess made me realize
a very valuable lesson. There is nothing better than a true and

honest friendship, and a good friend means all the world. . . .
It would be hard to become friends with Anne. I would have
to accept a lot of name-calling and teasing. But I felt if Anne
could handle it, so could I . . . I felt good, good enough to invite Anne over to my house.

Cathy has resolved her dilemma, her care voice and her justice
voice (Gilligan, 1982) coming together in harmony; her need to
assert herself and her need to maintain her connection to others
are reconciled to some degree.

In writing her process piece, reflecting on her story, Kristin
says, ". . . I know that sometimes it is easier to get your fiction
ideas from real things that have happened in your life. You have to
make sure you don't start writing the true story . . . I finally got
my idea from thinking about my old school and how I always felt
sorry for a girl named Beth. I didn't at all have the amount of
courage that "Cathy," my main character does . . ."

Kristin has found her story idea in her past experience. However, I would also maintain, she does more. In allowing Cathy to
demonstrate such "courage," Kristin tries on a new behavior,
stretching her wings to soar beyond the comfortable limits of peer
pressure. She uses her writing to live, not merely in retrospect, but
in projection. In this story Kristin charts what may well be her
own future development.

Gilligan writes, "The sequence of women's moral judgment
proceeds from an initial concern with survival to a focus on goodness and finally to a reflective understanding of care as the most
adequate guide to the resolution of conflicts in human relationships." (1982)

"This sounds a lot like our class," comments Wallis after reading Kristin's story.

"At times I've wondered what it would be like to do that myself," says Caroline. "Would I lose all my friends? This story leaves
me thinking."

Choice

Hallie's Story

Hallie is a serious young woman, tall, thin, and quiet in class, more
concerned, it appears, with school work than with her social life.
She often walks from class to class with her friend Vicki, although

she has lots of friends; the others seem to admire her for her level-headedness, her common sense. She is, they know, someone to trust.

While Kristin explores possibilities for her present relationships and interactions among her classmates, Hallie chooses to look farther ahead. Her story centers on the choices a woman makes as she attempts to balance job and family.

Starting Over

The phone rang in the office. It was the principal of my son's school, calling to tell me to rush to school right away. My son Rick, a sophomore, had never been in trouble and was close to being the perfect child. I had no idea what Mr. Robinson wanted me for. Had Rick done something great? But the tone of the principal's voice did not sound that way. My boss isn't understanding, so it was hard to convince him to let me leave.

This was my third year back at work. I used to work at a large law firm, the only woman attorney there, along with twenty-four men. I had Rick, my first child, five years after getting this job. Three years later I had my second child, Suzanne, who is now thirteen. After she was born, I decided to quit my job to stay home with my children.

Hallie sets up a common dilemma. Mom loves her job but feels the need to be with her young children. The girls see this drama played out in their own lives; many of their own mothers have careers outside the home. They read stories about women who have exciting, challenging jobs. They know that their future will be full of options.

. . . I was driving to the school thinking about what kind of trouble Rick could have gotten into. It must have been something little, but that wouldn't explain my having to go and talk to Mr. Robinson immediately.

As I walked into my old school it brought back many vivid memories, most of them happy, but some very embarrassing . . .

I opened the red door that read "Principal," my hands all sweaty. I was very nervous. I stepped into the office and saw my son sitting in a chair being lectured by Mr. Robinson. The principal got up and pulled out a chair for me.

As the story unfolds, we hear that Rick is being accused of cheating on a history test. At first his mother insists there must be some mistake, as Rick, being such a strong student, would have no reason to cheat. The principal reveals that several of the boy's teachers have expressed concern lately about his falling grades.

> "Why haven't you notified me earlier," I questioned.
> "I've tried calling you a number of times, but you've either been at a hearing or out to a late lunch," responded Mr. Robinson.
> "You could have called me at home. I get home at about six most nights."
> "When I tried you at home, you weren't there."
> "I've been very busy. . . ."
> "I understand you're busy, but shouldn't your children come first, Mrs. Clark?"

Oh, we can almost feel the poor woman's shame. Hallie has created a plausible situation—court hearings, late lunches, long days, phone messages not delivered. She is setting the stage for the mother to take the blame for her son's fall from grace. Things go from bad to worse.

> I couldn't believe I had to hear this from a man who obviously finds pleasure in lecturing children. It didn't bother me much, because I reassured myself that my children would always come first. The only reason I was working so hard was for my children's sake anyway. . . .
> ". . . and so I think that your son has a drinking problem," said Mr. Robinson.
> "I know my son has a problem, but I don't think it is alcohol, and you have no right saying so without proof," I replied.
> "But Mrs. Clark, just ask any one of his teachers and they'll tell you he's been stoned in class more than once."
> "And the next thing you're going to say is that he has a drug problem too," I retorted angrily.
> "A drinking problem yes, but I doubt that he has started with drugs yet, although he has been exposed many times."
> I looked over at poor innocent Rick, and I knew that the principal was wrong. After all, Rick was a great kid. Right? I didn't know what to think. This was all too confusing for me. I wished my husband was still around to help me out. . . .

"Your son is close to being an alcoholic," Mr. Robinson said gently.

My son the alcoholic. I knew it couldn't be true. I'd heard that a child's actions are caused by the way his parent treats him. I was a good parent. After all, what mother would spend every minute she has to give her child more than the every-day necessities of life?

Hallie's character becomes more and more agitated as she is forced to consider the fact that the principal may be right. She returns to work, has to skip lunch to make up for the time she lost at the school, and feels more and more flustered.

I got home that night at 6:35 and threw dinner into the microwave right away. Susie was upstairs watching television as usual, and Rick was upstairs. I tip-toed up and leaned my head against the door to his room. I heard him listening to the radio, but I had a feeling that that wasn't all he was doing. I flung the door open to find him at his desk doing his home-work.

"Hi, Mom, what are you doing up here? You know I hate people in my room, especially you," he said.

I hated it when he talked to me like that. It's as if he has no respect for me.

"Oh, umm ahh, I just wanted to tell you to come down for dinner in five minutes," I stammered.

"Yah, right. I bet you were checking up on me."

We ate dinner in the usual manner, Susie talking and asking lots of questions, Rick very silent. After dinner I tried to talk to Rick, but we hadn't gotten very far when I got a call from my boss. He had just heard on the news that my client had robbed a liquor store. His hearing on another crime was scheduled for tomorrow, and this meant I had to totally redo my preparation for his testimony. This would take all night. . . .

Days go by, the mother makes several attempts to talk to Rick, but is always called away to work. She keeps late hours, trying to work on her client's defense, spending little time at home. Things get worse with Rick.

When I got home, Susie told me that Rick was at Rob's house, where he went every day after school. I had never heard of

> Rob before, and this upset me. Three years ago I knew all
> of Rick's friends, and they knew me. I started crying. Susie,
> staring at me, said, "Hey, Mom, what's wrong? Don't you like
> Rob?"
>
> "No, honey, I haven't even met him."

Later, when Rick comes home, she smells liquor on his breath
and is forced to admit, finally, that her son has an alcohol problem,
as the principal had suspected. The mother feels terrible guilt and
decides to change things, demonstrating, in Gilligan's words, "a
concern with goodness—with being a good woman as defined by
the willingness to take care of, or to take on the cares of, others, a
willingness often to sacrifice oneself for others. . . ." (1990, p. 8)

> Right after dinner Rick and I had a long talk. I told him that I
> loved him, and that I hadn't meant to ignore him and Susie. I
> said I'd be glad to help him with his problems and that I'd
> always be there for him. I would quit my job. After that, he
> opened up and told me how frustrated he was with school.
> Exams were coming up, and since I hadn't been there to help,
> he had turned to drink. He had learned that drinking would
> make him feel better. . . .

But when the mother tells her boss she wants to quit, he immediately offers to shorten her hours. She is too good an attorney,
he insists, to leave the profession entirely.

> "I have kids also, so I understand how hard they can be to
> handle. It's just too bad that your child had trouble coping
> with your work schedule. . . ."

So, the mother spends more time with her son, Rick goes to
Alcoholics Anonymous meetings, and the family is closer than
ever. A happy ending. Hallie, in writing such a tale, reveals her
awareness that the notion of a woman's being a high-power professional and a devoted full-time single mother may be problematic. "Having it all" may be attractive, but Hallie recognizes that
it is not easy for women to cope with all the demands of family
and career.

It is interesting to me that she chooses to make her character a
single mom. In her story, the husband has died, leaving the family
in need of a breadwinner. Hallie and many of her classmates often

speak of their intentions to be financially secure, independent of husbands' incomes. Is Hallie considering possibilities? Her story, like Kristin's, provokes conversation. "It's not all the mother's fault." "She should have been paying more attention." "If you're not a criminal lawyer, you can have better hours." "Alcoholism is a disease. He probably would have gotten in trouble even if she had stayed home." "Maybe she shouldn't have gotten such a hard job."

In our class being an attorney ranks right up with being a physician as a dream career. But, Hallie knows, such a job will come with heavy expectations. She uses her writing to rehearse her life, just as Kristin does. Even though her story may have a "happily ever after" tone, I know her examination of this issue has been important to her. She will continue to think about it.

Carol Gilligan writes, "The knowledge about relationships and the life of relationships that flourish on this remote island of female adolescence are . . . like notes from the underground." (1990, p. 24)

Girls need to write, and they need to share their writing and feel its impact on others. As teachers of girls we need to help them find ways to break the silence and tell the real stories, the stories from the island: What does it feel like to be twelve-years-old, yearning for independence, while needing at the same time to sustain relationships? What is it like to suddenly doubt your own conceptions of right and wrong, as these may tend to put relationships in jeopardy? What is it like for you? I want to ask my girls, again and again, day after day. I am more aware now of your struggles. What is it like for you?

Working on fiction with these girls, I remember why I am a teacher of writing. I want my students' stories to tell them something about themselves, about the world they must live in and become a part of. I want them to pay attention to that. And I want them to know that writing can change them. Writing improves because we are committed to it, and we are committed to it because we are getting something out of it, beyond someone else's approval, beyond a high grade, today, right now.

4

The Curious Ballast:
Why We Read Books

———

The Bookstall

Just looking at them
I grow greedy, as if they were
freshly baked loaves
waiting on their shelves
to be broken open—that one
and that—and I make my choice
in a mood of exalted luck,
browsing among them
like a cow in sweetest pasture.

For life is continuous
as long as they wait
to be read—these inked paths
opening into the future, page
after page, every book
its own receding horizon.
And I hold them, one in each hand,
a curious ballast weighting me
here to the earth.

—Linda Pastan, *Heroes in Disguise*

RECENTLY A reporter from *Educational Leadership* called to interview me about teaching middle school students. "What exactly are your goals in teaching literature?" he wanted to know. I was between classes, expecting the bell to signal the next period any moment. "Just briefly," he said, "what is it you are trying to accomplish?" Well, there was no way to tell him in thirty seconds or less, what I hope will happen when I share books in the classroom. Answering that question would take much longer. Answering that question has taken me my whole teaching career. Answering that question has taken me my whole life. And the answer is constantly changing. There are, right now, a whole panoply of answers. Charlotte Huck says that when we teach literature to children we are, in truth, educating their hearts. I like that. Katherine Paterson says that when we bring our children wonderful books we are really giving them "life, and growth, and refreshment." (1981, p. 6) Indeed. In the film "Shadowlands," a student of C. S. Lewis tells him, "We read to know we are not alone." Aha!

To Love Literature

There is no way to overstate the joy and sustenance reading has brought me from my earliest days. An employee of Doubleday and Company for nearly thirty years, my grandmother delighted in bringing boxloads of free books to our house at regular intervals. I was a charter member of the Junior Literary Guild, but these wonderful titles that arrived in the mail once a month were just part of the treasure trove that created my world as a child. I learned to read sitting on my grandmother's lap, somehow making for myself the magical discovery that the squiggles on the page corresponded to the words coming out of her mouth, that the words made the stories that captivated me entirely. It was *Heidi* I read first, taking over spontaneously when she paused for an instant. I will never forget it.

Once I was in school, one of sixty in a first-grade classroom at St. William the Abbot, I discovered that reading meant something quite different to Sister Joanne. Here there were such things as "a consonant blend" and "a vowel sound" and "a silent e." I don't remember any stories in first grade. And, as the years went by, for survival's sake, I would carry one of my books with me to school. I'd slip it inside my desk, open, and while other students read aloud in turn from the basal, I would brazenly read my own real book. I read *Little Women* and *Under the Lilacs* and *The Five Little Peppers and How They Grew* and *Cheaper by the Dozen* and *The Wind in the Willows* and *Alice in Wonderland* and *The Little Princess* and *Black Beauty*. Reading these books enchanted me; no longer was I bound to the desk or the room or any part of my own world. Instead I was transfixed, transported, and transformed. Reading these books awakened in me the irrepressible knowledge that life was more than my own daily routine, and while my own real life was safe and warm and nurtured, the world of reading filled me with a new excitement. I read the entire Bobbsey Twins series this way, and later all the Nancy Drew and Cherry Ames books, marveling at how brave and strong these women were. (I loved series; when I'd finished the first book, I'd have to have all of them.)

My heart thumped sometimes, fearing ominous consequences if I were ever caught, but the joy was worth the risk. I managed to escape detection until eighth grade. Even then I was not "caught in the act," but discovered after the fact. An autobiography of Eleanor Roosevelt carelessly left on my desk after school gave me away. I was pulled out of choir practice, so alarmed were the nuns. Did my mother know I was reading such a book, they wondered? Of course she knew, I assured them. (She would not have approved, however, of my deviation from classroom procedures!) The principal called my house, where, to my relief, my mother informed everyone that this book was fine with her. I still wonder what it was that caused such a stir. Was it the fact that Mrs. Roosevelt was so candid about her fears, dreams, and convictions throughout her life? Or could it be that she broke the mold of "the perfect woman" by questioning the status quo? This was, in fact, why I loved the book so much.

I remember Betty Smith's *A Tree Grows in Brooklyn*, and Maureen Daly's *Seventeenth Summer*, but other titles from my sixth, seventh, and eighth grade years come back to me a bit fuzzily: *Cross My Heart*, *The Pink Dress*, *The Tender Time*. I don't remember who wrote these books, but I do know that they were all about young girls caught in the web of social intrigue. Who would get asked to the dance? Whose boyfriend was cuter, smarter, nicer? Whose heart would get broken in the course of the story? These books were *hot*. They made the rounds in our class, from one girl to the next—"Can I read it after Terry?"—my own unique currency for acceptance and inclusion. Suddenly, I was more than the shy nerd with the big glasses; I became the person with terrific books.

It's sad that I can't recall a single thing we read in school together. I have a strong sense that two of my teachers, Sister Anastasia and Sister Raphael, were women who loved literature, but I
don't know why I am so sure. What did they read to us? What did
we talk about when we talked about stories? It is gone. When I
think of how and why I became a reader, it is my grandmother
I credit. These days, when I dive into a new novel or pick up something at the bookstore for a child, I think of her, grateful for this
legacy.

How could I explain all this to the man on the phone? Reading
has been and continues to be essential in my life. When I was
young and newly divorced, I spent days reading Marilyn French
and Gail Sheehy and nights reading Emily Dickinson and William
Butler Yeats. It was the night reading that saw me through. These
days I turn to Linda Pastan, Mary Oliver, Anne Tyler, Kaye Gib-
bons, Toni Morrison. Their worlds and my own intermingle,
merge, coalesce. These days my biggest fear is that my eyes will
give out and I won't be able to read into the night the way I always
have.

Scout in Harper Lee's *To Kill a Mockingbird* says it well, "Until I
feared I might lose it, I did not love reading. One does not love
breathing." We read to educate our hearts, to find life, growth, and
refreshment, and to know we are not alone. We read in order to
become better human beings, more knowledgeable, more compassionate, more courageous, more accepting. We read to find and
build connections, to enter into relationships with the people we
encounter in the world of story. These people become for us, in
the best sense, our mentors, our colleagues, and our friends. We
discover that others have experienced and survived grief, guilt,
tragedy, and fear. We discover that our capacity for understanding
is greater than we could have dreamed. We discover that our
books change us. How could I explain all this to the man on the
phone?

And how do I explain it to my students? In recent years,
thanks to the groundbreaking work of Mary Ellen Giacobbe and
Nancie Atwell and the further discoveries of Linda Rief, middle
school teachers throughout the country have introduced choice
into the literature curriculum. Atwell makes an eloquent case:
"If we want our adolescent students to grow to appreciate literature, another first step is allowing them to exert ownership and
choose the literature they will read . . . As we adult readers can
turn to fiction for portrayals of the universalities of our condition,

our students can find their perspectives reflected and explored in a body of fiction of their own, books that can help them grow up, books that can help them love books." (1987, p. 161)

Learning to Choose

Atwell credits Mary Ellen Giacobbe for recognizing first that a dynamic reading-writing classroom should be based on three fundamental elements: Time, Choice, and Response. (1987, p. 54). Thus, they are at the heart of the curriculum in my classroom. After all, no one likes to be "assigned" a book. As readers, we appreciate suggestions, but we resist being strong-armed into anything. Like Atwell, Rief, and many other teachers, I fill my room with Young Adult paperback books and encourage my students to read whatever appeals to them. And like Nancie and Linda, I know that this is just the beginning. As teachers and more experienced readers, our job is to offer guidance.

I often read compelling leads or excerpts from books that I believe the girls might enjoy. We talk about all the ways readers choose books; we make suggestions to one another; we track down favorite authors' other titles in the school library. Choice is not always wide open. Concerned with making connections to their history class, I push historical fiction. When we are writing memoir, I ask them to read something in this genre by a writer they love. When we focus on intergenerational relationships, a study designed by Linda Rief, (1992) I give them her long list of books and ask them to read at least two. Throughout the year, we may read one or two books together, but the bulk of their reading is self-selected.

And whether they are reading historical fiction, memoir, romance, science fiction, realistic fiction, or contemporary short stories, they do find their own issues reflected in their literature. As they read they do all the things I do with books: they identify with characters, they enter into foreign settings, they laugh, cry, get angry, and feel afraid. They wonder why things are the way they are, why characters behave as they do. They make predictions and inferences; they critique writers' techniques and find qualities to emulate in their own writing. What I also notice, having looked at Gilligan's research, is that they express themselves in all the ways she identifies. Reading their notebooks, I hear their "justice" and their "care" voices. I see their perennial preoccupation with relationships—familial, boy-girl, girl-girl, girl-group. I hear their need to discover identity and to examine what the future might hold for them as adult women.

Some feminist teachers decry the fact that few YA books today seem to foster strong self-images for girls. At a recent workshop at an NCTE conference, I heard that even *Charlotte's Web* (E. B. White) can be seen as a sexist book! There was not one book the presenter felt comfortable giving to her female adolescent students. Authors, she explained, give us female characters who behave in courageous, strong, creative ways, traditionally male ways—the girl soldier, for example, or the female detective—thereby implying, "Aggression is the ideal,"—or who behave in traditional nurturing ways, caring for those who seem to need them. One depiction urges girls to be more like boys, this woman insisted, while the other perpetuates a dangerous stereotype. Many in the audience agreed, lamenting the paucity of good books for adolescent girls.

Lois Stover, who has made a study of gender issues in the teaching of literature, is not quite so pessimistic. There are titles available, she insists, if we are willing to seek them out. "We must choose books which provide young men and young women with strong, admirable characters who manage to move toward the kind of integration of "male" and "female" morality described by Gilligan." (McCracken and Appleby, 1993, p. 103) Stover goes on to suggest resources for finding such titles and offers suggestions on how to manage discussion of their themes. "We can," she says, "change our literature programs to indicate that we value and respect diversity and that we appreciate both the similarities and differences between the sexes as one small step toward building a future citizenry that accepts individuals on their own terms rather than imposes roles and unrealistic expectations upon them because of their sex." (1993, p. 106)

Committed to the ideal of choice, I do not censor what the girls want to read. However, I am impressed with their apparent ability to take virtually any text and examine it on their own terms. Do they read books that perpetuate stereotypes? Probably. Does it harm them? I hope not irrevocably. In class discussions and in my individual responses to their reading, I ask repeatedly, "Who is telling this story? What difference does that make? Why has the author chosen this point of view? Are there any stereotypes operating here? Why is the character acting this way?" We talk about the fact that women writers tend to portray girls and women as strong and capable of anything. Some male writers do this too. But it is never my intention to spoon-feed my girls only books about strong, brave, female protagonists; indeed, I want them to read also about women who find joy in nurturing their friends and families. I want them to understand that women have choices, that career paths and personal paths are more open than they have ever been, and that the value females place on being in relationship with others is something to celebrate. At times it is a tricky balance: Yes, be independent, be all you can be, but remember that sustaining connections to others is also a strength. Most of all, I hope they will find in their books, girls and women who struggle with these choices, because these are the characters who seem most like them, and like us.

Reading is, with writing, the heart of the curriculum from the beginning. I would meet with the girls six periods a week: once a day, plus a second class that we came to refer to as "Extra English," which was given over entirely to quiet, individual reading. In addition to this, one day a week we would have a reading workshop, exchanging notebooks, sharing excerpts from books we love, discussing elements in our stories that seem important to us. Sometimes we read stories or poems together during this time, write a bit in response, and then have some conversation. Most of the girls come into seventh grade already loving to read, thanks in large part to the passion and intelligent commitment of Mary Nodar and Ann Esselstyn, their fifth and sixth grade teachers. What I want them to do is to use their writing to reflect on what they read (Newkirk, 1988), and to share surprises and insights with one another.

The regular class requirement is to read thirty minutes each night (Rief, 1991) and to write three notebook entries each week, examining what they read. The entries are in the form of letters (Atwell, 1987), one addressed to me and two addressed to classmates. Having the letters in the notebooks prevents inevitable loss and destruction of loose papers. Thus, we are able to look back on the whole trimester, and eventually the whole year, and see change and growth. The notebooks become the "text" for the course: places for girls to do writing practice, draft pieces, reflect on poetry, copy bits of poems they discover, make lists of books they want to read next, etc. (Calkins, 1991) They love trading notebooks in class, writing responses to one another on facing pages. Although these entries are diverse—the girls analyze, criticize, and interpret authors' intentions regularly—it is their personal connections to their books that interest me here. What are they learning about themselves through the act of reading? How is their reading changing the way they view the world?

Voices of Justice and Care

Wallis exhibits a strong sense of justice when writing about Patty Bergen's decision to hide a POW during World War II, in Bette Greene's novel, *The Summer of My German Soldier.*

> Dear Mrs. B.,
>   I don't think Patty made the right decision in helping Anton. No matter how you slice it, he was one of "the enemy." At the POW camp, he wasn't being mistreated. In fact, he would've had a rougher life in Germany among all of the battles. Had Anton been mistreated, it would have been Patty's human duty to help him because you simply don't mistreat people. However, I believe that Patty's helping Anton had nothing to do with her sense of right or wrong.
>   Patty was frequently abused and degraded by her parents. Ruth was the only person who truly loved her. In desperation Patty was trying to find another person to be close to. Anton happened to be around and she knew he appreciated her, her sense of right and wrong diminished in her dire need to find a friend.
>   I can't say I wouldn't have done the same if I were Patty, but in terms of right and wrong, her actions were definitely wrong, in my opinion.

Wallis considers all the factors involved in Patty's decision; she knows that this is not an issue that can be defined in absolute terms, black-white, yes-no. She understands that other concerns have affected Patty's choice, and she ponders this in her commentary. In the past I would have seen Wallis's response as evidence of her careful attention to the book, of her empathy for the characters; now I see it as part of Wallis's own journey of defining herself as a female, as a signpost in her own moral development. She knows that "you simply don't mistreat people" and insists that, had Anton been mistreated, she would have had another opinion of Patty's behavior. In recognizing Patty's "dire need to find a friend," she is constructing an interpretation of the story.

She knows how vital it is to have friends, to feel close to someone else. She believes that this need affects Patty's ability to distinguish right from wrong. Most astonishing to me is her last paragraph, where Wallis admits that, indeed, given the same need, she might have made the same decision as Patty, even though, objectively, she sees it as wrong.

Sara also finds Patty's behavior objectionable, mostly because it gets her in hot water, and, although she admires Patty, she would act differently herself:

Dear Mrs. B.,

I feel that Patty made the wrong choice by helping Anton. Patty knew how much trouble she could get into and I feel that that should have changed her mind. By the middle of the book, you could really tell how close their relationship had gotten and if Patty would have decided no, and not to hide him, she would have had a much easier time letting go of him when he left for New York. She also wouldn't have been as sad when he got shot and died.

I felt so bad for Patty when everybody found out about her sin and called her names like "Jew Nazi-Lover." I never thought that people would do something that mean to a 12-year-old. It was also hard for me to believe that Patty was only 12. She seemed more mature to me. It would have been very hard for me to hide a German soldier like she did. I would have had trouble getting Anton food and I probably would have gotten caught long before Patty did.

Another part that made me sad was when Patty was in Reform School, how her parents never came to visit her. Patty might have done the wrong thing and made her parents very upset, but they should still come to see their daughter.

Overall, I feel that Patty was very brave. It seems to me that she cared about Anton a little bit more than herself. There were such serious consequences for what she did, and that is what would have stopped me from doing what Patty Bergen did.

Sara the pragmatist! Sara does not address the issues of right or wrong or of duty at all. For her, the question revolves around the consequences. Loving Anton as Patty does, causes her pain, and keeping her distance might have allowed her to escape being hurt. Sara considers the practical issues of feeding Anton, recognizing that she might not have been up to the task. But no matter what a

child does, Sara believes, parents should love and support her;
Patty's parents behave badly. Finally, the fact that Patty "cared for
Anton a little bit more than herself" impresses her. This is the fem-
inine ideal—to put the other before oneself. Sara may aspire to it,
but right now, she sees too many obstacles to make it feasible for
Patty.

Jamon sees the whole issue very differently:

Dear Mrs. Barbieri,

I think that Patty should have helped Anton because he
was nice to her and just because he was a German soldier, it
doesn't mean that he was mean by himself. He may have just
been fighting for his country, and he personally didn't like
what the Nazis were doing to the Jews. I think it's good that
Patty helped Anton.

Jamon is sure of herself. For her, this is not a matter of practical circumstances at all, nor is it a question of duty or need or of
putting someone else first. For Jamon it's simple. Anton was "nice
to her," and that fact overrides everything else. Anton's behavior
towards Patty indicates to her that he was, in all probability, not
even a Nazi. Anton deserves Patty's help, according to Jamon, because he is a good person. In this instance Jamon is what Nel Noddings terms "one-caring." (1984, p. 33)

In a 1988 white paper titled "Translating Girls' Voices: Two
Languages of Development," based on early work with the Laurel-
Harvard Study, Carol Gilligan and Annie G. Rogers note: "The seventh graders speak a clear, straight-forward language of love and
care. They notice suffering, feel compassion for others and for
themselves and want to help out. They do not evaluate this wish
to help. . . ."

My girls do exhibit such a language, but Wallis and Sara also
evaluate their wish to help, weighing the consequences, the special circumstances, and the complexities of the situation. They remind me that, for women, moral choices involve understanding
the bigger picture. Right and wrong are seen, not as absolute objective principles, but in terms of the need to care for others whenever possible. "Faced with a hypothetical moral dilemma," writes
Nel Noddings, "women often ask for more information." (1984,
p. 2) Jamon fills in—"he personally didn't like what the Nazis were
doing to the Jews"—and makes her judgment accordingly. Thinking and writing about their reading in this way offers the girls an

opportunity to rehearse the moral decisions they will inevitably be faced with in their own lives.

Defining Self in Relationship to Others

The girls often like to work together in small groups, choosing pieces to read and talk about from class sets of short story collections. While I provide the books, each group chooses from among them and decides which stories to read.

According to Brown and Gilligan's findings, girls' sense of identity is deeply rooted in their perceptions of relationship, which they see as a "way of knowing, an opening between self and other that creates a channel for discovery, an avenue for knowledge." (1992, p. 28) My girls explore this avenue in their reading.

Following Atwell and Rief's lead, I try to reply to their reading responses thoughtfully and specifically. After reading a Robert Cormier story with her group, Christine looks at her female character's behavior.

> Dear Mrs. Barbieri,
>
> In "Mine on Thursdays" by Robert Cormier, I was surprised at first about how happy the girl was all the time, but then I realized that you can't end your life and mope around because your parents are divorced.
>
> I liked how in this story Robert Cormier uses the rollercoaster to symbolize the times that are coming up when the father wouldn't want to be with the daughter.
>
> My feelings when I read this book were more toward the father. I felt sorry for him when she came off the ride and would not talk to him because he didn't go on with her. Even though I realized what this girl was going through, I don't think she should have been angry at him, risking their father-daughter relationship.

In past years, I would have supported the fact that Christine sympathizes with the father, whom some other readers see as the villain in the piece. Indeed, this reflects a high degree of empathy on her part. However, my understanding that the notion of "the perfect girl" and of "ideal relationships" often leads to the denial of authentic feeling and knowing (Gilligan, 1992) gives me another way to respond:

Dear Christine:

Many children have to cope with parents' divorces, and it is really, really difficult. My feeling is that this man has "risked the relationship" by his drinking and his selfishness. I am glad you're so compassionate towards the father who is such an unhappy man. But I wonder if you may be letting him off the hook here. I think he has some responsibility too.

Although I don't want to push the girls into my way of looking at a particular story—at least I try to guard against this—I do share my honest reactions to their comments. In this case, I was moved by Christine's assumption that the little girl should hide her feelings to avoid upsetting her father, and I wanted to challenge it, gently. Wallis, on the other hand is much tougher on the father in the story:

Dear Mrs. Barbieri,

My group and I read the story "Mine on Thursdays" by Robert Cormier. I think the father is a scum. (He's like Arnie Becker on *L.A. Law* except for his alcohol problem.) I can't say I feel for him as a person because "feeling sorry for" is one of those phrases that can mean multiple things and can be interpreted different ways.

In this context, I think feeling sorry for him means something like, "the poor man, Allison should have stood by him through his hardships. All he needs is love." He has problems and until he's attempting to fix them or admit there is a problem: STAY AWAY. The guy's an alcoholic, and a womanizer. He needs professional help. No amount of love from a wife can cure that.

I am sorry the issue occurred, because innocent people like Holly suffer the consequences of a broken home. I'm not sure what to say about Allison. I'd be interested in knowing if Allison thought she could change him with her love. This idea of "changing" your spouse with love, when a serious or developing problem is evident, is dumb, not to mention unsuccessful. A spouse is not a "project" like an old house one is restoring.

I think the father used Holly and with her growing maturity she started realizing she was second fiddle to her father's "other" interests. I think the Rocket Ride made her realize her father wouldn't be there to stand by her, nor regarding beer or blondes. I'm not sure if Holly realized exactly what her father's "other" interests were, but I think she sensed something. This is part of the reason it's good that the change in Holly and her father's relationship happened early. If it hadn't, Holly would've realized more and more truth, to the point that she would hate her father. Especially if Allison was encouraging the feeling at home.

In the future, I hope Holly's dad will try to gain her love, not her spirit of adventure, or he might eternally lose both.

P.S. I think the father used Holly as a possession, not a person, in the sense that he used her as someone to feel loved by.

Reading Wallis's comments, I understand that, for her, issues of relationship are tied in with issues of moral decision-making. She condemns the father in the story for neglecting his relationship with Holly. She wonders about the mother's intentions, cynical in her opinion that "love" does not conquer all. Since I cannot sit in on all the girls' discussions of their stories—I move from group to group—I do not know how Wallis's point of view affected the group or vice versa. It seems, however, that Wallis is clear about what she knows. It is a relief to me that she does not place the responsibility for salvaging the family on the mother or the daughter; she understands that life is more complicated than that, and she appears to support Holly's right to back away from her relationship with her father.

For Brady, suppressing real feelings is sometimes okay:

Dear Mrs. Barbieri,

I am reading *Checking on the Moon* by Jenny Davis. I feel sorry for Cab, she is moving to a town with unknown people. I can't imagine that. Cab certainly is strong, independent, and confident . . .

Earlier, when Cab was driving to Whasco, she said, "everything I knew was speeding by, dropping off, disappearing around some corner, into some fog." Then she started to think that people were starting to slip away like her friends. I think this really hurts Cab, but she's scared to confront her mother about it.

I believe Cab will face up to the facts sooner or later and realize it's life. Sometimes life is easy to live, and at other times you need to wait and let things get better, but in the meantime, it doesn't do any good to get frustrated, which a lot of people do. I have confidence in Cab, and I believe if she is patient with her new way of life, she will be a successful and fun person to be around. If a person overflows with optimism, they will go much farther in life, than a person who is overwhelmed in pessimism. I strongly believe this and this is where Cab shines through with her neverending fine qualities. I admire Cab for her self-control about this radical change in her life.

I cannot disagree with Brady's belief in having a positive attitude, but it worries me that she so wholeheartedly endorses Cab's decision not to talk to her mother about her feelings. Does Brady think that the way to cope with sorrow is to "grin and bear it?" "For girls to remain responsive to themselves," writes Gilligan, "they must resist the conventions of feminine goodness; for them to remain responsive to others, they must resist the values placed on self-sufficiency and independence in North American culture." (1990, p. 10) Is Cab responsive to her own needs here, I wonder? Is she responsive to the needs of her family?

> Dear Brady,
>   Are you like Cab yourself? What do you do when you feel sad about something, such as losing a friend? What you say about optimism is important and true. We all have to endure difficult circumstances in life—you know that Erin and I were sad to leave New Hampshire—and it's good to be positive and trust that things will get better. Can Cab feel better by denying her real feelings? Maybe her mother feels bad too. It's often better to be honest about sad feelings and, when possible, to talk about them. What do you think?

Brady does not comment on my response, but a few weeks later she reads Robert Cormier's *We All Fall Down* and writes:

> Dear Mrs. B.
>   . . . Out of all the characters in the book, I feel like I know Jane the best . . . I think she has drawn closer to her sister and brother, because Karen is in the hospital, and Jane has always thought she was a brat, but now she's realizing how dull it is without her . . .
>   I think that once Karen leaves the hospital, the family will be closer, but for them to accomplish this, they need to discuss their real feelings about what has happened, and then proceed in present day life. If the family doesn't share their

thoughts together, they will never become closer. Jane and Artie have expressed their opinions together and they're already closer.

I give Jane a lot of credit. She is the one trying to bring the family together and talk about what has happened in the past. Obviously, she is a very shy and sensitive person, willing to listen to others ecspecially others who she loves and cares about. She, I believe, is the one who is going to bring this family closer than they've ever been before!

Brady has been thinking about sharing real feelings, a shift from her earlier attitude. It is her literature that gives her varied perspectives and allows her to reconsider her ideas. The Cormier book is one I have difficulty with, due to its graphic violence, but for this student, it is a powerful vehicle for thinking. Another argument for choice and against censorship.

Dear Brady,

This book is shocking, even though we do hear about violent crime every night on the news. Cormier has a real knack for making readers' hearts pound. He makes it real.

Sometimes, when people are victims of violence, they suffer long-term psychological damage that makes talking about the incident difficult. You are wise to recognize that talking together is precisely what this family needs. It is sad that they are not pulling together, but, to me, it seems plausible. Sometimes people think, if we don't talk about it, it will be less than real or it will become undone. I read a book called *The Prince of Tides* by Pat Conroy where the mother refused to talk about the violence her family had endured. It was a type of denial.

Let's hope that Jane will influence her family to begin the healing process that will enable them all to go on with their lives. Honest talk, as you say, is the only way to go.

Rachel also examines relationships in her books, entering into each story in a personal way:

Dear Mrs. B.,

I am reading *After the Rain* by Norma Fox Mazer. I think that (so far) this book is a good blend of romance, reality, fantasy, and generations. I feel very sorry for Rachel, as her brother Jeremy is gone and hardly writes to her. I think that

Rachel definitely hides too many of her feelings. I think Lewis
will be good for her . . .
    I'm getting mixed messages about Lewis. He seems to be
shy a lot, then he gets on the phone with Rachel and goes
crazy.
    Rachel will be a big help to Izzy with his cancer, and I fore-
see a special relationship between them.

Right away, Rachel moves to discuss relationships in the character's life—ones with her brother, friend Lewis, and grandfather
Izzy. She notes that the fictional Rachel "hides her feelings way
too much" and hopes that the new friendship will help her be
more open. She recognizes the universal need to be understood,
accepted, and valued; she, like most of her classmates, longs for
this kind of relationship herself. Her last comment about Izzy's
cancer shows her belief that the young girl in the story has the potential to be a true "one-caring" for her grandfather. She makes a
prediction based on her belief that such caring does indeed build
and strengthen relationships.

In my response to Rachel, I suggest that she focus on her observation that the character (also named Rachel) hides feelings a
lot. To what extent has she noticed this in herself or in others?

Dear Rachel,
    Great book! Rachel does hide her feelings, as you've no-
ticed. Is this believable to you? I notice it sometimes in real
life. What makes people do this? I'm thinking of the man in
the Anne Tyler story, "With All Flags Flying." Do you think
boys and men hide their feelings more than females? What
makes Lewis so different?

In her next entry, Rachel reacts to another book, but finds
time to reply to me about Mazer's book too:

Dear Mrs. B.,
    . . . Now to your questions, I think that people hide feel-
ings because they are afraid of what others will think of them.
I do think that males hide feelings more often than females
because they're still thought of as the "stronger" sex, and
they are afraid that showing feelings will look "weak," therefore making them seem more like a girl. I think Lewis is different in the way that he changes, but not according to the

people he's with. He is talkative towards the people who are quiet (Rachel) and silent towards talkers such as Helena and Mikey. This is plausible, I think.

Of course, since their friendships are central to their lives, it is natural that the girls appreciate stories of friendship in their literature. I am always excited and pleased to know the extent to which my girls enter the world of story. Coming from a writing perspective myself, I urge the girls to look at their texts as products of other writers' crafts. My good friend Karen Smith has pushed my own thinking here, helping me see other priorities—such as recognizing stories as means of knowing ourselves—and as I read Danielle's entry, I think of Karen as well as Carol Gilligan.

Dear Marlana,

I've finished *Going on Twelve* by Candice F. Ranson. Kobie in this book quits the mural contest and her class loses. She thinks she has no talents. People often think when they are put down that they have no qualities, but everyone has qualities and I wish I could have been in the book and told her that. She has a best friend, though, who she shares all her secrets with, and I think that it's neat, no matter whose side is right, that Gretchen will always stick up for Kobie, but sometimes she gets angry at Kobie. It helped Kobie a lot to have a friend. Kobie thinks the most popular girl is a jerk. Often in every school there is a girl who is "popular" but almost more people don't like her than do. Kobie at times gets stressed out and sometimes I feel like her where everything is going wrong for me that day. One day she gets so angry at a boy and does something mean to him she later regrets. We often let our body work faster than our mind and it doesn't do exactly what we told it to do.

How intuitive Danielle is! Brown and Gilligan discuss the issue of "popularity" and see it as Danielle does. "Understandably, popular girls are outwardly doted on at the same time they are privately envied or despised," they write. "Other girls watch the popular girl closely since she has the potential to "use" or hurt people and also to elevate them in the eyes of adults. Girls wonder who she is aligning with and why—is she showing off, looking for the approval of adults, or is she in relationship with other girls, a collaborator behind the scenes?" (1992, p. 101) Kristin (See Chapter 3) addresses this dilemma in her fiction writing; Danielle looks at it in her reading. Both are rehearsing their own choices, their own behavior.

Neeti explores another issue: What happens when a friendship changes?

> Dear Molly,
>
> I am reading *Middle School Blues* by Lou Kaṣsem. It is about a girl named Cindy who is in her first year of Middle School. First of all, the girl had a best friend, but her best friend seemed to "mature" faster and became friends with a different group, who, by the way, Cindy hated. This hurt her a lot especially since she was "competing" with the head of the group. Both girls were very smart, but Cindy wanted to make friends, not be a competitor of her own classmate. This may sound confusing, but it is something that happens. In fact, this sort of thing happened to me during my first year in Middle School. I thought I had a "best friend," but she dumped me for someone else. It really hurt, but I think it also helped me. I realized that people aren't always what they seem to be, but there are many other good people who may not appear nice.
>
> There is so much to talk about friendship. Maybe that'll be my next idea for a story—Friendship.

What interests me here is that Neeti not only echoes the frustration girls experience in trying to differentiate between friendships that are real and those that are artificial, but she also seems to accept the character's belief that competition is not a good thing. Being accepted and valued, being in harmony with one's friends, is more important than being superior in any sense. Deborah Tannen finds this same inclination in adult women. (1990, p. 218)

Of course, in addition to reflecting on family situations and friendship, the girls are interested in how boys and girls behave in relationships. Sarah is one of the most prolific readers in the class—I believe she read more than fifty books during her seventh grade year—and she has a special interest in historical fiction. Here she focuses on a special friendship:

> Dear Mrs. B.,
>
> This weekend I finished reading *The Good Side of My Heart* by Ann Rinaldi. This book is a piece of realistic-contemporary fiction, and in a lot of ways different from Ann Rinaldi's other

books of historical fiction. This book is about a girl who finds friendship in a boy that was kicked out of military school. He helps her work through her problems such as: her father, the editor and her brother, the priest . . .

I like how Ann Rinaldi makes the main character in some aspects a vulnerable little girl but in other ways a young-adult because I think in some ways we are all like this, sometimes I want to rush home and hug my mom and cry over all the bad things that have occurred and other times I want to be an adult and handle my problems myself, I guess this is what growing up is about.

I admire Sarah's willingness to be so honest, and, in this case, my response is little more than an acknowledgement of her feelings.

Dear Sarah,

How right you are! Growing up is exactly what you describe, at least it was for me. It was confusing and painful sometimes. Writing about your feelings can be helpful, as you know.

Rinaldi is certainly prolific, isn't she? She has more books than I realized, and you are finding them all. Thanks for telling me about this one.

Ann Rinaldi is one of Sarah's favorite authors. Even when reflecting on historical fiction, she looks at issues of identity and admires this writer for breaking down stereotypes:

Dear Mrs. B.,

I read *Time Enough for Drums* by Ann Rinaldi. I loved this book; I love this author. This book takes place during the Revolutionary War and is about a girl who is forced to change from a mischievous, immature girl to a mature, responsible woman. This book has all the elements to cater to my liking: danger, adventure, and even Romance, while situated in a well-researched historical setting. My favorite part is the romance, and I know this is typical girl stuff. I guess that doesn't matter; maybe I like romance in the books I read because I'm otherwise very practical, except for when I read. I like reading because I get put in situations that I will never experience.

I like how in Ann Rinaldi's books the hero is a heroine and that the guy the heroine loves isn't perfect. Normally in a romance book the girl is helpless and the guy is always there to save the helpless girl, but not in Ann Rinaldi's books. She makes the girl strong and I like that. The guy isn't perfect either, he's not necessarily dashing, he just has a kind heart and a good personality. I think this makes the book realistic.

Danielle writes about the pitfalls of getting involved with boys too soon. An avid skater interested in serious competition, many of her reading choices reflect her passion for the ice.

> Dear Bernice,
> I have finished *Winner's Waltz* by Barbara J. Mumma and *Thumb's Up* by Elizabeth Manely. Both of these stories were about ice-skating. In *Winner's Waltz* the plot is mainly about an ice-dancing team who constantly fight, but they manage to pull themselves together before the major competition. I think all the pair teams at the Olympics have to admit that there were times when they fought. Also, a big problem in skating and in those two ice-skating books I read recently was both of the skaters because they had boyfriends didn't care anymore about skating. This happens to a lot of skaters. There's a saying, "Once you kiss a boy, you can kiss the boards," meaning once you kiss a boy, forget about skating. A lot of coaches and parents get angry because they spend all their money in skating and then it gets all wasted on a boy. I don't think having a boyfriend is work risking your career until like after the Olympics. People go too far to have their career wasted on boys.

Visions of Womanhood

The girls often discuss their impressions of the adults in their novels, of course, defining in the process their dreams and expectations for the future. They are aware that they have a whole range of opportunities ahead of them, and they attempt, in their reading, to look at different sets of values.

Danielle speculates on what her future holds when she reads, "Do You Know That Feeling?" by Cynthia Rylant:

> Dear Mrs. Barbieri,
> I read this story from *A Couple of Kooks* by Cynthia Rylant . . . There must be a lot of love for the girl to bake brownies and make soup every day at exact times. That also shows she's lonely. I wouldn't do that for my husband.

Maybe only for a week. I would go to work. I could not stand not working everyday. I would get so bored at home. I think the boy looks pretty ugly, but the girl seems to like him and it shows you she likes him for what he is on the inside.

Most of the girls in the class feel as Danielle does. They expect to have families—definitely children—but they also expect to have exciting careers outside the home. Ironically, few of them would consider teaching as a viable option, although Torey Hayden's books are among the best loved in the room. Wallis admires her honesty:

Dear Mrs. B.,

I'm reading a book by Torey Hayden called *Somebody Else's Kids.* So far, I've met two of the four children, Boo and Lori. . . .

How Edna, an older teacher who is Lori's first-grade teacher annoys me to no end! She is like an icicle—has a glowing, shimmery look, but is cold and insensitive. She claims Lori is hopeless and should be cast away because of her injuries that have damaged her brain.

I like how Torey Hayden portrays herself in this book as a human. She seems very real and not overly patient and loving to the point of being fake. She mentions times of frustration and triumph, not just triumph.

What is important to Wallis, as she contrasts these two teachers, are qualities of warmth and honesty. While caring is important, as opposed to being "cold and insensitive," it is also essential that a woman be "very real" and "a human."

Rachel has different expectations as she reads *My Antonia* by Willa Cather:

Dear Elizabeth,

I have really enjoyed reading *My Antonia,* so far. I'm really reading a lot to try to get this book read! Antonia sounds like a really nice person, and a great friend to Jimmy. They are both very lucky to have eachother for friends. I feel really sorry for Antonia when her father dies. I guess it was kind of good, he didn't have to live in a place that his heart wasn't in. I've grown to not like Antonia's mother very much, because she tends to only talk about what she wants, what other people have and she wants, and what she used to have and wants.

Here Rachel evaluates the behavior of the adult woman in the book, seeing Antonia's mother's "wanting" as a character flaw. Indeed, in many of her reading responses, Rachel articulates her admiration for selflessness in women, something Brown and Gilligan see as dangerous. Girls' fear is that selfish attitudes or behaviors will lead to loss of approval or even loss of love. (1992)

Rachel has written this letter to her friend Elizabeth, and I do not write a response. However, shortly after noticing her comments, endorsing selflessness, I initiate a class discussion on the topic, bringing in several poems for the girls to consider. (See Chapter 5.)

I love reading the girls' notebooks, where they seem so comfortable being frank: sharing doubts, changing their minds, or even getting angry. Reading their words gives me unique insight and helps me know what they are thinking and what they may need from me next. It is, after all, their classroom, and I want the agenda to be theirs too.

Like so many women of my generation, I remember my childhood classrooms quite differently. Thanks to my family, I had plenty of choice in what I read, and I made (stole) the time to read voraciously. But that was another era; Mary Ellen Giacobbe and Nancie Atwell were children themselves. So what I didn't have was response, the chance to share my reactions to books with other readers and to hear and learn from their interpretations, enhancing the experience for all of us. There were periods when I read a book a day—I was insatiable—with little or no thought about what my books might mean to my own real life. For me reading was pure escape, and joyful as it was, I can't help but wish things had been a bit different. For now I believe that it is not only in reading but also in writing and talking about books that we come to define who we are and what it is we hope our lives will be.

5

Dissonance and Harmony: Talking Things Over

_____

And mostly I'm grateful that I take this world so seriously.

—Mary Oliver, *The Gift*

Aversion to Violence

SCENE: FIRST week of school, Room 311, seventh-grade English. Nineteen girls, bright-eyed, full of energy, and eager to please, file in and choose seats in the circle ringing the room.

"I know you are probably a very good teacher and all," Marlana says gently, "but I have a question for you, if that's okay?"

"Of course, that's okay," I reply, delighted.

"Why did you make us read a book about war?"

For a minute, I am confused. War? Make them? She is referring to the traditional summer reading list which includes *My Brother Sam is Dead* by James Collier and Christopher Collier. I stammer something about choice. Haven't they picked three from the list that appealed to them? Well, Marlana explains, she has read them all. So have many others. "It was pretty gory," she insists. "It really upset me. Why is it even on the list?"

As I explain the book's relevance to American history, I see, in some faces, bewilderment. On the one hand, they are not used to challenging a teacher, but, apparently, this book has bothered them.

"What do the rest of you think?" I ask.

Silence.

"Anyone?"

"I liked the book," says Emily. "It makes you see how the family felt and all. It's a good book."

"Okay, how does the family feel? How do they cope with it?"

"Well, it's very personal to them. They have to make a lot of sacrifices," another girl offers.

So early in the year, I cannot blame the girls for feeling shy. I ask them to write for a few minutes in their notebooks, giving their reactions to the book or a comment on what Marlana has suggested. As they write, I write too, surprised that the issue of violence has come up so soon.

Soon volunteers share their thoughts, the first expressing sympathy for the Meeker family. Sara wonders how they can go on living. Emily expresses admiration for their valor.

Wallis says, "We should think about all these sacrifices when we are watching the fireworks on the Fourth of July."

"I think it was hardest on the mother," says Caroline. "Her son was away being a soldier, and later on in the war her husband was killed. Then when her oldest son is killed, the war is over for her. This war has hurt her and will affect her for years to come."

"I'm glad our family didn't have anything like this," someone says. Murmurs of agreement. "It must have been horrible." "I don't think about all the little sacrifices when I think about the battles." "It wasn't only the soldiers. . . ." "But it wasn't fair what happened to Sam. . . ." They are warming up to the subject, beginning to offer personal reactions.

"When Sam died," Emily reads from her notebook, "Tim probably felt alone and devastated. His brother and father were both dead and his mother had gone numb in feeling."

Empathy reigns; they acknowledge the tragedies the war has caused this family and others. Few express an opinion on whether or not the war was necessary or justified.

Molly reads a notebook entry:

> In my lifetime I have lived through one war, and I hope that never changes to two. Operation Desert Storm did not affect my daily life at all. Therefore, it never clicked in my mind that the United States was truly at war. But if Desert Storm was fought in the United States, who knows, I might not be here now.
>
> In reading *My Brother Sam is Dead*, I realized how devastating wars can be. There are so many good and innocent people whose lives are destroyed. If people would just settle their differences by talking things over and compromising, it would be so much better. I don't think we could have done anything about Operation Desert Storm or World War II because in both cases we were dealing with mad men. But in the Revolutionary War, I do think that there might have been another way besides war.

Other girls nod. Someone says, "I agree with that. . . ."
Sarah raises her hand, eager to read next:

> I think that the Revolutionary War was important. I usually don't believe in violence, but in this case, it was important for our freedom. Benjamin Franklin tried negotiating but nothing worked. If we hadn't fought the war, we might never have gotten our independence.

"I don't think violence is ever good," says Molly.

"But if we hadn't gone to war, where would we be?" Sarah asks. "Think about that. I'm glad they had the war."

"I don't know, but. . . ," Molly stops suddenly.

"I agree with Molly," offers Ali, "There might have been a way to settle it without killing people."

Silence again.

I try to stay quiet, remembering the suffering in the novel and my own New Englander's pride in the American Revolution. The girls are making me face it from a new angle. Is violence ever justified, I ask myself?

"Any response to Sarah? What do you think? Was the war necessary? Was it worth the violence?"

There erupts a general hum in the room as the girls consider the question. "Well, they did try to get concessions from the king and all." "And we had to get away from England. . . ." "Maybe they could have, I don't know, talked more or something. . . ." "Was that really true about the cows? Could that happen?" They interrupt one another, apparently comfortable with overlapping comments. (Tannen, 1990) After a few minutes, the period is nearly over, so we come together as a big group. Feelings are high, and opinions are mixed. Several girls speak eagerly: Violence should be avoided, yes, but isn't a free America best? Maybe violence was the price exacted. Maybe there could have been another way. Catherine, a British subject, in this country for four years, listens and nods pensively. I wonder what she is thinking.

I ask the girls to reflect on the discussion that night in their notebooks, and Marlana writes:

> I had a lot of feelings about today's discussion and the book *My Brother Sam is Dead*. I think my biggest feeling was anger. All through the book I knew Sam was going to die and I figured that he would be killed in action, so I was surprised that he would be executed for stealing his own cows.
>
> My parents never let me watch scary things. They even made me cover my eyes when I was little and horror movie previews came on t.v. They pounded it in so well that now I don't even want to watch scary things. That's why I hate watching the news. Even though it is reality, I hate hearing all the cruel things people do today. I wouldn't have minded Sam's dying, facing the enemy, but he was facing his friends. I am not saying this because Sam was right and he didn't steal the cows, I feel that way even about murderers. Life is a precious thing, a gift from God, and you shouldn't have to give up your gift because you do something bad. Rot in jail maybe, but not die.

> Last year during the war my dad told me if we won the war, Saddam Hussein would be captured and executed. When we wrote about the war I wrote that I think even he deserves to live. This doesn't mean I think he's right, I just think he deserves a life.

Marlana is confident expressing herself in her notebook. Writing has allowed her to expand on her original impulse and to figure out what she really means. Other girls write other opinions, equally heartfelt. It is not necessary that we look at everything the same way, but it is necessary that everyone try to articulate her convictions. It is necessary that in reading books we learn more about ourselves. We do not need to reach consensus when questions come up in our discussions; many issues are just too complex for that. What matters more, to them and to me, is that each person have a chance to consider the questions, and then, to make herself heard and understood.

Ethics

Scene: November, Room 311, seventh-grade English. Priya arrives early, eager to make a request. "Would it be all right if we talked about something from *Merlyn's Pen* today? I read this story last night, and I really want to have a discussion about it."

"Fine," I say. "What is it you read?"

"It's called 'Law versus Morality,' and it's all about a boy and a baseball card and what happened, and I think everyone will have opinions on it."

"Oh, I know the one. Good idea."

The girls arrive, boisterous. When I tell them we're going to switch gears, in light of Priya's request, a few grumble, and one or two run back to their lockers to get their copies of *Merlyn's Pen.* We settle down and read for about ten minutes.

The piece, written by seventh grader Evan Moffic of Bayside Middle School in Milwaukee, Wisconsin, is a commentary on a news account of a young boy who sees a $1,200 baseball card in a shop and asks the inexperienced clerk, "Is this worth $12?" When she says yes, he buys it on the spot, knowing its true value. The boy, Brian, is an aficionado himself, while the clerk is just filling in as a favor. Later, the owner approaches the boy and offers to buy the card back for one hundred dollars, but the boy refuses. The case goes to court, and the boy's father argues that Brian has done nothing illegal. The question, according to writer Evan Moffic, is one of morality. While Brian may be within his legal rights, is he behaving morally here?

Soft gasps as the girls realize the dilemma. Then we write for five minutes before talking. Writing is natural to them now; they do not balk. Writing is safe, a place to figure out what we think, a place to be real. Jamon reads aloud:

"I think this case shows that kids are taken advantage of in card stores, and this time it was the other way around, the kid took advantage of the store. I do take the side of the store in this case. I mean he got it for less than 1/80 of the price! Also, I think that the store shouldn't have had an inexperienced salesclerk, and the saleslady shouldn't have agreed on that price because she knew she was inexperienced, so she should have asked the manager."

The next girl to speak agrees: "Right, and I think when the boy went to court, the judge can't prove that Brian knew the real value. I think the person should've sued Ball-Mart because she's the one who sold the card in the first place. If I were Brian, I wouldn't give the card back for $100 either. I think that it wasn't Brian's fault, but it was the lady who sold it to him and Ball-Mart's fault for having the lady sell in the first place."

"Yeah, that's what I think," says Jenifer. "The lady shouldn't have done it."

"But what about Brian? Do you think he was innocent here?" I ask.

"Not me," says Wallis. "I think he is a pig. Can I read?"

"Of course."

"Brian said people bargain all the time, but he knew he was getting something for much, much less. I don't consider downing the price by $1,188 to be bargaining. Bargaining is when both people are fully aware of what is occurring. In this case, Brian took advantage of an inexperienced sales clerk.

I suppose, when you come down to it, Brian has lost more than his financial gain of $1,188. If he keeps this attitude up, people will team against him, he'll never succeed, and he'll be a lonely old man sitting at home with his baseball card."

"That could be true," says Liz.

"But he really hasn't done anything wrong," says Priya. "He's just smarter than the lady in the store."

"Yeah, that's what I think!" "They shouldn't have let the woman next door take care of the shop if she knew nothing about baseball." "I agree with Priya." "The store should let the boy keep the card." A few frowns. A few shaking heads.

"What do you think, Christine?"

"I think the boy should be able to keep the baseball card."

"Why? What makes you think that?" I ask.

"He does have a receipt that proves its purchase . . . I'm not sure, but I think they should sue the woman at the counter instead of the boy. I think it is the store's fault they lost money, not the boy's. He did ask the salesclerk, didn't he?"

"She was doing the owner a favor by being there, so why should she get sued?" asks Loren. "I don't think that would be fair either. I also don't get the boy's father. Most fathers would probably tell him to take the reward and give it back."

"Maybe not," says Rachel. "The boy really hasn't stolen it. I agree with Christine."

It is a bit like a ping-pong match: back and forth go the comments. "I agree with ———," offered as tribute to another's thinking, but enough dissension to be healthy. Agreeing, finally, to disagree, several nod solemnly.

"Hey, Priya," Haley says, as the day wanes, and the girls pack up their things, "Good class. Do you really think that Brian . . .?" They leave the room talking.

Prejudice and Revenge

Scene: November, Laurel School Chapel, early afternoon.

The room is hushed, dark, as we wait for the play, "Ice Wolf," to begin. We are seated in chairs around a platform in the center of the room, and it is here that the action will unfold. The mythical story takes place on a frozen tundra, and the careful lighting somehow makes us shiver. Anatou, a young girl, is tormented and eventually banished because she does not look like the others in her community: a story of prejudice and cruelty. Later, we watch, astonished, as the main stage is revealed as an eerie forest, full of danger and ritual, full of fear. Anatou has become a wolf and returns to her village to seek vengeance on those who have hurt her.

The hour flies by, and we are enthralled by the excellent acting, the stark and unusual costumes, the extraordinary set design. I am grateful to Middle School director Andrea Archer for suggesting that we come up here for this production by older students, as I know it will give us lots to talk about back in Room 311. As usual, we turn to our notebooks first.

"I loved this play," reads Emily. "I thought that the ending was sad, but it showed us much about people. I don't think that Anatou was right to turn into a wolf and then kill some of the Eskimo villagers. By doing that the Eskimos thought that all wolves and woodland animals were bad. I can understand how Anatou felt with all of the hurt, anger, and sorrow kept up inside of her. But I do think that she should forgive and forget. If she couldn't forgive them, then she should have forgotten about them and left them alone.

When I left the chapel after the play, I felt badly about how I had treated some people when I shouldn't have. I should have tried to understand them just like Anatou should have tried to do that with the villagers . . ."

General assent in the class. The Eskimos are definitely cruel to Anatou. They have no right to treat her the way they have. It seems a reflection of our society, the girls believe, where prejudice is everywhere.

"I've noticed that when people are different or don't have any other friends, they're really nice inside," says Molly. "When people don't have any friends, they begin thinking "what's wrong with me?" Really nothing is."

"The message here," offers Bernice, "is don't judge a person by what he or she looks like. They shouldn't have judged her badly because she looked different."

"That's true," says Sara. "People should never hate or be mean to someone because they are different. These days people won't make fun of you because you are a different color, but they might make fun of your clothes or the way your hair is done. I really don't like it when this happens. Most of the time I feel bad for the person who is being made fun of."

"One thing that surprised me," offers Marlana, "was the angle of the prejudice. I know that there is prejudice from Caucasian people to black people, and as a result black people separate themselves from white people. But in this play, the Eskimos made Anatou leave because she DIDN'T have dark skin. That's why she is cruel to them later."

Any other reactions to the play, I wonder?

"Well, you can't escape your problems by running away," someone comments.

"Lots of times people want to run away, but they have to face their problems. I agree with Bernice," says Christine.

"But later she gets even. Everyone hurt this girl so much," says Bernice, "that it was only natural for her to hurt the Eskimos."

"Yes," says someone else. "They had kicked her when she was down. They refused to feed her, and they wouldn't talk to her."

"Right," another girl pipes in. "Even Turto, her best friend, wasn't allowed to talk to her. When she was first born, people wanted to put her out in the snow!"

"Violence isn't right," Sara admits, "but even the gentlest person gets angry and can lash out. They were so mean to her."

"I don't think it was right for Anatou to kill the Eskimos," Caroline reads from her notebook. "She should have listened to her friend's warning and stayed in the forest. She wanted revenge on the people but could have done that in other ways. Anatou could have stolen the "catch of the day" at night. Before killing all those people she should have thought of how the people would react. I think that Anatou is trying to be a wolf but is really more like a human. No wolf would go to the village unless mad from hunger. I don't think Anatou made the right choice . . . "

Others disagree, reminding her that Anatou was the real victim. She had every right to kill those who had banished her from her home as a child. General agitation in the room; the girls are disturbed by the play. We write again.

Caroline amends her entry, and volunteers to read again: I have mixed feelings after I heard everyone's responses. I changed my mind. I probably would have killed the people but would have thought of my friends first.

Sara writes:

I know that anti-Semitism means hatred of Jews. Sometimes people are that way because they don't know any better. Maybe that is the same with the villagers. They probably didn't know anything about Anatou or white people. And that is where the problem comes in. The villagers didn't know enough to understand Anatou. They thought everyone had to be like them and if someone wasn't they were strange and something was the matter with them. Besides having the play teach you about this, it is also making you really think. It wants you to decide for yourself if Anatou did the right thing by going back to the village and killing someone. The play teaches you and makes you really think.

Sexuality and Identity

Scene: Early spring, Jabberwocky Bookstore, Cleveland Heights. The lake-effect gray gives way to snatches of blue sky, there is a new hum in the air, and I am here celebrating. I grab a few new paperbacks for the classroom along with a new book by Bette Greene—*The Drowning of Stephan Jones*. The girls love *Summer of My German Soldier* by this same author, so I am excited. In a hurry to get back to school for my next class, I do not read the jacket to see what the story is about; I just buy it.

Back in Room 311 I sit waiting for the sixth period class to arrive. I begin to read the plot summary of Greene's new novel: "For Carla, Rachetville, Arkansas, would be heaven on earth if only handsome Andy Harris would show some interest in her. While attempting to attract Andy's attention at work, Carla notices two men shopping in his father's store who are not locals. As the men discuss their household purchases, it becomes evident that they are gay . . . Andy's reaction to the men surprises Carla, but she is so blinded by her infatuation that she manages to overlook his faults. But when Andy convinces his pals to help him harass the "sodomites," explaining that his cause is just because it is rooted in his religious convictions, Carla finds it harder to deny Andy's darker side . . . Bette Greene's hard-hitting exploration and condemnation of prejudice in the name of social conformity will deeply affect readers, as the quest against oppression and the cause of justice is championed."

Something begins to throb right behind my eyes. What will I do about this book? Since the girls select their own titles, we have hundreds in the room. Whenever a girl wants one, she puts her name on the sign-out sheet. Should I say nothing and add this book to our collection?

The girls spill into the room, full of gossip and spring fever. They begin to trade notebooks, ready to reply to each other's reading entries. But I interrupt them.

"I went out during lunch today and picked up a new book. I didn't read the jacket or a review. I just grabbed it because it's by Bette Greene."

Then I read them the blurb. They sit wide-eyed.

"I think this sounds like a great book," I say. "But I was wondering what you thought. I know you like to read different kinds of things, but this is pretty nontraditional. How do you feel about it?"

"Mrs. B.," comes a small voice, "can you get your money back?"

"Well, probably I can, but is that what you think I should do? I want to read it myself, and I can just keep it at my house, if nobody's interested. Do you think anyone in here would like to read it?"

"Yes," says Eve. "I think my mother would want me to read it. We have a lot of friends who are gay, and they are really nice people." Suspecting some level of discomfort around the issue of homosexuality among the Laurel middle schoolers, I admire Eve's candor.

Silence. All eyes on me. Has Eve ventured too far? What do I want them to say? What is the right answer here? I wait for them to make the next move.

"I don't think the whole class should have to read it," says Jennifer. "My father is a minister, and I don't think he would want me reading a book like this. We don't talk about it, but that's just my impression."

"Well, we don't have to read it as a class," I say. "Are there other options here?"

Pros and cons abound. What will happen if anyone who wants to read it borrows it? Whose parents might object and why? What is censorship and how do we feel about it? Should some books be saved until readers are older and more mature? Some hands are waving, but many voices call out spontaneously. "Let's read it in groups." "Read it to us." "Don't make a big deal of it. Put it on the shelf." "My parents don't care what I read." "Can I read it first?"

Most girls feel strongly about their right to read whatever they choose. They thrive on this freedom, and believe it is their right. I believe it too.

"Put it on the bookcase," says Brady. "That way anyone who wants it can sign it out. It sounds like a great book."

"Or maybe you could put it on your desk and that way you could decide who should read it. And then you'd know who had it," a more timid soul suggests.

"How would I decide who should read it and who shouldn't?" I wonder.

"You know who can handle it and who would be shocked," one girl insists. "You should keep some kind of control over this."

"But I don't do that with other books," I remind her. "You sign out whatever you want. You never have to ask my permission. Tell me why this book is different."

A flurry of reaction. "It isn't different!" "We should read what we want to read." "Let's make a sign-up list!" "My mother will probably want to read it too."

I suggest they go home and discuss this matter with their parents. I want them to open up the same sort of dialogue at home that we are having now in class. Some parents, like the minister, might prefer that their children wait a bit before examining issues like homophobia, and I want to respect their right to be involved in the decision.

"We're not babies, you know," says Amy. "I think we should all read it. We don't know enough about this, and it is a big issue in our society. We need to learn more about it."

Silence again. I watch the girls seek out the eyes of their close friends, as if searching for the "right" thing to say next. I wait.

"I don't know anyone who's gay, but I think if that's that person's choice, it is nobody else's business," says Emily.

"Right," says Sarah. "Why do some people think they can tell other people how to live their lives?"

"Well," Jennifer ventures, "some religions say it's a sin to be gay."

"I don't think it's a sin," says Eve. "And I know my mother doesn't either."

As we talk, the girls pass the book around and read the cover and a few excerpts, intrigued.

"Okay," I say. "Who would like to read this book?"

More than half the hands in the room shoot up. "Can I have it tonight?" asks Emily.

"Well, no, I think I'd like to read it first myself, Emily," I tell her. "That way I'll be able to have a more informed conversation with you about it."

I take the book home and read it in one sitting. Carla, the main character, feels familiar to me at once. She could be a girl in our class.

> I want everyone to like me! So what if once in a while I don't like or pretend to dislike people that I really like. What's the big deal? It's just that simple: "I want to be liked," she insists to her mother. . . . There's nothing more important than being liked. (48)

It is the aching need of every seventh-grade girl I know. Carla knows that harassing the gay couple is wrong, but she cannot bring herself to defy Andy; she wants too much to be his girlfriend. It is the same dilemma I watch my students face often.

> It felt as though the right side of her body was ripping itself away from the left and soon there would be two separate but equal halves. One of those halves wanted to defend the men because she really liked them. She just felt they were nice, gentle people who didn't hurt others. In her heart, she knew it was the right thing to do. But the other part of her wanted to stand by her man, no matter what damn fool thing he said or did. After all, suddenly she felt she belonged. She was Andy's girlfriend. Right or wrong, it was the womanly thing and loving thing to do since Andy would expect that behavior. Wouldn't that draw Andy and her that much closer together? Didn't she want to be a couple more than anything else? (58)

My heart goes out to Carla. How sad to feel so trapped, desperate, and helpless. Where is Carla's self-esteem? Why can't she speak out against this tyranny? Discouraged, I know the answers to my own questions.

Emily reads it first, then Brooke, Eve, Brady, Sara, and Caroline. Before long the word is out: This is one terrific book. The clamor to borrow it is so great that I go back to the bookstore for copies. They remain in constant circulation, and the girls' responses remind me of Katherine Paterson's assertion that reading is really rehearsal for living.

The issues in these students' lives are not identical to Carla's, but they, too, struggle daily to voice their honest feelings and to keep the love and respect of their closest friends. Too often, the price of safeguarding their friendships is keeping their convictions to themselves, just as Carla does. But not speaking has a high price too. Carla is tormented by her duplicity, as readers of the book are quick to note. What is difficult or impossible for them to see in themselves, they see clearly in her. Many write about the dilemma in their notebooks.

Dear Mrs. Barbieri,

I'm reading *The Drowning of Stephan Jones* by Bette Greene. The main character Carla seems very insecure and unsure of herself. She really likes Stephan; he seems nice, no matter who he likes. Yet she is in a big crush with Andy who hates gays.

When Andy gets fired up about gays, Carla tries to defend them, but she loves Andy too much to contradict him. I think she should speak up. Her mother is trying to be good role model, but Carla can't see that. Carla is ashamed of her opinion.

Before I came to Laurel, I was not ashamed of my opinion, but careful to always give the "right" opinion. If everyone thought something was right and I thought it was wrong, I usually kept my opinions to myself. Laurel's environment helps that. I thought a girl's school would be awful, but it's great. I'm not careful of my opinion, right or wrong.

Carla should not be afraid of what people think and share her opinions.

While I am not sure about Caroline's assessment of her own willingness to express her opinion, I see that this book is helping her clarify her thinking. She values honesty, at least hypothetically. She wants Carla to speak out; she wants to speak out herself. Other readers have similar responses. They condemn Andy's behavior and express their strong convictions that Carla should defend the men under attack. Here is Rachel:

Dear Mrs. B.,

I really enjoyed this book, *Drowning of Stephan Jones* by Bette Greene. Actually, enjoyed is not a good word for it. I couldn't stop reading it once I started it. It scared me that it was so realistic and it could really happen, to see that this is the way people really ARE, that people could persecute someone like this! The thing about it that bothered me was that Carla, know what the "Rachetville Five" were doing was wrong, her "love" for Andy kept her thoughts from coming out. This happens a lot in real life. This is one of the most thought-provoking books I've ever read.

Female Priorities

Scene: Late May, Room 311, windows wide open. Seventh-grade girls bend over three poems and take turns reading aloud "Poem of the Mother" by Myra Skalrew, "A Kitchen Memory" by Roy Scheele, and "Baking Day" by Rosemary Joseph. Concerned lately with how the girls view adult women's roles, I want to think with them about choices. Carrie reads:

> "My mother, who thought her life had been narrow, did not want
> Her daughters to be bakers of bread. I think she was wise . . ."
>
> (Rosemary Joseph)

When each poem has been read two or three times—everyone who wants to read aloud has that chance—I ask them to jot down quick reactions to any or all of the poems.

Bernice comments, "The mother must have had limited schooling, but she is desperate to give her children more."

Do educated women ever stay at home and bake and care for their children, I wonder?

"I wouldn't want to be just a housewife," says Priya. "I would want to go and work and be somebody. Maybe I would take some time off to be with my kids for a while, but I wouldn't want to be a housewife."

"Yeah," says Naeta, reading from her notebook. "In "Baking Day," the mother made the decision to be a housewife and to spend her life catering to her husband and children's needs. I think the daughter chose a different way of life because she knew her mother was not very happy with her life, even though the mother probably loved her very much. The mother wants more out of life than cooking and cleaning and taking care of kids. The daughter understands this and wants more too."

Danielle reads next: "The woman in "A Kitchen Memory" has chosen to cut the apples by herself without the help of a man which means it was expected that she would do the cooking while the man worked. I think this is not correct and both women and men should have equal shares of the household work. She peels more than one apple, which may mean she is cooking for more than herself. If it is her husband I disagree with this. I believe the husband and wife should both cook and have their own careers besides parenting."

"Yeah but if the husband gets a new job, who has to move?" "Who gets to say who does which jobs around the house?" "What do you do if your husband won't help you?" "It would be good to have a husband who did some of the cooking, but I don't know if it's realistic. . . ."

Puzzled, I think of their weekly reading responses where the girls often express admiration for selflessness in women characters. I think of Hallie's recent fiction piece portraying a woman who gives up a law career to stay home with her teenage son as a heroine. How do they really feel, I wonder, about the choices that lie ahead of them?

"I want to be a physical therapist," says Carrie, "but I worry sometimes about whether it will disrupt my family. I don't know. . . ."

Others think about this too. "Maybe it would be better to work part-time." "But then you don't get ahead. I don't know if you can be a part-time doctor anyway." "I don't plan on being a housewife ever. Period."

Priya comments, "I'm not a mother, but I think that you can't always be watching for your children. You need to do something else or you will be worrying all the time, like in 'Poem of the Mother.'"

"Yes, but, I love this poem," says Haley. "Saying "her heart goes out ahead/scouting for him" makes me think that her heart will always be looking for him, even though he is far from her. Even though he won't need her as much as he matures, she will still be there like the "clock on the mantel." I admire her choices."

Nods, frowns, shifting bodies. Hands wave eagerly.

"In 'Baking Day,' I don't really see a lot of choice," Jennifer says. "I think it was more of a duty. It says, 'my cultivated brains chafes at kitchen tasks,' meaning the daughter. And then 'all bent towards nourishing her children.' I think the speaker wants to be like her mother, admires her mother for doing her duty."

Is this always a woman's duty if she has children, I ask them? Where is it written?

"If she loves her family, it's her duty," says Jennifer. "She makes a commitment, and she has to live with it."

"Oh, I see choices," offers Sarah. "The woman in 'Baking Day' gave up any chance for a career so that her children would have a mother, but she also encouraged them to get something out of life before getting married, have some independence. I think in a way she feels regret that she never did anything, but in other ways she never had any regrets over being a wife and mother because she loves her children. The daughter never did learn to make bread, but she didn't have as narrow a life as her mom."

I read them Marge Piercy's "What's That Smell in the Kitchen?" and they laugh. "All over America women are burning dinner. . . ."

"Sounds like my house. . . ." "I can really see this happening." "I think this woman doesn't want to cook any more." "What's Spam?" "Different from the women in the other poems. . . ." "Choices are complicated, I don't know. . . ." "What is this woman so angry about?"

"What do you think she's angry about?" I cut in.

"Maybe that a lot of women feel stuck in the kitchen or that they have to cater to their husbands," Wallis says.

"Do' you think it's okay for women to feel annoyed about that?" I ask.

"Well, if they have a family, they shouldn't feel annoyed," replies Jennifer.

"I don't know but. . . . I think the husband should do some of it," says Danielle.

"Do you think it's wrong for women to want other things too?" I ask, thinking of some of their reading entries.

"No!" "Of course not." "Not if it doesn't hurt anyone else." "Sometimes it is. . . ." "Women are supposed to take care of the family, but so are men." "It depends on how old the kids are. If the kids are little, the woman should think about them first." "I would think of my career first." The whole gamut.

"I wonder what boys think. . . ."

"A lot of boys still think a woman belongs in the kitchen;" says Brady, "that men are superior and all that. They can be so immature."

"Could we have a joint discussion with U.S.?" Ali asks.

I agree to call Mr. Obendorf, the seventh-grade English teacher at the neighboring boys' school, to set up a meeting of the two groups. We decide to brainstorm questions to get ready to host the boys, beginning tomorrow.

Connections

In the book *Women's Ways of Knowing: The Development of Self, Voice and Mind*, Mary Field Belenky, Blythe McVicker Clinchy, Nancy Rule Goldberger, and Jill Mattuck Tarule present a vision of what they call "a Connected Classroom," a classroom that is, in fact, a real community. This is what I hope my classroom will become: a place where every girl is honored, where ideas are freely shared, where students see me as another learner and themselves as confident teachers, where we may act perplexed, annoyed, or angry—perhaps even raising our voices on occasion—as we negotiate the meaning of a published text or an emerging draft of writing; or as we digress to examine what we think and how we feel about issues that come out of our literature or out of our lives. I hope my classroom will be a place where we celebrate literacy with passion, comfortable with the richly diverse interpretations our community produces, and welcoming ambiguity. "It is assumed that evolving thought will be tentative," write Belenky and her colleagues. ". . . teacher and students collaborate(d) in constructing a new interpretation. . . . In a community, unlike a hierarchy, people get to know each other." (1986, p. 221) Getting to know these girls seems a worthy, if challenging, goal.

When I was a new teacher, I had lots of goals, so I made lots of lesson plans to hand in to my department head. Each week I'd map out activities for my five class periods, complete with specific literature, mini-lessons, and in-class writing exercises. But I was frustrated. At first, I'd make arrows on my plans, indicating that much of what I'd wanted to do on Monday had been moved to Tuesday, then Wednesday, and sometimes right into the following week. Some of it—usually the lessons on adverbial clauses—never came to fruition at all. My lesson plans, after the fact, were downright messy, and I worried about them. Then Jane Kearns became my instructor in the New Hampshire Writing Project and assured me I was not doomed as a teacher.

"Make lesson plans, if you have to," was her advice. "But make sure you skip a lot of lines. You have to leave room for the kids." Aha!

At Laurel no one collected my lesson plans. At Laurel teachers are expected to have goals and implement them. At Laurel teachers are professionals. I start each year with an overall plan, attempt various themes every trimester, and maintain high expectations for my students. As a teacher researcher, I try to pay close attention to what the girls need as well as to how they respond to any work we do as a class. Whenever I adhere too rigidly to my own game plan, things get tense. When I am able to be flexible—drop everything and talk about Priya's story; abandon class to attend a school play; try a new book on a controversial topic—the girls' energy carries the day.

I know, reading Gilligan and others, that female students need to talk more, and that often their talk will be less than frank. "When they feel themselves too sad or too angry or too sexual or too loud," write Brown and Gilligan, "they may decide that it is better to bury their feelings." But even then, girls feel a need to express themselves somehow. "They remain on the lookout for others by whom they can be safely seen and with whom they can safely speak." (1992, p. 168) This is the kind of community I hope to nurture in Room 311. But when talking is not easy for students, fast, expressive writing can give them a way to get at their intuition, their hopes, and their fears. Thus, writing is our way of connecting reading and talking, our way to think for ourselves. Reading, writing, and talking come together, helping us examine the biggest question of all:

"Tell me, what is it you plan to do
with your one wild and precious life?"
                    —Mary Oliver, *The Summer Day*

6

Making Room for Truth: Lessons of Little Tree

———

What can I do when I feel the wind's harsh breath and know
That if I stay too long in its path
My path shall be burned up also. . .

—Nancy Wood, *Many Winters: Prose and Poetry of the Pueblos*

EVERY ENGLISH teacher I know insists that she wants her students to develop and express their own ideas about literature and about other issues in and beyond the classroom. Certainly, I am quick to take this stance myself. I object to the notion that students must figure out "the one correct reading" of a text just to feed it back on exams or in class discussions. The very idea appalls me. And as I became more aware of Gilligan's view of adolescent girls, particularly their apparent willingness to muffle their voices in an attempt to please adults (1992, p. 61), I believed I was trying harder than ever to promote honest, open discourse in my classroom. What was not evident to me, I learned from my Laurel students and from my own daughter, was my low tolerance for conflict of any kind. The lengths to which I would go to avoid it turned out to be enormous.

It started with a book. Even though I am a strong supporter of students' right to choose their own reading, once in a while, I believe we need to share a common experience. Once or twice a year we read the same book. Naturally, I am ambivalent about this, and making selections is a tricky proposition for me. Should it be an American classic? Should it be a contemporary book told from a cultural perspective different from any of ours? Should it be a book that ties in with what the students are doing in social studies or science? While all of these factors are relevant perhaps, the primary consideration must always be the story. Is this a good *story*, one that haunts us day and night until we've finished the book and for months, even years, afterwards? Do the characters live and breathe and make us rethink our own lives? Does the book shake us to our roots, making us laugh and cry and finally heave a sigh of satisfaction when we come, eagerly but filled with regret, to the end? Such a book, I became convinced, was Forrest Carter's *The Education of Little Tree*. I loved this book so much that I asked my seventh graders three years in a row to read it together. Things went swimmingly until the third year.

It's the story of a young Cherokee boy growing up with his grandparents in the mountains of Tennessee. We used it at Laurel in conjunction with our work on memoir, since that is what we believed the book to be. For several weeks we read and talked, with the girls raising issues of cruelty to others, prejudice, respect for the natural world, and familial love. How could white men have been so brutal to the Cherokee Nation? What can we learn from The Way? Why does Granpa hate Christians and politicians? Why doesn't he stop Little Tree from buying the calf that he knows is sickly? Why is Willow John always so sad? Do we have special talismans like the Dog Star in our own lives? What are they?

The girls' notebook entries that year were fluent and heartfelt. There seemed to be something in this book that touched them, made them look at themselves, the environment, and the whole notion of living and dying with new eyes.

> *Sarah:* Little Tree was a very moving book. It made me think about how we as a society treat the land and people with different backgrounds. When I read the part about Little Tree being taken from his grandparents, I was furious. . . .
>
> Once again Life and Death was described philosophically and in a way that lessens the fear. The way Granpa said, "It's time," and just went to bed never to wake up helped me realize that death isn't something to fear but just the next step and the cycle of life. I was touched by the way Granma just left a note. I think Granma and Granpa taught Little Tree a lot and after they left, their knowledge stuck with him. . . .
>
> This book made me think and I actually got into the situations and felt pain when L.T. did. I would recommend this book to anyone and everyone.

Other girls had similar reactions. Many claimed it was the best book they had ever read. Kristin called it "a book about nature, sadness, and most of all, love, a book that makes you think about everything all over again." I was gratified to hear how deeply affected they were by the book's simple message of celebrating the cycles of life.

We read lots of Native American poetry and talked about how far we as a society have moved from the attitude of respect Little Tree and his grandparents had for life and for the earth. What a book, we thought, to be able to generate so much good talk! When we wrote our own memoirs, we looked to the story for inspiration, noting how Carter made each episode in Little Tree's life an opportunity for insight and new thinking.

Rethinking *Little Tree*

It was a Sunday afternoon, just after we had finished *Little Tree,* when my father called. "You know that book you like so much, the one about the Indian boy?" he began. "Well, it turns out it's a fake." As he recounted a *New York Times* article revealing that Forrest Carter was in fact Asa Carter, a well-known segregationist who had worked under Governor George Wallace, I became dizzy. The book, my father insisted, was pure fiction. According to the *Times* piece, Carter was not Cherokee at all and had fabricated the entire story. It must be a mistake, I insisted. Why would a bigot write a book like this? It didn't make sense. Naively, I hoped none of my girls would get wind of this; I did not want their experience with the book to be tainted in any way; I didn't want them to be disillusioned. If I don't mention it, I reasoned, they won't have to ask themselves or me whether everything in the book is a lie. I prayed that the news could be kept quiet.

Not a chance. At the copier machine early the next morning no fewer than three teachers hit me with the news. One handed me a copy of the *Times* article. One laughingly asked how I planned to handle this with the girls. I was too confused to answer; I wanted the whole problem to go away. It couldn't be true, I knew in my heart; it had to be a huge mistake.

Of course the girls had heard all about it. The author of their favorite book was a fraud, according to the *New York Times,* and they raced upstairs to our room to tell me. What does this mean, they demanded? Is the whole book a big fake? Or is it the news story that's not true? While a few girls seemed excited over the controversy, eager to get to the bottom of things, when I took a careful look at the class, I noticed more sad eyes, downturned mouths, slumping shoulders. Clearly, they were hurt by this. As hurt as I was.

"He's a racist," Liz said. "He worked for George Wallace."

Carrie flinched, as if to avoid the sound of her friend's voice. And I made a bad decision. "We won't talk about this today," I said. "Let's wait until Friday and see what else we can find out."

That worked on Monday and even on Tuesday, as we plunged ourselves into writing. But by Wednesday, there was no way I could stem the tide of confusion, anger, and distress that threatened to engulf us. Knowing this would be a unique opportunity, I asked the girls if they would mind if I taped their comments. Nonplussed at this suggestion, they agreed. First, I read aloud two news articles—one from the *New York Times* Op-Ed page, the other from *Time* magazine—that seemed to summarize the current furor over the book. Dan T. Carter, professor at Emory University wrote the Op-Ed piece:

> Unfortunately, *The Education of Little Tree* is a hoax. The carefully constructed mask of Forrest Carter—Cherokee cowboy,

self-taught writer and spokesman for Native Americans—was simply the last fantasy of a man who reinvented himself again and again in the thirty years that preceded his death in 1979 . . . His real name was Asa (Ace) Carter. Between 1946 and 1973, the Alabama native carved out a violent career in Southern politics as a Ku Klux Klan terrorist, right-wing radio announcer, home-grown American fascist and anti-Semite, rabble rousing demagogue and secret author of the famous 1963 speech by Gov. George Wallace of Alabama: "Segregation now. . . . Segregation tomorrow. . . . Segregation forever . . ."

The *Time* magazine piece, written by John Leland with Marc Peyser, summarized the same allegations but included Forrest Carter's record of denying these allegations (which had surfaced fifteen years earlier) and a current defense of the author.

"Forrest Carter's agent, Eleanor Friede, who describes herself as "a New York liberal," doesn't believe the two men were the same person. "How can a person (like Asa Carter) write "Little Tree?" she asked. "Come on—that kind of honesty and truth? Could that come from a bigot?"

Betrayal

The girls produced other news clippings from various sources. Catherine recounted a report on National Public Radio. Could it be true, after all? Were Asa Carter and Forrest Carter one and the same man? And, if it were true, what did that mean about the book? We proceeded around the circle, each girl taking a turn. Did it matter who wrote this book, I asked?

> Sarah: If Asa Carter wrote it and it's not really his true story, I think it's okay because you learn a lot from a book . . . and I would hate to . . . I don't want it to be true that he's a racist, because it just seems like that would kind of make the story . . . because if it's not true, it *seems* true, it seems real. If he's a racist, that would be kind of like a contradiction in itself.
>
> MB: In what sense?
>
> Sarah: Well, a racist, we know they're for segregation and whites only, and somehow I think Indians and Native Americans fall into the category that they would want to be segregated from. That's kind of like a contradiction right there, see?

MB: Okay. If it's true that Forrest and Asa are one person, could it be that there are things in the book that are still true, points that were made in the book that still have some value?

Sarah (tentatively): I think so.

MB: Like what? What would some of those be?

Sarah: It made me think about how we as a society look at things. And The Way sort of made me see that we waste so much and the Native Americans had the right idea about it.

Was Sarah saying what she thought I wanted to hear? Was I pushing her into looking at the whole controversy in a particular way? In a way that did not threaten my own beliefs about the book, about my teaching and their learning what I considered important principles? But in addition to coercing her into thinking a certain way—anathema to any good teacher—wasn't I also refusing to acknowledge the real pain and confusion she was feeling? As the talk continued, I remember feeling nervous and uncomfortable. I refused to let Sarah see how angry and hurt I was by this whole exposé, and inadvertently, I put my relationship with her at risk. I refused to admit that, like her, I was bewildered and sick at heart. I refused to be honest, even with myself, about how guilty I felt for imposing a book on them that now seemed, in the face of these news accounts, so empty and shallow. But what exactly was I so afraid of?

Kristin: I love the book, I mean, I really love the book a lot. But the fact that when I was reading it and I was like, geez, the fact that it was all really true made the book that much more.

MB: Did you read *Where the Red Fern Grows*?

Kristin: Yes.

MB: Did you feel for the character in that book?

Kristin: Incredibly.

MB: Incredibly. Fiction, right?

Kristin: Yeah.

I wanted to get Kristin and the other students to look beyond the fact that this author had evidently deceived his readers by claiming that the story was a true one. When I played the cassette tape of our class discussion in the car on the way home that afternoon, my seventeen-year-old daughter Erin was surprised. "Mom," she said, "you sound like you want them to think exactly what you think. And you're not even saying what you really feel.

I can't believe this." As I got ready to deny it, I began to hear what she meant. I should have been listening for my students' deep concerns instead of insisting over and over that this was indeed a fine book.

> Emily: I think that the book is true, at least that's what I want to believe because the book was really moving to me, and whoever the author is, Forrest Carter or whoever it is, did a really good job, and I think he must have stayed with a family that was Indian and it taught him The Way, or he read a lot about it.
>
> MB: He seems to know a lot about it. Can something be true in a sense that is different from the facts being accurate? Can you say anything about that? What's the point, or what are some of the points that this book makes?
>
> Emily: That everything's equal and that nobody should be judging anybody else cause they're not any better than them.
>
> MB: Is that true, do you think? A true point?
>
> Emily: Yeah, I don't think anybody's better than anybody else.
>
> MB: So for you, that message is true, whether or not this particular little boy really lived this particular set of events?
>
> Emily: Yeah.

Emily loved the book, despite any criticism of its author. Emily loves reading and literature and will be a reader all her life, fulfilling one of my deepest wishes for her. It is precisely what I want for all the girls, and this whole mess seemed to threaten that. But listening to the tape, I felt more and more embarrassed at how obviously I had applauded Emily's opinions, while moving past those of other girls who were more ambivalent. I had not realized I could be so heavy-handed and controlling with my students.

> Brenna: I don't believe that Forrest Carter and Asa Carter are the same person. I don't think it's possible that a man who was part of the original Ku Klux Klan could just convert and write that. I don't think it's possible. So what, they had the same last name? I don't think it's true.
>
> MB: Well, there are these allegations, there are coincidences, and even Asa Carter's own brother is saying, "Yeah, when Asa wrote, he used a pen name." I would like to believe that they are not the same person, but there is a lot here. I'm sure we'll read more about it. And you know what, Brenna? Sometimes people change. You know, maybe he was in the

KKK, and when he got older, maybe he had a change of heart. And maybe that's partly why he wrote this.

Brenna: That's true. I really do want to believe that they're not the same person, but it seems like, it seems just like they were, but I don't want to believe it . . . I just don't know.

MB: It's such a contradiction, as Sarah says. The KKK and all the beautiful philosophy in *Little Tree*, it just seems so opposite. Who hasn't said anything?

More than anything else, I didn't want these girls to think that the person who created this book was inherently racist. I proposed the theory, in spite of a total lack of evidence, that Asa Carter may have repented in his old age and written the book to atone for past mistakes. It was a hard sell to such savvy young women.

Nina: Well, I still think it's really disappointing to think that it wasn't Forrest Carter who wrote the book, because the whole time I was reading the book, I kept thinking, I can't believe this is happening, it's so incredible. I don't know, it's just really disappointing that it's not a true story.

MB: Do you think it could have happened, maybe to someone else?

Nina: Yeah. It seems so real.

MB: AHA. It seems so real. Have you ever read a fiction book that you said the same thing about? Have you ever cried reading a book that was fiction?

Class: Yeah. . . . Yes. . . . Yeah.

MB: And why? They're made up characters! To have a writer make it "seem so real," that's dynamite writing. That is really effective writing.

Now I was back on a familiar theme, one that a huge portion of our class time was allotted to throughout the year: What is it that makes writing effective? Not only did I want the girls not to despise Carter, I now apparently wanted them to recognize him as a strong, effective writer, whether he had lied or not.

Kristin: Well, I kind of don't want to believe that he really didn't write it because everything just seemed to be so true. I mean everything, all the characters and the fact that, I don't know, just everything in the book. It just had to have happened for him to be able to write that well.

MB: Molly, what were you going to say?

Molly: I'm not glad that Forrest Carter's dead or anything, but I'm sort of happy that he doesn't have to be here right now listening to all these things being said because, if it was true, then he'd have to go through like a lot of hard times and all that.

Dear Molly. This was so typical of her, in all the confusion and chaos, to think of how the writer would have felt. It was Molly's sweet compassion that I wanted to preserve and protect. I wanted her and all the girls to believe that not only the book, but life itself, was filled with more goodness than treachery, that people, not just in the book but also in the world, were more decent than conniving. Somehow admitting that the book was not all we had believed it to be would threaten their visions of the world at large. I had an urge to hug Molly and tell her how I really felt. I wanted to let her know how I honored her sensitivity, how I hoped she would hold onto it. But I chose instead to move this discussion forward.

MB: You know, it's interesting that you raise that point. This accusation was made for the first time in 1976, and Forrest Carter denied it. He said, "I am not Asa Carter." He denied it. And his publisher stood behind him and several historians stood behind him. So this is not a one-sided debate. It's a controversy. Naeta, what do you think?

Naeta: I have something to say. A lot of people are going to be upset about this, if he really was a racist. When you read the book, Little Tree is the victim of prejudice and then to find out that the author is a prejudiced person, well, it makes you feel bad.

Naeta had hit on the essential point of the whole discussion: "It makes you feel bad." She and her classmates needed to express their sadness, anger, betrayal, and even bitterness, and they needed to have their feelings acknowledged. Instead, I kept trying to change the subject by insisting that there was still quite a bit in the book to value. I made excuses for why Asa/Forrest Carter might have lied to his readers. I did not listen to my students, and in my insensitivity to their needs, I gave them the message that the way to handle disillusionment is not to face it but to run away from it. I should have asked Naeta and Sarah and all the girls to talk more, or even to write for a few minutes about exactly what they were feeling in the midst of all the hubbub. Although not conscious of the fact, I was obviously trying to avoid true conflict in my classroom, conflict between the girls and the author or between them and the ideas this writer, a trusted expert, had proposed that I so cherish. For me, in this conversation, respecting fine literature and effective writing seemed to be a clearer priority than addressing the girls' confusion or sense of loss. I did not want them to be angry.

> MB: Yes, Naeta, but pretend you're Asa Carter and you've been in the KKK and you've worked for George Wallace and done a lot of terrible things. Now you're getting to be an old man. What would motivate you to write a book with the message of Little Tree? What might be a possible reason?
> Naeta: Well, maybe you felt guilty about what you did and you wanted to make it up to some people.
> MB: And maybe spread a message to a wide audience that racism is wrong.
> Emily: I really hope that if they are the same man. I really hope this doesn't affect the book, so that people will stop reading it. Because it is a story and there is a lesson there, and I don't think anyone should be cheated out of what was, you know, being taught there in that book. There's so much love. And it taught me things. You know, like it's easier to accept things and, you know, don't be so mean to others even though they're mean to you.

Wow! How sensitive Emily is! She continued to say precisely what I needed to hear. She was glad she had read this book; she thought other people should read it too. I felt vindicated, until I listened to the tape and realized I had no idea what Emily really felt. Was she being honest? Did she know how she felt? Brown and Gilligan write, "Voice training by adults, especially adult "good women," undermines these girls' experiences and reinforces images of female perfection by implying that "nice girls" are always calm, controlled, quiet, that they never cause a ruckus, are never noisy, bossy, or aggressive, are not anxious and do not cause trouble . . . (1992, p. 61) Was I doing this to the girls? Naeta was still skeptical. She wanted to get to the bottom of things.

Higher Stakes

Was the story true or not?

> Naeta: You know like how he was sent into an orphanage and everything? Couldn't that be checked?

MB: The professor is saying that he did check and that he can't find any records of it. Some historians dispute his claims. Carrie.

Here, I actually moved on to another student instead of following Naeta's line of questioning. I was tired of the nit-picking over details, as I was sure by now that the assertions made by the Emory University professor must be true. How sad that I couldn't have just admitted that to the girls!

Carrie: I really loved this book, and I think I was kind of appreciating the goodness I saw around me more since I read it. But it seems now like things would be kind of hard to believe, if it's true that Forrest was really Asa.
MB: It would be hard for you to believe that Asa wrote it?
Carrie: No, it would be hard for me to believe the things that are in the book, kind of, if Asa wrote it.

My worst fear—that the girls would dismiss the ideas in the book as untrue, irrelevant, a waste of their time—was being realized as she spoke. If we had to face that possibility, I would have to admit my own questions about our capacity to live in peace with one another, about the fundamental nature of humanity, about good versus evil in the world. Unequal to that task, I tried desperately to dissuade Carrie from this point of view.

MB: Well, except that truth is something that when we hear it personally, something happens inside of us. The big truths, like love is better than the absence of love, and respect for nature is better than destroying nature. Those are things that you know are true because of what's inside of you. Something inside of you says, "Aha, yes!" when you read that. Yes? Tell me what you wouldn't believe. If you became convinced that Asa wrote this book, what would you have to let go of?
Carrie: I don't know. It just seems that it would be a little different and that, I don't know exactly. . . .
MB: I want you to think about why it would be. Who hasn't . . .? Sara.
Sara: And also, what you just said to Carrie, I wouldn't believe that Granpa was like the man he was and that would really upset me.

Sara looked carefully at me and at her classmates and, I suspect, wondered if she had gone too far. Had she been too critical? She spoke again.

Sara: But also, if it wasn't a true story, we all still learned a lot from it because we all live in a home, drive around, go out and get food and just live so differently, and this just taught us what it would be like to live how he did.

MB: What about Granpa? You said you wouldn't like to think that he hadn't really lived. Have you ever known anyone or heard of anyone like him?

Sara: Yes.

MB: What were some of his qualities?

Sara: He was really caring and kind, and he taught Little Tree so much.

MB: What did he teach him?

Sara: The Way. How just to get through life basically. I think that was important.

MB: Could there be a man, even today, who is like Granpa, who is teaching the same things to children?

Sara: Yeah, but it wouldn't be the same because children also learn in school and not just from one person. . . .

MB: Uh-huh, but do you think that at some point in history there might have been a situation when a little boy and his grandfather walked through the mountains together and saw the sun come up and had those kinds of conversations?

Sara: Uh-huh.

MB: I think probably there were more than one.

I wish I could go back and apologize to Sara for badgering her like this. I kept at her and at her until she was forced to agree with me. What she wanted to do was grieve for the fact that Granpa was (probably) not a real live human being after all. For Sara this fact changed the story, no matter what. Loren had her own misgivings.

Loren: It's just sort of hard to imagine that a person who believes that certain people should live on this side of the country and other people should live on the other side of the country—that's what segregation is—would write about discrimination and everything the way the author did in this book. It just doesn't make sense.

MB: It's an absolute contradiction.

Loren: Well, the book still makes a good point, you know, about how we mistreat people, about how we don't see things for what they really are. But it's just hard to really think about that when you realize that this was written by a man who thinks that people should be separated according to their race or their religious beliefs, and things like that.

MB: But generally, when we read books, do we know a whole lot about the author? About the author's values? His politics and his past?

Loren: No. . . .

MB: We generally don't. And what becomes alive for us when we read books?

I twisted and turned in my arguments, still desperate to avoid any real pain, including my own. I wanted it to be all right. I wanted them to believe that good would always triumph over evil in their own lives. I wanted to feel that I had not made a terrible mistake in selecting a book like this for the whole class, and I continued to ask the girls to reassure me. But Naeta was not so easily persuaded. She poked holes in my arguments, and I carried on with all the subtlety of a steamroller.

Naeta: You can usually get a feeling about the person who wrote the book.

MB: You can make an inference. You may be right; you may not be right. What matters more to us when we read books?

Molly N.: That we enjoy them and that we learn something from them?

MB: Who's real when we read? More real than the writer?

Emily: The character?

MB: Yes!

Sarah K.: If it isn't true, how can it be so detailed? It seems so realistic.

MB: Katherine Paterson wrote about Rass Island. And she wrote it like a memoir, but it was all research. It's possible to be absolutely realistic when you're writing fiction.

Kristin: Well, I think about Little Tree and his grandparents, and I just keep thinking that there has to have been those characters, I mean there has to . . . I mean everything about them, I don't know, just seemed to be so real.

Haley: I feel kinda loyal to the book because I like it so much, and I don't know, this whole thing about Asa Carter, it makes me mad because I don't know whether to believe it or to stick with what I feel was true. But if it's Asa Carter's book, I think it was still a good book, but it's just not the same. You have to look at it in an entirely different way.

Haley was right. Naeta was right. Carrie was right. You did have to look at this book in a different way when you realized that its author had lied to his readers. And the others were right too, to hold to their assertions of insight, respect, and affection; *or* to react with feelings of betrayal, hostility, and distrust. The only one wrong here was the teacher.

It was no consolation to discover that Gilligan and Brown (1992) found similar behavior among the female faculty members they studied at Laurel. "For women to enter into relationships with girls means to break false images of perfection, to invite their most urgent questions into conversation, into relationship. One of the most difficult questions for the women teachers was whether it was legitimate for them to show girls their sadness and their anger." (1992, p. 230)

My own fears had spawned inauthentic conversation, further confusion, and a loss of trust among us. How could any of the girls resolve their real ambivalence over this book and the issues it raised, let alone risk disagreeing with the teacher in future discussions, given the disastrous model I had provided? How ironic that in a discussion ostensibly concerned with truth, I had avoided it so thoroughly! To my everlasting chagrin, I had done everyone real harm. But in spite of how much it still hurts to realize this, there's a line from the disputed book itself that continues to offer solace: "Next time will be better."

7

A Real Conversation

───

Blessing the Boats

may the tide
that is entering even now
the lip of our understanding
carry you out
beyond the face of fear
may you kiss
the wind then turn from it
certain it will
love your back   may you
open your eyes to water
water waving forever
and may you in your innocence
sail through this to that

—lucille clifton, *Quilting*

THE GIRLS convince me. If we are going to have a class newsletter, something that seventh graders have been doing for years, then they want full control. Instead of the curricular, sports, and school news that I feel is so important, they decide to focus on movie reviews, advice to the lovelorn, gossip, opinion pieces, and letters to the editor. I want them to practice interviewing people, to be learning how exciting it is to track down current and compelling facts. Aren't there new faculty members to be profiled, students from other schools recently come to Laurel who deserve our attention? Isn't anything going on in their classes that they want to share with parents and other readers? What is happening in sports, music, and drama? How about local news? Surely there are events breaking all around them that will concern the Laurel community. I urge them to think more like journalists. They listen with characteristic politeness—"perfect girls" all—and then they dig their heels in.

What is News?

"We're the ones who will be reading this," they argue. "We should be able to have whatever we want in every issue. You shouldn't censor our newsletter."

I decide to see this as healthy resistance.

Since we have three sections of seventh graders, we rotate publication of *The Seventh Grade Gazette*. Each month girls vie for the honor of doing a column or an article. Advice is by far the most popular feature.

Dear Nina and Brenna,

I have a friend in the eighth grade. She says that I'm one of her best friends. These days she has been really distant and not really wanted to talk to me. I'm afraid that next year, when she goes to upperschool, she wants to be in her own little upperschool life and wants me out of it.

Sincerely,

Worried

Dear Worried,

We suggest that you talk to her and tell her how you feel. Don't worry, she'll come around once she realizes what a

great person you are! And if she can't understand, find a reliable person to trust.
Sincerely,

                                              Nina and Brenna

Instead of gathering specific information and organizing it into coherent pieces with sharp focus, the girls are using their writing to examine their most basic fears. What is a real friend? Is this person honest? Reliable? When the newsletter was photocopied each month, this was what everyone turned to first. Where do I stand with other people? Is there anything I can do differently in order to be well-liked? Why do some girls treat me so badly? And, of course, the perennial fascination with boys:

Dear Brenna and Nina,
    I am having trouble with my boyfriend. He is moving way too fast for me. I can't tell him to stop because I don't want to lose him. Part of me doesn't want to say no. But I know it is wrong, and I feel uncomfortable. I also don't want to dump him.
Sincerely,

                                                    In Trouble

Dear In Trouble,
    If you don't feel comfortable, no guy is worth it. You need to tell him how you feel and if he doesn't understand, I suggest you be on your way.
Sincerely,

                                              Nina and Brenna

Having a boyfriend means instant status at Laurel. Whispered secrets before, during, and after school, more often than not, center on who is calling whom, or even who is planning to call whom. To be "going out" with a boy might mean that he has just told his friend that he likes you, that he might think about giving you a call when his parents aren't around. Talking about boys far surpasses talking to boys for Laurel seventh graders. Still, the notion of "going too fast" is on their minds. How would I handle this if it happened to me? Where is the balance between holding a boy's interest and feeling good about my decisions? What will my friends think of me if I go out with him? Will this mean I'm popular?

The mania over boys manifests itself in another column in the *Gazette—gossip*. Girls plead to be assigned this feature, waving hands frantically in my face, insisting it is their turn. Like Brenna and Nina, they work in pairs to pull together the scoop on classmates. To my dismay, the result is a series of lists.

Happy Couples

Sara and Jonah
Katie and John
Kerry and Dave
Brooke and Ryan
Carrie B. and Marcus
Emily G. and Paul H.
Catherine and Scott
Nina and Pete H.
Liz and Mike P.

Break Ups

Brady and Chris (Goddess and God)
Ali and Kevin
Nina and Paul H.
Brooke and Pete H.
Sarah and Nat
Catherine and Marcus
Jamon and Scott
Kerry and Brig
Carrie and Mike P.
Molly M. and Brig

Future Couples

Kristen and Zach
Jennifer H. and Brandon
Heather and Mike Peters
Carrie M. and Kevin
Ali and John M.
Brenna and Yoson P.

This column causes titters throughout the class as girls run their fingers down the lists. Invariably, by this time the names have shifted again. A week is a long time for a "couple" to remain intact, and there seems no way to stay current and accurate, given the nature of these friendships. From time to time, I raise the issue of embarrassing a girl—or a boy—who might not wish to have such affection made public. The girls outvote me once again. "This is what we're interested in," they tell me.

I insist that, if I see evidence of hurt feelings over this column, we will have to discontinue it. The rotating gossip editors go to some pains to ensure that people whose names are listed under "Happy" or "Future" Couples or "Break Ups" have no objection. Several girls wonder whether those whose names never appear feel left out.

"We seem to have the same names every month," says Brenna. "It doesn't seem fair."

We never resolve this dilemma, since no one wants to admit feeling sorry not to see her name in print. Whenever we take a vote about continuing this feature, it is clear that they want it to stay, whether they are part of it or not. Perhaps it is a matter of hope's springing eternal.

My own hopes that the girls will elevate the nature of their reporting—I have visions of *The New York Times,* while they seem mired in *The National Enquirer*—are occasionally gratified, although never to the point that I distribute our newsletter to the rest of the faculty, as I have done in past years; I am too mortified. What will my colleagues think of the way I use class time? What, they will demand, am I teaching the girls about writing anyway? Isn't this just fluff?

But then Carrie writes an article about the Olympics, with particular emphasis on the figure skating competition, since she and many of her classmates are avid skaters themselves. Eve writes a Laurel sports update, and Sarah fills readers in on an upcoming simulated Women's Suffrage Meeting in social studies. Priya writes about her trip to India, the places she's seen and the holidays she's celebrated with her relatives there. Jennifer writes about the recent debates in science class, reporting, "There were not really any hard feelings, and overall both teams did very well," demonstrating even here that her priority is harmony, or at least the appearance of it, in the class. Bernice and Christine submit an opinion piece entitled "Shopping for A Better Future" in which they urge consumers to be more conscious of the environment when making purchases. Things are definitely looking up. I begin to feel that my decision to give the girls free reign is turning out to be a good one. They are using their writing in diverse ways, all self-selected. They are writing for their own, and not my, purposes. They have real readers, one another, who seem to appreciate their efforts.

Passionate Editorials

And then come "J and J Editorials." Jennifer H. and Jennifer M., two girls in my last period class, suggest that they do an opinion column. For starters, they propose to survey the seventh grade, soliciting classmates' attitudes about attending an all girls' school. They will publish the most interesting findings, they promise, whether positive or negative. The class seems enthusiastic, and J and J begin in earnest.

There is real electricity in the air on the day the copy is due. Jennifer H. has a "hold onto your hat, Mrs. B." look on her face, as she hands me her folder first thing that morning. "This is our column," she says proudly. "Tell us what you think." As I scan the various "letters to the editor," I realize we are setting off into new territory.

J & J EDITORIALS

This is J & J here with your opinions. We have been talking to people about how they feel going to an all girls' school and how this affects your social life. We've gotten many different responses, such as the ones Danielle R. and Christine B. gave:

"I think that going to an all girls' school is good; you don't have to worry about boys, and you can be yourself. We have dances and they're not that bad. We can answer questions without being embarrassed. You wouldn't go to a coed school and find couches. If there were some, you probably wouldn't lie on them."

Thank you for your response! Here's another from Jenifer C:

"I like Laurel. I don't think it affects my social life because we see the guys at U.S. I don't want to go to a public or coed school, almost all the guys there are snobs."

Jenifer, Christine, and Danielle have given "the party line," making me wonder whether they could discuss this subject with any degree of candor at all. Do they even know how they really feel? Admissions counselors make precisely these points—boys are distracting; girls can be more independent in a single-sex environment—when giving tours of the school or talking to prospective students. The girls, intentionally or not, are parroting what they've been hearing for years. I think again of Carol Gilligan's belief in silencing; adolescent girls' go underground with real feelings and opinions realizing how little value the dominant culture places in these. (1992, p. 166–168) Christine and Danielle's comments seem to epitomize Gilligan's theory that girls hold a notion of an "ideal girl" in their heads, a girl who is polite and caring, a girl who appreciates what others do for her, a girl who does not make trouble by complaining. The comment on the couches, however, is purely original. Do they really like their couches, I wonder, or are they merely trying again to be polite?

> We appreciate these fine comments about Laurel. But in addition to this, we have received some rather negative comments, and some suggestions to improve our school. Let's read our first letter.

> Dear J. & J.
>   I think going to an all girls' school does have some problems. For one thing, homework is a lot more than for normal kids our age, but this is a college prep school, so I understand.
>   Another problem is the fact that there are not boys. True, boys do divert the attention of girls and make them less independent, but there are problems without them. If guys aren't there for girls to focus on, girls focus on themselves, causing a lot of self-centered people, lots of gossiping and cliques.

Well, I think, here is a person who is at least trying to be honest. She's uncomfortable with the amount of homework she's asked to do, but tells herself it must be good for her because she has dreams of college. Instead of questioning the validity or the purpose of her various assignments, she decides to trust the system in this case. However, when it comes to boys, she is more courageous. Acknowledging that boys may be distracting, she sees both an up and a down side to living without them in school. I applaud her thinking and her willingness to express these ideas in print.

> Because the school is so small, a huge problem is the fact that everyone knows everyone else's business, or dies to find out. If you're having a bad day, and you walk down the hall, you can't go by without someone asking what's wrong. I know it's because they care, but that someone is probably not a good friend, and they are probably going to tell someone else, who will tell someone else, etc. etc. etc. etc.

Here this writer puts her finger on one of the essential facets of life at Laurel. There is virtually no privacy. While caring for others is certainly highly valued, it too has its costs. I am pleased to know that my student has used her writing to articulate what she sees as a major problem. What is the answer? Would she give up being in a school where she is known and cared for in favor of a larger one where she has the freedom to be more anonymous? Sometimes, as Rilke told us, it's the questions themselves that are important. And sometimes we have to acknowledge the fact that there is probably no ideal answer, no ideal school, and no ideal world. These girls are beginning to realize that.

The Silence of Anonymity

Another issue presents itself: Laurel's student body is diverse, but the majority is still white. How do girls of other races feel about their school? Brown and Gilligan address this in their work: "The daily reality of difference gives these girls sharp eyes for shallowness, for false commitments, "phony" relationships, and abuses of power, and gives their voices a strength and a clarity we found stunning." (1992, p. 226) For some African-American girls, coming to Laurel means having to live in two worlds, the researchers discovered. At school they feel a pressure to "act white," but they also feel a strong loyalty to their black community as well as a responsibility to break negative stereotypes. (1992, p. 225–227) I think of this as I read on:

> My final problem is the small amount of exposure to people less fortunate. You really learn a lot being exposed to the less fortunate, (which I think is the real world, considering it's a majority). Yes, we are exposed to other cultures, but the real world that is less fortunate is of all cultures. I bet if our class was dumped in the worst part of Cleveland, less than half of us would know what to do, proving you can't learn everything in a classroom.

She may be asking what she is doing in a private school. She may be feeling ambivalent about what the strong push to "get ahead" will ultimately cost her in terms of identity. Or she may be asking this question of all of us. Shouldn't we be out there—after all, we believe in democracy—where all kinds of people experience diversity, face problems, and learn to help one another in our day-to-day lives? It's an issue I struggle with myself, one I would love to explore further with the girls. I'm pleased to know all of this is on this writer's mind, and I begin to wonder how to make her questions part of our curriculum in seventh grade. By this time, I'm filled with admiration for the young woman who has touched on so many issues in one short letter to the editor. I want to congratulate her. I want to hear more of her ideas. I want to know who she is. But I am shocked to discover at the bottom of her heartfelt letter the lonely word *Anonymous.*

And hers is not the only one:

> Hmmm . . . now this is quite strong and argumentative. This writer has made some very interesting points here. Do you sometimes feel this way? Take time to reflect on this. Well, we have to move on to our next letter.

> Dear J. & J.
>
> I'm glad that you care about the way we feel on different things. Laurel is an OK school, I guess. I mean it would be better if it was a coed school. I've noticed that before, when I was around boys all the time, I didn't think about them, but now with nothing but girls, that's the talk of the day, this boy, that boy.
>
> The school uniform: The colors navy blue and a regular or forest green and white is fine, but I think they should say, "Wear whatever you want in that range of colors," because these uniforms are too expensive, and as long as we are all in the same range of colors, what's the problem? I also think that civvies should be every other Friday, and shouldn't be taken away, no matter what.
>
> Lunch: We pay to go to this school. In that tuition we are supposed to have lunch. Ha! About two times out of five we have something good for lunch. My suggestion is that the people who have a problem with what lunch we may have should be able to bring their own lunch.

Another girl with strong opinions! I marvel at the intensity of her protest: "Ha!" and "no matter what" add such heart to her voice. She knows her own mind, and she wants to convince others. I could not give the class a better model of persuasive writing. Who is this girl? I skip to the end of her letter and am stunned again at the cold *Anonymous.* I continue reading:

Students and Teachers: Some students are not very considerate of each other. I always thought that a classroom should be like a big gang of people who stick together. We all have bad times, but this is ridiculous! Most of them, if you took them to a school in the lower part of Cleveland, only about one-third would probably get through it.

Teachers: I feel that teachers should be split up more race-wise: Black, Spanish, Puerto Rican, Hispanic, Asian, etc. . . . I think this would help a lot. Students won't become prejudiced or disrespectful around their classmates of a different race. I believe that teachers should also give us a break on Friday's homework. Just because we have two-and-a-half or three days off doesn't really mean we have the time. Also, I think teachers ought to listen to what students say and not just push them aside.

Her words make me flinch. I think of how hard the administration tries every year to bring qualified teachers of various races and cultures onto the faculty. But we don't always have applicants for available positions, I want to explain. The homework issue again. I agree that we need to have an honest re-examination of our whole approach to homework. Our director, Andrea Archer, is working on it, deeply concerned about the high stress level among seventh and eighth graders. But which teachers "push them aside?" I bristle at this. Laurel teachers are without question the most sensitive, dedicated, caring people I have known in my life. I have never seen a teacher brush a student off for any reason. But still I wonder, what does this girl mean? Where do her feelings come from? Who has hurt her to this extent? Could I have done it myself?

Education: I feel that what we learn in class should be given time to soak in, and not just rushed and pushed by. I also have a suggestion that has been a special, very special, tradition at my old school. It starts on February 1 and ends on February 28. This month is what's known as Black History Month. This month lets us know about black people who have done some magnificent things which nobody knows about, because sometimes someone else took credit for whatever it was, since blacks weren't considered human when they made their inventions, etc. I believe it would be interesting, and what you'd find out, you'd be shocked by.

OK! I gotta go!

P.S. But overall, Laurel is a good school!

The qualifier at the end startles me. Finishing this letter, a reader is forced to ask, "What's so good about it?" Is the last comment, complete with exclamation point, the writer's inevitable need to stay connected, to be, even after all her criticism, "a good girl?" Perhaps.

Much as I applaud both writers' ideas and the clarity and force with which they express them, I am uncomfortable with the anonymity of these letters. I bring the matter to the class. Tradition demands, I say, that writers who want their opinions published in newspapers must state their names. Both letters are so well written, I say, that anyone should feel proud of them. It's not easy to criticize an institution or the people who are a part of it, I say, but there is self-respect at stake here. Be proud of your convictions. Own up to them. Take a risk. It will be enormously satisfying to stand up for your ideas.

For several long seconds the class sits silent. A few eyes turn downward; some peer out windows. Bodies shift restlessly in chairs, and I can feel them drawing themselves in, away from me, suddenly the stranger. The chasm between us seems unbridgeable, frightening, enormous. Finally, Jennifer speaks. "The people who wrote these letters don't want anyone to be angry at them."

"I know that," I say, "but it is my strong feeling that, as far as teachers are concerned, none of us will be angry. We need to know what out students think," I insist. We need to re-examine things like homework and uniforms and Black History Month. Most of all, we need to be in touch with what really matters to the girls. "Teachers may not always agree with you," I explain, "but we do want to know what you are thinking."

The room erupts in a frenzy of agitation. "It's not worth it if anyone gets mad." "You could lose all your friends." "A lot of this is not exactly flattering to people in this class." "Some people could get their feelings hurt." "I don't think you should make anyone sign their name, if they don't want to."

Everyone is talking at once, and my feeble reassurances seem to be falling on deaf ears. I am in a quandary. Should I run the letters the way they were, unsigned? Or should I pull rank and refuse to include them in the newsletter until the writers came forward. Once again, I argue that both letters are articulate, convincing, provocative. The writers should feel great satisfaction and self-respect, I say.

I look around the room for one shred of acquiescence. Doesn't anyone see my point? Should I let this go? Finally Bernice puts her hand up. Brimming with tears, her eyes stare right into my own.

"You just don't understand," she shouts. "What good is self-respect if you lose all your friends?" Others mumble assent. More angry faces glare back at me. I feel small, humbled, and alone. The chasm gets wider. I think about how to respond, allowing silence to reign for what seems like many minutes.

"I want to understand," I say. "I think I understand. But there are other issues to consider here. Who are your friends, your real friends? Do you know?"

"My friends don't hate me for what I believe in," Jamon offers. "Real friends let you say what you think."

"But last year Sarah started saying what she thought about everything, and then no one liked her." Another voice in the room.

"You have to be careful with friends. It's not always easy to . . ." Liz stops in mid sentence.

It is then that I notice a hand from the corner of the room. "What do you think, Amy?" I ask.

"Well, if I don't say what I really think because I'm worried about how my friends will take it, when I just pretend to agree with everyone else, and if I do this all the time, if I do it a lot, then pretty soon I forget what I actually think. And then I start to forget who I really am. . . . So I'm not sure it's always worth it. I don't know."

The next hush lasts longer. My head is spinning. I want to freeze the moment in time, a moment when my own awareness of their lives is sharp, painful, and clear, and I hate the thought of losing it. For this moment I am in their skin, remembering. It is terrifying and exhilarating at the same time. My students have presented me with such gifts—their anger, their fear, and their open hearts. What should I do with them?

"I wrote the first letter," rings out across the room. "Do you really think it's well written?"

We are back to "normal." Student eager for teacher's praise. Part of me feels relieved, reconnected, reassured; they still trust me, and they are willing to take the big risk of being honest. But something has happened that cannot be undone: A glimpse into their worlds, lonely worlds where relationships, true or false, are paramount and where self-knowledge is in constant jeopardy. Jennifer and Jennifer have set the stage for provocative thinking. Marlana and Kim, the two gutsy letter writers, have given us all a lesson in risk-taking and in the power of writing to change thinking. Bernice and Amy, caring enough about themselves and the group, have provided the tenacity for a real conversation. The newsletter turns out to be a vehicle for true expression, and it will remain in their competent hands. The girls convince me.

8

A Place for the Genuine: Living with Poetry

——

For poems are not words, after all, but fires for the cold, ropes to be let down to the lost, something as necessary as bread in the pockets of the hungry.

—Mary Oliver, *A Poetry Handbook*

THE CHAPEL, traditionally named although our school has no religious affiliation, falls quiet as the middle school student body waits for the program to begin. Several parents line the side rows, eager to see their seventh-grade daughters perform. My students whisper last-minute instructions to one another as the minutes tick by. First there is the pledge of allegiance, then weekly announcements: A sixth grader has received an award from a science foundation; the basketball team has beaten its chief rival; Friday will be a civvies day. And I swallow my anxiety, confident that the girls will do well.

For weeks they have worked towards this, gathering in groups to decide which poet's work to study and perform. For days they have rehearsed, choreographing every motion, practicing every inflection, nuance, and projection, to be sure that the audience will feel the effect of each poem. And for hours they have brushed hair, tucked shirttails, gulped deep breaths. Nikki Giovanni is their hands-down favorite, and three groups will perform her work.

Brenna, Kristin, Kristen, and Naeta walk solemnly onto the stage. Each girl stands in a different corner, and one by one they speak the poet's lines, twirling their bodies, waving their arms, and bowing their heads as they finish. Without a single prop they bring flowers, trees, books, and webs to life before our eyes. The words ring out clearly, poignantly, and the whole audience is stunned.

Woman

she wanted to be a blade
of grass amid the fields
but he wouldn't agree
to be the dandelion

she wanted to be a robin singing
through the leaves
but he refused to be
her tree

she spun herself into a web
and looking for a place to rest
turned to him
but he stood straight
declining to be her corner

she tried to be a book
but he wouldn't read

she turned herself into a bulb
but he wouldn't let her grow

she decided to become
a woman
and though he still refused
to be a man
she decided it was all
right

They have chosen Giovanni's "A Poem of Friendship" next, moving towards one another, then away, finally standing close together, arms entwined, projecting this poem not only with their voices but also with the simple grace of their movements. I am awed. These are my students, but they have done this without me. They have looked into the poetry and into themselves to find ways to depict the emotion they feel, the emotion they want others to know too. Thinking back over the weeks we've spent getting ready for this day, I am relieved.

Working in groups is not always easy—digressions, gossip, noise, arguments, tears, and chaos creep in—for teachers or for students. But in this case, it has clearly paid off. Giving the girls the prerogative to choose their own poems and to handle their own stage direction has worked too. As I look around the room and see younger students as well as eighth graders and adults mesmerized by what's going on, I am reminded again of the power in poetry. It is February and we've been immersed in poems from day one, as we will continue to be. I couldn't have it any other way.

Poetry as Lifeline

Growing up, my life was filled with poems, spoken casually; part of ordinary conversations. On long car trips my father would repeat these lines from an old one by Joyce Kilmer:

Whenever I walk to Suffern along the
    Erie track
I go by a poor old farmhouse with its shingles
    broken and black.

I suppose I've passed it a hundred times, but I
   always stop for a minute
And look at the house, the tragic house, the
   house with nobody in it.
                          ("The House with Nobody in It")

There were others he liked, too, but this was his standard. It
touched us children with its mystery—who had abandoned this
house and where were they now?—and its sadness. Something
about it foretold a future of unanswered questions, terrible loneliness, unfathomable grief, and while it frightened us a little, we
were intrigued.

I can't recall poems as part of everyday school life, although
the nuns had us memorize a few each year. What is clearer to me
is my grandmother's voice in the playground of her apartment
building:

How do you like to go up in a swing,
   Up in the air so blue?
Oh, I do think it the pleasantest thing
   Ever a child can do!

                                          ("The Swing")

Later, back in her kitchen we would eat cinnamon toast, and
indulge in more Robert Louis Stevenson:

I have a little shadow that goes in and out with me,
And what can be the use of him is more than I can see.
He is very, very like me from the heels up to the head;
And I see him jump before me, when I jump into my bed.
                                          ("My Shadow")

Even as a very young child, what struck me most was the
emotion in the poems. I was swept away, awash in the drama of
"The House with Nobody in It" or the delight of "The Swing." And
today, when Emily Dickinson's words echo on summer mornings
unbidden, I hear them in my grandmother's voice: "I'll tell you
how the sun rose, a ribbon at a time . . ." (Dickinson's poems are
untitled)

Beyond the pleasures that filled ordinary days, I discovered
poems in moments of crisis and tragedy. When John Kennedy
died, I was a sophomore in high school and felt for the first time a
sense of disequilibrium. Life would never be the same again, and

I was overcome with despair. But a simple poem by Senator Mike Mansfield helped me reconcile what had happened and go on with the business of school and friendships and growing up. The lines come back to me even now—"And so she took a ring from her finger and put it in his hand . . ." Sitting paralyzed in front of the television, sharing the anguish of the President's funeral, I heard Robert Kennedy quote Shakespeare's *Romeo and Juliet*:

> Take him and cut him out in little stars
> And he will make the face of heaven so fine
> That all the world will be in love with night
> And pay no worship to the garish sun . . .   (111.1.22–25)

A nation mourned its lost leader in ways both eloquent and profound, but it was these two disparate bits of poetry that consoled me in a way I could not name. Somehow the words put the event in a much larger context, and I knew this loss would not annihilate us, as I had feared.

As a middle school English teacher, it struck me at first that I was lucky. My job was to help young people discover how language could touch their lives. I was sure my enthusiasm for poetry would be contagious, and often it was. Soon, however, my conscience began to nudge me. Was I teaching enough? Maybe reading Robert Frost and Emily Dickinson and Eve Merriam and Langston Hughes aloud was not a valid way to use precious class time. We ought to study rhythm and meter and metaphor in more depth; we ought to do more complex analyses. Then there were all the other "ought to's" that plagued me. Vocabulary workbooks. Spelling lists. And what about adverbs? Adverbs took so much time that sometimes our daily poetry reading was squeezed out, leaving me feeling righteous but sad.

We English majors once loved poetry with something akin to reverence or awe as we puzzled out the "correct reading" in our literature classes. If we were lucky, we got beyond that to a real sensation of reveling in the immediacy, impact, and surprise, the humor, precision, and emotion—all the things I had known as a child. What allows us then to excuse ourselves from making it central to our curriculum when we become teachers? What are we so busy doing? And what is it all for anyway? We forget how fleeting each moment is, and we encourage our students to forget it too, so intent are we on preparing them for what comes next. We think of poetry as nonessential, extra, or "fluff," and we neglect it in our classrooms. Nancie Atwell says, "Either we read it and love it, as I did, but can't imagine how to begin to help children experience it fully and so end up lecturing about it or assigning cute formulas for our kids to write; or we don't read it and don't love it and relegate it to an enrichment unit that we'll assign in June if we don't run out of time." (1991, p. 79)

The longer I teach, the more I learn, both from my students and from others in the field. I sensed that poetry was important, and, as I pursued a master's degree at the University of New Hampshire, I heard my professors confirm my belief. Donald Murray read his own poems to us in a summer workshop class, and confessed that it was this genre that intrigued him most. I heard other teachers' accounts of how much poetry meant to their students. I took two poetry classes with Mekeel McBride, poet and English professor, and discovered that writing poetry not only enhanced my reading of poems but also made me look at things around me with more questions, more attention, and more concern. I read books by Lucy Calkins, Georgia Heard, Myra Cohn Livingston, William Stafford, and Donald Hall, all chock-full of good reasons to read and write poems with students.

In *Climb Into the Bell Tower*, Livingston writes: "Perhaps it is the curse of our scientific age; that we are so beset by labels and definitions, so busy fitting things into compartments, dealing with facts and figures, cataloging and computing, that we fail to feel the meanings behind the things . . . perhaps a good part of the answer lies in our strangled emotions. . . . Do we shrink from emotion, afraid that we will be thought immature, weak, should we cry, foolish if we laugh?" (p. 7)

Each year I've been in the classroom I have found ways to bring poetry in too. My conviction that it is essential for students—and for adults—grows only stronger with time. I'm with William Stafford when he describes what reading and writing poetry can do: "You'll be invited; things will happen; your life will have more in it than other people's lives have." (Janeczko, 1990) In the end we teach from our deepest beliefs; we make the time for what is important to us.

As girls reach seventh grade, it seems to me, they are ripe for poetry. They are certainly struggling to hold onto what Jungian psychologist Irene Claremont de Castillejo describes as a level of awareness separate from the focused consciousness of most of their school endeavors. "Most children are born with and many women retain, a diffuse awareness of the wholeness of nature, where everything is linked with everything else and they feel themselves to be part of an individual whole. . . . Here lies the wisdom of artists, and the words and parables of prophets, spoken obliquely so that only those who have ears to hear can hear. . . ." (*Knowing Woman, A Feminine Psychology,* p. 15) Like Gilligan, de Castillejo laments the danger of a loss of relational knowing girls experience as adolescence approaches. The level of knowing that is not valued in school—where focus and logic and clear thinking are paramount—is one girls seem all too willing to relinquish.

Certainly, as girls enter adolescence, the adult world signals the priority of thought over emotion. At what price do girls suppress all they know through their senses, their imaginations, and their intuition? Could it be that more poetry would help them stay in closer touch with these parts of themselves, even as they progress through an educational system that clearly values other ways of knowing? This is my hope for them.

Poetry as Permission

I surround my students with poetry so that they will come to love language and so that they will look at their worlds in new ways. I want them to know that every minute we are alive is packed with something to discover. The content of what we read is important to me and to them, as we become aware that poems do shed light on the lives we are leading; the connections are strong. Poets show us that small experiences as well as big questions can be examined and appreciated. Poetry, it seems, is uniquely suited to such examination. Elliot Eisner, who has made frequent pleas that teachers develop greater regard for their students' imaginations, has this to say: "Language is diverse: the kinds of meaning that can be represented and secure in poetry, for example, are simply unavailable to those limited to prose." (1991)

And so I fill bookshelves with my own personal collection, from Lucille Clifton to Robert Frost to Marge Piercy to William Butler Yeats. We have poetry anthologies compiled by Paul Janeczko and Arnold Adoff and Seamus Heany and Lee Bennet Hopkins. We have dozens, more than dozens, of books by individual poets: Maya Angelou, Nikki Giovanni, Emily Dickinson, Linda Pastan, Walt Whitman, Cynthia Rylant, Arnold Adoff, Gary Soto,

and so many others. I want there to be something for everyone.
Then I cover the bulletin boards with copies of poems that students have read, written, and loved in years past. We read it aloud;
we search for new poets; from time to time we write responses in
our notebooks; we write our own poems; and we perform our favorites for larger audiences.

As the year begins in my class, we are busy setting up writing
workshop. For the first few weeks, I read poems aloud, with minimal comment, trying to present a good enough variety to keep
things lively and playful. Judith Viorst's book *If I Were in Charge of
the World* is a treasure, as are Paul Janeczko's *The Place My Words
Are Looking For*, and Eloise Greenfield's *Honey I Love*. We often listen to a tape of Eve Merriam or some other poet reading her own
work, a real treat. I play or read Linda Pastan and Mary Oliver and
Lucille Clifton right from the start, too, so the girls will know who
my current favorites are.

Pastan's "Egg," which we listen to on tape, helps us realize that
even the most familiar things deserve careful attention:

> In this kingdom
> the sun never sets;
> under the pale oval
> of the sky
> there seems no way in
> or out,
> and though there is a sea here
> there is no tide.
>
> For the egg itself
> is a moon
> glowing faintly
> in the galaxy of the barn,
> safe but for the spoon's
> ominous thunder,
> the first delicate crack
> of lightning.

One of the things that the Harvard researchers discovered in
their study at Laurel was the propensity of girls to interject the
phrase "I don't know" in many of their conversations. (1992,
p. 174) I began to notice the same phenomenon in many of our
class discussions. It was almost a reflex on their parts, a safety

net against saying the wrong thing, in spite of my assurances that all opinions were valid and welcomed. But in their notebook responses the girls would show how diverse are their ways of knowing, their methods of making meaning of the poet's words. We would often take five or six minutes to write initial ideas.

Jenifer writes:

> I think this poem "Egg" is kind of odd. I don't quite understand exactly what she means or the point she is trying to get across. I do like one line though: "and though there is a sea here, there is no tide." The pale oval is the egg shell, and it seems like you can't get in or out. The first delicate crack is the crack of the shell. That's about all I can get out of this poem. I don't understand it all, just parts.

Jenifer is reacting to a bit of the poem that stirs her imagination. The poet has made a connection to two elements that most of us don't consider alike in any way. The fact that even this much of the poem has touched Jen is significant. If this happens enough, and if she is encouraged to notice specific images, she will come to value poetry as a way of expanding her thought processes and develop greater confidence that she does indeed know.

Sara is philosophical about the poem:

> This poem to me means that sometimes when you see the outside of someone or something, it seems dull and boring and plain. The poem tells us to look inside and forget what's on the outside, it doesn't matter.

Although I never ask the girls for "the main idea" of a poem, some feel comfortable discussing their perceptions this way. There are as many ways of looking at a poem as there are readers. Depending on what the reader brings to the poem, each reading will be unique. (Rosenblatt, 1983) Helping them realize this, helping them let go of the notion that they are somehow incompetent when faced with complex material, is one of my primary goals as their teacher.

When classmates mentioned aspects of a poem that Marlana had not noticed, she grimaced. "It seems as if every time I think I understand a poem I'm wrong. I think I have a comprehension problem." Yet writing in response to "A Kitchen Memory" by Roy Scheele, she is quite sensitive:

> I really can relate to "A Kitchen Memory." I remember when I was little I would love to watch my mother cook. Her hand would be dirty with seasonings but I thought it was beautiful and couldn't wait to grow up and cook. "The apple fattens in her hand" confuses me if she's already peeled it. The descriptions of an apple aren't like other poems.

My job is to help Marlana see that her personal associations have real value and that we all benefit from hearing others'. Often we feel what a poem is saying—as I did hearing "the tragic house"—before our minds make logical sense of it. We need permission to feel before we can think, and so sometimes we jot down what we feel, writing practice-style, before we attempt to do any analysis. Writing responses to complicated poems helps us see more than we would otherwise and gives us opportunities to work out our own meanings, the way all readers do.

As the year progresses, I ask the girls to bring in poems to share with the class, and many of these are new to me. I share with them my own responses and meaning-making processes, so they will know how personal, messy, and intriguing it can be to embrace a poem. Tom Newkirk explains this phenomenon in "Looking for Trouble: A Way to Unmask Our Readings," (1984) and helps me realize that we must never hide our own reading processes from students. Rather, we need to let them see all the ways readers go about constructing meaning when we read literature that seems, at first blush, inaccessible to us. Maressa does this when she writes about Galway Kinnell's "St. Francis and the Sow."

> This was quite a beautiful poem and it surely was more sophisticated than all of our other poems. St. Francis is telling a female pig that she is lovely and it makes her feel good. And all things are like a rosebud. For some reason this poem doesn't have a point. But I liked "the spiritual curl of the tail." That was a really neat line, but I'm not exactly sure what it means. Oh! I just got the poem. When you're really kind to a

person and lift their self esteem, their bud blossoms and the person (or animal) becomes even *more* beautiful!

Like many girls in the seventh grade, Maressa tends to doubt her own opinions. Twice here she comments that the poem is eluding her, although there are sections that she does admire. As she writes, however, a larger vision develops in her imagination and she experiences real insight. "Oh! I just got the poem." Her willingness to look at certain lines and think about them in her writing yields deeper understanding of "sophisticated" writing.

Of course, students will also see their own experiences in the poems we read together, making associations and connections that no teacher—or poet—could predict. Erin writes:

I loved "You Are There" by Nikki Giovanni. It just reminded me of how I feel about Firedance, my first horse I had for two years and who is now retired. She makes you think of what's going to happen in years to come, also when I have to leave home and when my animals die. I will miss seeing them, but their memory will be there. I sometimes want to cry about what this poem is about because Brutus, our family's dog is getting old and will die someday and he's done so much and he has always been there for me to cry on.

When I read responses like Erin's, I remember that we are all connected to one another in a large and a real sense, and that poetry is tangible proof of this. The pain, fear, and loneliness as well as the determination, delight, and joy we experience has all been felt before. We are not alone after all.

I bring in poems that seem to fit in with what we're studying or with what's going on in school. We read Stanley Kunitz's "End of Summer," and Emily Dickinson's "Morns Are Meeker Than They Were," and Linda Pastan's "September," at the beginning of the year. We listen to Eve Merriam's "New Love" and "Metaphor" and "I Am Looking for A Book" on tape. When Amy writes about a child searching for an escape to a magical place, I bring her William Butler Yeats' "Stolen Child." In winter we read snow poems, cold poems, holiday poems, and then write our own class anthology. As we read *The Education of Little Tree* together, I share poems from Nancy Wood's *Many Winters* and from Howard A. Norman's collection, *The Wishing Bone Cycle: Narrative Poems from the*

Swampy Cree Indians. Later in the year, as we do our theme study of generations (Rief, 1992), we collect dozens of poems about relationships, many from the Paul Janeczko book *Strings: A Gathering of Family Poems.*

The girls save their own favorite poems in folders and share them with us in class. Once every five or six weeks we take a whole class period to copy and illustrate new discoveries on posterboard and hang them all over the room and on the walls in the corridor. We are a room and a middle school bursting with poetry.

Linda Pastan's new book *Heroes in Disguise* delights us. When we read "A New Poet"—"Finding a new poet is like finding a new wildflower . . .," I ask the girls to search out new poets or new poems to share in class, widening and enriching our repertoire. Bernice brings us Edgar Allan Poe's beloved "Annabel Lee." Emily brings e.e. cummings, and we laugh at his freedom with the rules of punctuation. Jennifer discovers *Dancing on the Rim of the World: An Anthology of Contemporary Northwest Native American Writing,* replete with poets none of us know. Part Cherokee herself, she reads a poem by Jo Whitehorse Cochran:

From My Grandmother

You were talking to my blood
in those years before my memory
was awake. When I had no one's language
yet not Lakota not Salish
not English

You were talking me into life
and knowing. Giving me colors
the thin gray of pin feathers
on a redtail hawk for blizzard sky
I would never see. Dakota sky
just before a white out.
Your midnight blue blanket each end a light
with a mountain design yellow to red,
these were candle flames and the August night.

You were making sense of things
in image and textures
stories of Old One Changers
and the Lakota I can only find
in dreams in visions.

> Grandmother are we searching
> out each other you and I?
> Or am I just remembering
> from you from my blood.

How lovely her voice sounds, how strong and proud. We talk and read and write quite a bit in the seventh grade about family stories, intergenerational relationships, and our own histories. This poem touches all of that and is unique at the same time. Whenever I trust my students to shape their own curriculum, I am never disappointed. A quiet engulfs the room as Jennifer finishes her poem.

And, of course, we write our own. Sharing my poems is difficult for me. Studying with Mekeel McBride, I learned that writing poetry is a way to pay closer attention, to think more seriously, and to be more a part of life. She urges students not to compare themselves to others in the class. "Think of a garden," she says. "All the flowers are so different; each one is lovely in its own way." I want to be the kind of teacher she is! For me it's a real challenge to forge meaning out of memories, images, and words. I am shy about my attempts for the same reasons the girls are shy about theirs: my writing reveals what matters to me, and often it is personal and private. When I share my writing, I acknowledge that I can be clumsy when I try to find what I mean to say. But I want my students to know I love the process, and so I read my work aloud:

Love's Seasons

> At the intersection of Van Aken
> and Chagrin, in Shaker Heights, Ohio,
> black fumes spew through new snow
> heaving itself down in great gusts.
> Tangles of commuters' cars
> slow to halts in all directions.
> Horns cry out; a bus shrieks to a stop.
> The old woman climbs down first,
> twine-handled shopping bag
> holding new groceries,
> black face defying white fury.
> She reaches for her man who nearly stumbles,
> leans on her.
> The wind wants to knock her down,
> but she is stronger, looks instead to him,
> pulls the red muffler tighter

around his neck, claps his shoulders
before hooking her arm in his.
All the world is dusky snow and blowing.
Cold, she gasps, lifts her chin,
takes a minute to get her bearings,
moving her head—left, then right—
finally ready to lead him
home. She listens
to his words in the storm.

Summer is short in New Hampshire,
so old folks come down to the shore
early, not to miss it.
The woman in the white cap, navy-skirted
bathing suit has veined legs;
one gnarled hand clasps her husband's.
They walk side by side across wet sand,
noticing sandpiper's tracks,
a piece of driftwood. The beach
is theirs alone.
But soon he's in a hurry,
pulls her forward, cajoling.
His shoulders, red from yesterday's
sun, stooped from eighty-odd
years' labor, rise against icy water.
Surf up to his chin now,
he rides waves with abandon, laughs out loud.
All the world is salty sea and buoyant.
He forgets her completely,
left standing at the shore,
dipping her fingers in the water
to make the Sign of the Cross.

Sometimes the girls ask questions—"Why are you writing about old people you don't even know?" or "What is the Sign of the Cross?"—and make comments—"The first part is really just like a Cleveland storm." or "The first couple seems more in love than the second." Their responses are helpful to me, as I continue to rethink and rewrite my poems, in the same way that I hope my responses to their work will be helpful to them.

Of course we find help all around us too. The professional poets we admire become what Shelley Harwayne (1992) calls our "writing teachers," not only in mini-lessons, but in more unpredictable and ubiquitous ways. After reading Lisa Schoenfein's

"Loneliness," (Grossman, 1982, p. 4) we try to capture some other emotions as a quick exercise.

Loneliness

Loneliness comes from a lost
Childhood dream
And a boy who never called
Empty walnut shells
And a breeze too cool for summer
From parents who couldn't understand
And a grandmother who died.

Bernice writes:

Hatred

A burst of anger!
Fire
A punch in the face
A bloody nose.
Like a hot flame
A power inside
that is undescribable
uncontrollable.
Annoying, bothersome, disturbing,
stubborn, ignorant.
An attempt at suicide
Death row
Contempt
Rapists, thieves.
A slap in the face
A burning red color
of rage
A liar, deceiver
Loud shouts, screams
tight fists,
squeezed jaws
fierce eyes
HATRED.

What touches me about this poem is the fact that its writer is a prime example of "a perfect girl." (Brown & Gilligan, 1992, p. 180) Conscientious about her schoolwork, fastidious in her preparation for class, tuned in to every group discussion, Bernice has her heart set on achieving great things in school. Rarely does she moan or complain about the amount of homework or extra projects that seem to plague the others. And her writing—most of it—is error free. One of her goals is to use more sophisticated vocabulary, and this, combined with her commitment to perfect form, contributes to correct but predictable pieces. This poem stands out for its anger—a punch in the face, suicide, rape, burning red color of rage, tight fists, squeezed jaws and, best of all, fierce eyes. I suspect that this is one piece where Bernice has allowed herself to be a little less constrained than usual, a little less perfect, a little less silent.

This is what matters to me, breaking the silences that can suffocate adolescent girls. Thus, I do not ask them to concentrate on specific forms when they write. In her book, *For the Good of the Earth and Sun,* poet Georgia Heard describes her process this way: "Many of my poems begin with a feeling, some deep urge. Sometimes it's so strong I actually feel something inside me move. It can happen any time; it happens about ideas, memories, things I see every day. Often I start with an image, a picture in my mind. I use this as a resource to guide me in the making of the rest of the poem." (p. 10) Because I want my students to be aware of different writing processes, I share Heard's words with them. We also read extensively from the Paul Janeczko books, *The Place My Words Are Looking For* and *Poetspeak in their work, about their work,* to hear what contemporary writers have to say about the craft of making poetry. Both books are treasures, and I turn to them again and again throughout the year.

"We hear so many voices every day, swirling around us, and a poem makes us slow down and listen carefully to a few things we have really heard, deep inside," writes Naomi Shihab Nye (Janeczko, 1990, p. 7)

As we read poetry, we see that nothing is off-limits; that the things poets notice, wonder about, believe in, cherish, fear, or dread can all be brought out onto the page and examined. One of the things they seem to love to examine is poetry itself. Eve Merriam helps us understand the value of the concrete with "Reply to the Question: How Do You Become a Poet." In "How to Eat A Poem" and "It Doesn't Always Have to Rhyme" she dispels some of our preconceived notions about appreciation and about form. We turn to William Stafford's "A Course in Creative Writing" and Mary Oliver's "Writing Poems" and Linda Pastan's "Prosody 101" to learn more about qualities of surprise and mystery. We look at

Marianne Moore's "Poetry" and realize that even she has ambivalent feelings about her own work.

Neeti responds to Moore:

> There is a place for everyone in the world of poetry, but you have to find it for yourself. There are different sorts of poems—ones with surprise, sad ones and ones like this that make you think. I think "a place for the genuine" is the body of the verse. It is saying that some time or other you will discover that you fit in with poetry, and it is a place you can say whatever you want, things you couldn't say in other ways. It's like another world.

It's a world where girls are freer to be themselves. "Sometimes there's no one to listen to what you really might like to say at a certain moment. The paper will always listen," writes poet Naomi Shihab Nye. "Also, the more you write, the paper will begin to speak back and allow you to discover new parts of your own life and other lives and feel how things connect. Poets are explorers, pilgrims." (Janeczko 1990)

Marlana did lots of exploring in writing practice as she vented her frustrations over the new demands in her life. She felt overwhelmed by all that was suddenly expected of her, but at the same time, intoxicated by the privileges and freedom her position as a seventh grader offered. During writing practice a list emerged in her notebook:

being twelve   being misunderstood
complaining
doing a lot of homework
talking on the phone
smiling
having braces
unwanted growth spurts
big shirts
white jeans
being a Christian
black jeans
white jeans
loving guys
guys not loving you
now knowing what you want
retainers

    having the choice of almost
        anything
    gaining new friendships
    eating
    all girls school
    being organized
    talking on the phone
    being an individual
    loneliness/tears
    aggravation
    mood swings
    too young for teenage stuff
    unwanted pimples
    strict parents
    short skirts
    too old for kids stuff
    more responsibility
    more fun
    starting makeup
    being lonely
    changing schools
    losing friends
    playing clarinet
    accepting life
    being responsible

Next she read her list, crossed out "responsibility" and "fun" and "laughter." She circled "being twelve" and starred "all girls school" and "talking on the phone," (which she had listed twice.) A draft of what she hoped would become a poem emerged later that week:

Twelve

    Hear the laughter
    taste the tears
    Lots of fun
    endless homework
    Years of braces
    getting pretty, straight, white teeth
    Liking guys
    guys liking you
    Talking on the phone
    being misunderstood
    You don't know what you want

But the world is at your fingertips,
so fly away with it.

In our writing conference we talk about poems she likes. Nikki
Giovanni is high on her list, as is Linda Pastan. "nikki rosa" is a
good poem, she says, because Giovanni uses the details of her life
to show the reader that she was a happy child. In her poem, Marlana wants to convey something different. She wants the reader to
feel her confusion, and her ambivalence. She chose a simple
form—images listed in two-line stanzas—to make her point; she is
living in a world of contradictions.

Twelve

Hear the laughter;
taste the wet, salty tears.

Parties with friends,
endless homework.

Years of braces,
a beautiful smile.

Your first boyfriend,
Your first broken heart.

Talking on the phone,
being misunderstood.

You don't know what you want.
But the world is at your fingertips,
so fly away with it.

In our workshop, writers usually choose their own topic and
genre (Murray, 1982), unless we are working on a specific project
together. I do not ask the girls to write poetry, although I do publish class anthologies throughout the year and encourage everyone to contribute. Later in the year, we also compile a middle
school literary magazine which includes lots of poems from students in grades five through eight. In seventh grade the girls learn
that poetry is not a quick, easy way to complete a writing requirement. Rather, its demands are tough—economy of language, fresh

imagery, evocative metaphor, and sincere emotion. The poets we read together in class are our colleagues in the process.

Nikki Giovanni taught Marlana about specifics and about contrasts. Later in the year, after many readings and rehearsals of "Woman" as we prepared for our Chapel performance, Marlana wrote another poem:

1

I asked you to trust in me
but you said you had no faith—
I asked you to let me fly like a butterfly
but you put me on a leash
I asked to talk to you
but you said you were busy
I baked you a cake
you said it needed more salt
I scrubbed your kitchen floor
but you said you saw a spot.
I told you I needed your support
but you left me stranded and alone
So I'm silent now.

2

I told you a funny story,
but you said you weren't in the mood
I wrote you a letter,
but you never wrote back.
I came to see you
but you left me stranded in the night.
You became colder and meaner,
like strong wind in winter,
And I became you: disappointed, brokenhearted,
frostbitten from your harsh actions,
So now I'm silent.

The whole subject of friendship comes up again and again in poems, as the girls struggle with the ever-shifting loyalties among them. It is easy to see that they long for earlier days when they could say what they meant and trust that their friends were doing the same. Their anguish pours itself onto the pages of their notebooks and sometimes ends up in an anthology for others to read. The need to be connected to one another in a real sense is something that just grows stronger, as Kelly shows here in her poem about a shattered romance:

Nothing

Nothing can fill up this space in my heart
 Nothing
  No one.

I thought that we'd be together forever,
 Then you left me,
  Alone.

Now I cry all day and night,
 Wishing you were here
  With me.

I loved you so much that I gave you my heart,
 And you picked it up,
  And you broke it.

Now I sit here thinking of you,
 And I don't know where I
  Went wrong.

No one can fill up this space in my heart,
 No one,
  Nothing.

For me the poem is poignant because it speaks of a truth in these girls' lives. They idealize relationships, particularly romantic relationships, and the pain they feel is very real. Jennifer writes of a similar experience:

Abandoned

I've been thrown around
like an old rag doll,
Beaten and uncared for.
But I've stood firm.
You've leaned on my shoulder
through painful times
But I'm here crying now—
Where are you?

I let you in
when you were crying in the dark.
And now I'm out here
where you were,
But there isn't a soul
to help me,
to pick me up,
and show me where
the light is.

So I've been
left alone,
like a child
in the dark.

In spite of their repeated experiences with disappointment, the girls maintain the hope and trust that ideal friendships are still possible. They long for relationships, Gilligan believes, where they can be candid and even flawed, and still loved. (1992, p. 168) Liz writes of the solace such a friendship can bring:

Together Forever, Friends

We've been through everything
Together.
The good times, the bad times,
Yet we're still
Friends.
We've had friends—
We've lost friends
Together.
When I met you, I knew we'd be
Friends.
Now we'll be together
Forever,
And that's what we are—
Together Forever. Friends.

But in her next poem Jennifer captures what I think is the essence of a young girl trying to hold on to what she knows and what she is, even though the forces of her world seem to be pulling her in other directions:

That Feeling

Ever had that feeling
when you don't know what it is?
You're sort of hurt
and angry
You want to cry
but not a single tear
will fall

You're wondering
what it is,
what can make it stop,
and you shout,
"Go away!"
in the dark
as you sit on your bed
trying to cry
trying to be angry
trying to feel ——————— something

You wait and wait
but nothing comes
So you're left alone.

Years ago, I would have been touched—perhaps—by her candor in expressing this "can't put my finger on it" kind of aching that all adolescents experience from time to time. But Gilligan's work makes me take it more seriously. Jennifer's poem seems a response to the pressures in her life telling her what to value, what to think, and what to be. As she becomes acculturated, she begins to lose something vital. She cries out in protest, longing to recapture a time when she could "feel—something," anything at all. Brown and Gilligan write that, during this time in their lives, girls can become confused about their real feelings and often turn to others to tell them what they think and feel. (1992) Jennifer is struggling with disconnection, and cries out against the emptiness. By the end of the poem, she is defeated and "alone." It is a poem to break your heart.

As I read the girls' poetry, I am reinforced in my conviction that writing is a sure way for them to stay in touch with the deepest, most candid parts of themselves. Any kind of writing can do this, of course, but poetry has further value. In elevating our emotions to an art form, it reaches out to the imaginations of readers and has the potential to make the connections that females so yearn for. There should be, I am convinced, poetry in all classrooms. "We need a more generous conception of what it means to know and a wider conception of the sources of human understanding," writes Elliot Eisner. "The poet, the painter, the composer, the playwright, as well as the physicist, the chemist, the botanist, the astronomer have something to teach us. Paying adequate attention to such forms of understanding in schools is the best way to make them a meaningful part of our students' intellectual lives." (1991)

Now, sitting in Chapel, I hear the girls speak the words of Langston Hughes, Paul Laurence Dunbar, Eloise Greenfield, Nikki Giovanni, and Lucille Clifton. Emily, Marlana, Jennifer, and Amy, all dressed in black, wave red, purple, yellow, and blue scarves above their heads, then around one another's waists as they chant Caribbean poet James Berry's "When I Dance." They give us the poem not only in words, but also in movement:

When I dance it isn't merely
That music absorbs my shyness,
My laughter settles in my eyes,
My swings of arms convert my frills
As timing tunes my feet with floor
As if I never just looked on.

It is that when I dance
O music expands my hearing
And it wants no mathematics,
It wants no thinking, no speaking,
It wants all my feeling
In with animation of place.

When I dance it isn't merely
That surprises dictate movements,
Other rhythms move my rhythms,
I uncradle rocking-memory
And skipping, hopping and running
All mix movements I balance in.

It is that when I dance
I'm costumed in a rainbow mood,
I'm okay at any angle,
Outfit of drums crowds madness round,
Talking winds and plucked strings conspire,
Beat after beat warms me like sun.

When I dance it isn't merely
I shift bodyweight balances
As movement amasses my show,
I celebrate each dancer here,
No sleep invades me now at all
And I see how I am tireless.

It is that when I dance
I gather up all my senses
Well into hearing and feeling,
With body's flexible postures
Telling their poetry in movement
And I celebrate all rhythms.

They are graceful and proud gliding across the stage, their
voices and their bodies conveying joy in the poem that has become
joy in themselves. I let myself envision them years hence, still
dancing, still shouting, still themselves. Where will they go from
here, and how will they make sure that they are heard? It is impossible to know. But I am grateful for this day, for their glowing
faces, for their earnest voices raised in hope. On this day there is
no silence.

9

Let's Remember:
Stories of Our Lives

———

"It's about waking up. A child wakes up over and over again, and notices that she's living. She dreams along, loving the exuberant life of the senses, in love with beauty and power, oblivious of herself—and then suddenly, bingo, she wakes up and feels herself alive. She notices her own awareness. And she notices that she is set down here, mysteriously, in a going world."

—Annie Dillard, "To Fashion A Text"

WALKING BACK from a poetry reading at an NCTE convention one night in Baltimore, Bill Johnson, a seventh-grade teacher from the all-male University School in Cleveland, began telling me about the writing his boys were doing. "It is livelier than anything I've seen in a long time, and better than a lot of what I've heard at the presentations here," he said. The boys were writing memoirs and family stories.

As he described the process, I became fascinated. They had done warm-up exercises in class: Write about a time you taught someone something. What do you remember about kindergarten, its smells, sounds, routines? Write about a time you felt afraid. Using the writing practice technique—write very fast; don't erase—they jotted down their early memories. At home they asked parents and grandparents many of the same questions, and came back to school with compelling stories to tell.

"It's the thought of those interviews taking place that really gets me," Bill said. "Can you just picture one of these guys asking their dads to tell them about when they were young?"

Since I found myself in a constant struggle to provide adequate scaffolding for the girls' learning while assuring them that it is their voices, not my own echoes, that I valued in the classroom, I became intrigued with Bill's idea. He talked about the mobility of today's society and what the loss of extended families means to our students. Stories, he feared, were being forgotten, and these stories were really "the landscape of the human heart." We discussed the need to examine our lives as we are living them and about the value of looking at small moments and finding meaning there; we talked about celebrating these moments instead of merely rushing through them. I thought of Don Murray and Natalie Goldberg and Annie Dillard and all the other writers who make sense of life through writing, and I knew that this was what I wanted for my students and for myself. In addition to that, the family story gathering might give the girls the chance to reestablish and strengthen their connections to their own families. By the end of the evening, I was hooked. Could we make this a joint project, I asked him? Would he bring the boys to Laurel to read their work to my students?

When I broached the matter with the girls, they were dubious. Memoir? "Nothing good ever happened to me." Family stories? "My family doesn't have any stories." They shifted uncomfortably in their seats, skeptical, nervous, and annoyed. I told them what Willa Cather had said—"Most of the basic material a writer works with is acquired before the age of fifteen." (Murray, 1990)—but still they grumbled. Finally, when I mentioned that the U.S. boys would be coming over to share their stories, their reaction was a bit different. Maybe they could keep an open mind for a few days; maybe this wouldn't be so bad after all.

In the meantime, we tried some focused writing practices, using Bill's suggestions and adding a few of our own. Write about a time you were hurt. Include as many sensory details as possible. Write about something you treasured as a young child, something that you couldn't be without. Write about a family ritual or tradition. Write about something you did for the first time. If someone drew a blank on any of the prompts, she was free to digress, as long as she stayed in the general category of memories. I read them Cynthia Rylant's beautiful book, *The Relatives Came*, and we wrote about our own experiences with family visits. Later, we looked at *Waiting to Waltz* and *When I Was Young in the Mountains*, as Rylant quickly became one of our favorite authors. When we had dozens of quick writes collected in notebooks, we reread them, searching for threads of connection. (Calkins, 1991) What were some issues or themes that seemed to surface repeatedly during these exercises? Trust what you see here, I urged them. On the wall I hung a quote from Joanne Greenberg: "Your writing is trying to tell you something. Just lend an ear." (Murray, 1990) Your story will become clear to you eventually, I promised, if you listen hard enough.

When the boys came to our room, we crowded the chairs together and sat around long tables. I don't know who was more nervous, the girls or their guests. There was lots of whispering and giggling and shifting of seating arrangements. But as soon as Bill began to talk, things settled down. He described the work they had been doing, the in-class writing and the gathering of family stories, and then asked David to read. David hid his anxiety by clowning around—rolling his eyes, smirking, commenting in code under his breath—but once he began to read, we were all startled.

"Pieces" was short. In it David told of his attachment to a baby blanket that had actually disintegrated into shreds from being so well-loved. It was lost on a trip to Disney World, and he wrote of how devastated he had felt at the time. The class laughed, and David grinned bravely. I looked at the girls' perplexed faces. This was a memoir? David stood there—no feeling is more lonely—waiting for a response. Suddenly the room erupted in a series of "Oh, I had a blankie too. . . ." from the girls, as they began to realize that this memoir project would not overwhelm them. I asked David to describe what he went through writing this piece. "Well," he said, "at first I couldn't think of anything to write about, but when I asked my mother she told me this story, and then when I started, the more I wrote, the more I remembered."

Aha! This is precisely what I had promised my girls would happen. Writing triggers memories long dormant. It is positively astonishing the things that surface when we commit ourselves to the writing. When students discover this on their own, as David did, they develop a new attraction for and confidence in writing.

Other boys read pieces about a grandmother who made her own ice cream, a stolen kiss in a kindergarten coatroom, a red coat handed down from one brother to the next. We were all impressed with the variety, the imagery, and the gentle humor. We said goodbye with promises to come to their school when our pieces were finished. And then we began in earnest.

A memoir, I explained, was not only the retelling of an event, but, more importantly, the reflection on the significance of this event. Here is what happened, and here is why it matters in my life. (Calkins, 1991) I told them that when I was growing up, the nuns who taught me used to say that our lives were like tapestries, very intricately woven. While we are alive, they said, we could only see the back side, the messy side, of the tapestry. When we died, God would show us the fine side, the good side, the finished side, and then we would know what our lives had meant. It was a metaphor that irked me even then. I wanted to take a peek from time to time at that fine side, I wanted to know what my life meant then and there, and I wanted to make it something significant. Memoir writing, I told the girls, was our chance to do that. We would look at small events and find threads of meaning, and then we would speculate on what the whole tapestry might turn out to be. We might even, if we chose, find new and different ways to weave the threads.

One night's homework was to look through family albums to find a picture that surprised them; the next day in class they wrote about their discoveries during writing practice. I hoped that perusing the photos would stir dormant memories, and that the writing would preserve these memories in a unique way. Robert Coles in his book, *The Call of Stories: Teaching and the Moral Imagination*, quotes Alyosha in Dostoevsky's novel, *The Brothers Karamazov*:

"My dear children . . . you must know that there is nothing higher and stronger than some good memory, especially a memory of childhood, of home. People talk to you a good deal about your education, but some good, sacred memory, preserved from childhood, is perhaps the best education. If one carries many such memories into life, one is safe to the end of one's days, and if one has only one good memory left in one's heart, even that may be the means of saving us." (1989, p. 183)

Molly found such a memory and wrote in her notebook:

> There is a picture of me as a baby with my grandfather holding me, feeding me a bottle. This picture touches me and makes me feel sad because my grandpa is dead now and this picture reminds me of the great times we had together. I didn't know that there were very many pictures as there are of my grandfather and me because when I was one and a half years old my grandfather became very sick and there weren't pictures of him when he was sick. The last reason I like this picture is it is when my grandfather is healthy and hearty and the last I remember of him is very pale and sick in his hospital bed.

In this simple exercise, Molly had discovered something about her family. She might choose to write about her grandfather for this project, or she might come up with another idea. The purpose of the exercises was to give students options.

From June Gould's book, *The Writer in All of Us*, we discovered a new way to explore point of view: Write about an incident that happened when you were very little, very quickly, but in as much detail as possible; now write about the same incident from the point of view of another person who was there with you; now describe the scene from the perspective of a person looking down from an airplane.

Family memories are obviously an essential part of the tapestry, part of the "waking up" process we long for. And so, we began to collect stories, calling grandparents in Florida or making special trips across town to listen to reminiscences of times past; for this project was multi-faceted. I wanted to leave lots of room for choice, but I also wanted each student to explore all the various options available by participating in class as well as homework exercises. The long-term assignment was: Write either a memoir based on an incident in your own life or a story that is important in your family.

June Gould was a big help to us: "Whether we like it or not," she writes, "we are the beneficiaries of the memories and messages our relatives leave behind for a future they will not see. Their childhood reminiscences can be inspirational and instructive, remnants of our collective heritage. Unfortunately, because many of us are too busy or too frightened to listen to them, our collective legacy has begun to wither and die.

"But you will receive a multitude of gifts if you are willing to listen to these memories. Embedded (here) are the hopes, victories, and defeats not only of your loved ones, but of the human race. Beneath the surface of their stories are the subtle clues that can guide us toward the actions that we must take in our lifetime." (Gould, 1991, p. 29)

I shared with the girls a story from my own family. My father's mother was an elegant if imperious woman. Never warm or effusive in the manner of my other grandmother (the one with the books and the poems), she seemed aloof, distant, and sometimes critical during the early years of my life. But there was a story about her as a young woman that helped me see her differently. The film "Gone with the Wind" had just been released when she arranged with a friend to go together to see it on a Saturday afternoon. Well, she waited at the agreed-upon corner for twenty, twenty-five, thirty minutes, and then realized her friend would not show up.

Undaunted, she proceeded to the theater alone and for the next three hours immersed herself in the panorama of the Old South and the passions of Scarlett O'Hara. Scarlett, you will recall, gives poor Rhett quite a difficult time. In the very last scene she realizes she does love him after all, but it's too late; he's leaving her. She cries out to him, insisting that she cannot go on without him, whereupon he retorts, "Frankly my dear, I don't give a damn," one of the most famous lines in all of film.

Well, the music blared, the curtain closed over the massive screen, and the lights came up. But my grandmother—this young teenager—refused to budge. The film, she was sure, was not over. The projectionist must be changing reels. Rhett would came back to Scarlett, and they would be together, joyously, forever. She sat through another showing of the movie, then part of a third, so certain was she that Rhett would change his mind. It was late that night when she finally left the theater.

I loved this story as a child, and I love it today. When I remember my grandmother, I see her polished fingernails, her rigid posture, her veiled eyes, but I also see a vulnerable girl weeping in a movie theater, devastated in the knowledge that things do not always work out for the best. This story helps me understand her—she was a woman who did not let people close—and it helps me understand myself, for we are more alike than we are different.

Developing Empathy

Telling the girls this story gave me the opportunity to explain something else about memoir. Sometimes we remember details that others dispute. How old was my grandmother? How long was she in the movie theater exactly? Why didn't her friend ever show up? We, the writers, decide which details are significant and which can be eliminated. We also have the option of doing what William Zinsser calls "inventing the truth." What matters is what comes back to the writer, the details that allow her to discover the meaning—the reality—of the event. We can fill in the appropriate images to get to the real essence of what we want to say. It is not imperative to have every last fact straight, when indeed, our memories come out of our perceptions and our perception of a given event will be uniquely our own, in any case. The girls were skeptical about this. Was I saying they could write fiction? No, I insisted, write the truth, but remember that your own interpretation of the actual events is the key. Coles writes, "A memory is an event endowed with the subjectivity of our imaginative life." (1989, p. 183) The essential question is, what does this mean in your life? And the true answer to that question is always larger than just the facts.

As David, writer of "Pieces," had promised, the more we wrote, the more we remembered, and soon any initial skepticism had dissipated. As Rachel commented, "One of the main things is that if you start writing about something that happened a long time ago, the more you write, the easier it comes. Once I started thinking and writing, I started remembering what my grandmother looked like."

Students who had initially complained of not having anything to write about were soon pouring their hearts into their journals. "Ideas kept popping into my head the more I wrote," they told me. Soon we were facing a new problem: which story to choose to write up as a finished piece. Some decided to recapture important moments in their own lives, often developing new insight about what had happened, through the act of writing.

In a conference on her piece, Amanda had this to say: "'The Paddling Nun Affair' means a lot to me because it ended up totally different than I thought. I had always thought that this nun was really mean, but when I wrote this piece, I began to understand that I was wrong about that. Writing made me see that I had a young kid's idea of her, not a right idea."

Amanda now sees this adult in her life with more compassionate eyes. It is a facet of her development, of course, but it is the writing that allows her to discover and express her new attitude. Like Amanda, many others changed their minds about people and incidents from the past.

Just as my memory of my grandmother's story gives me empathy for her and changes the reality of my present life, so, too, did the girls come to know and understand their family members—and themselves—better.

Hillary said, "I learned that my family isn't as normal as I thought it was. I also learned that the funniest things happen before you're born. Now I know how my family used to act."

Drawing on our work with point of view, several girls chose to write their pieces from someone else's perspective. Bernice tried telling her story about moving from Russia to America first from her grandmother's point of view:

. . . When you were almost three years old the family decided to move to America. I was so worried that you wouldn't leave without me. Your Dad had started taking short walks with you, so you'd be used to him and being without me. Surprising enough, when you were already loaded to leave, about to drive off, I kissed and hugged you, and you simply waved and left. No crying, no anything, just a simple wave . . .

In her next draft she decided to tell the story in her own voice:

. . . From the time I was one year old until the time that we moved when I was almost three, I lived with my grandparents in a small town. They took care of me and raised me very well during that one year. My parents both worked, and I guess they couldn't find a longterm babysitter, so they let my grandparents look after me. I was a cute baby and hard to refuse. My grandma acted as my mother. I called her "Babushka." I became very tied to her . . . So what was going to happen when we had to move to America from the Soviet Union without Babushka? Babushka was pretty scared I imagine, that I wouldn't want to leave without her. . . .

Neither draft satisfied her and when she discussed them with me in conference, I suspected that what she really wanted to write about was her relationship with her grandmother. She wasn't enthusiastic about this, however, and after two tries abandoned that aspect of this event altogether. As she read through her writing practices from the beginning of the year, it was easy to see that Alex, her brother away at college, was the most important person in her life. Working through drafts of her piece, focusing on what was probably the biggest change the family had ever been through, Bernice began to imagine what it must have been like for the others, particularly for her beloved Alex. Once she came up with the idea of telling the story through his eyes, she was off and running:

Alex froze and wiped the cold sweat off his forehead as he put down the telephone receiver. Today he had come home from school early because he hadn't felt too well. He had on a sweater and grey sweat pants that matched the color of his eyes. His hair was dark and curly and looked uncombed. His face, now scared, revealed more freckles.

Alex sat down on the bed and shivered. He reviewed the telephone conversation he had just had with his mother in his head once more. She had called him and asked how he felt. She told him to hurry up and feel better because in a few weeks they—meaning his little two year old sister, his parents and him—would be leaving for America. All he could think of was leaving all he had behind and starting all over again. As he thought about it over and over again, sad memories sprung to his mind.

America?! That explained why his parents had been packing for weeks and weeks, having tutors come over and give them lessons on how to speak English. That was why they had been receiving hundreds of letters from his aunt and uncle who lived in America.

Alex slowly put on his jacket, trying not to let tears start flowing down his face. But one by one, they dribbled down from his eyes. He took off his jacket, washed his face, then put the jacket on again, took the key to the apartment, and went outside.

"Hi," said Alex to his best friend Drew. Drew ran over to where Alex was standing and threw a football to him.

"Think fast," replied Drew, laughing as Alex's eyes widened and he nearly fell over trying to catch the ball. He would really miss his best friend's corny tricks. A bunch of boys ran after Drew and started playing football too. When they were dead tired and out of breath, tears started falling out of Alex's watery eyes. He would miss his close buddies terribly! His friends looked at him but didn't laugh because they understood this was something serious, for Alex barely ever cried.

"Guys," he said, wiping his eyes and trying to keep his voice steady. "I-I . . . um . . ." His eyes watered up again. "I'm—well,—um—I'm moving to America in a few weeks," he spurted out quickly. He then started running for his apartment. They followed after him and soon caught up. They all, especially Drew, understood and wanted to help him and tell him it wouldn't be so bad. After all, they could still be friends writing back and forth to each other. . . .

While we were writing, we were also reading. As a class we read excerpts from Russell Baker's *Growing Up* and from Annie Dillard's *An American Childhood*. Another selection that had real impact on the girls was Maya Angelou's "Graduation" chapter from *I Know Why the Caged Bird Sings*. Very often reflection on these pieces—which all dealt with specific incidents, brief snatches of time—led to thinking that had much broader implications.

Hallie: The Annie Dillard piece about the dances from *An American Childhood*—I loved the first sentence, "The boys were changing. . . ." Especially since I have recently realized the true meaning of this. I don't know when this was written, but I know that everything she said about her dance is absolutely true, how you pick out boys to dance with and which are cute. I think that the author did a really good job of showing the boys change and develop, from gross things to cute.

She also hints at a very serious topic here. There is a dancing school like hers here in Cleveland. They won't let you in unless you are Christian, white Christian. It's not right that some people are turned away like that.

Shana wrote about "Graduation:"

This experience has probably been one of the events that inspired Maya Angelou. She wanted to prove to the world (and
to herself) that she was talented enough and had enough
courage to let all people see beyond her skin color and see her
poetry. She was brave and confident enough (because of the
lessons of her graduation) to put herself to the test. By having
a white, critical speaker, they put themselves to an important
test—whether they were able to distinguish prejudice and
real inferiority. There is a difference. Inferiority, like superiority, has no color. When times are difficult, she can look back
to 1940 or even further into her ancestry and see how far
she and the world have come; this is an opportunity not to
be wasted. She also knows not to use her color as an excuse.
During the man's speech, she was saying to herself, "I am
black, therefore inferior." She now knows to say, "I am black,
therefore proud. I know anything I accomplish that is worth-
while will be because of hard work." She knows that she
should try to express these feelings in her writing so that others will be able to overcome prejudice and tolerate others'
values.

The literature got us thinking about big issues; we saw what
insight can be gained when we look at specific moments in our
lives and reflect on how these moments change us. And this, of
course, is why we read in the first place, to figure out how to live
our lives, to learn to be better people than we are now. "Literature," says Mem Fox, "provides essential sustenance for the soul."
(1993, p. 94)

When Christmas came, I read aloud Truman Capote's *A Christmas Memory,* the story of a young boy's special relationship with an
elderly relative, replete with all the sights, sounds, and aromas of
the holiday. Enraptured, the girls exclaimed, "He makes my
mouth water when he describes how the kitchen smells."

I also read Gloria Houston's *The Year of the Perfect Christmas Tree,*
a story handed down to the author from her own grandmother,
and several tales from *My Grandmother's Stories: A Collection of Jewish
Folktales* by Adele Geras. It seemed that memoirs presented themselves at every turn. Cynthia Rylant's *But I'll Be Back Again,* which
I read a few pages at a time, became the most popular read-aloud
I've ever done; the girls literally raced into the room after lunch
demanding to hear more. We read Forrest Carter's *The Education*

of Little Tree together as a class and fell captive to the charms of the young Cherokee growing up in the mountains with his grandparents.

Because we are constantly working to understand the craft of writing, I asked the girls to choose a memoir by a favorite writer to read and respond to in their notebooks. I provided a good variety of titles in my classroom and asked our school librarian to be sure she, too, had plenty of these on hand.

Lois Duncan and Beverly Cleary are authors they know well, and the memoirs of both were quite popular. Several girls chose to read Baker's *Growing Up* or Dillard's *An American Childhood* in their entirety, after having their curiosity piqued in class. And Maya Angelou's autobiography was in constant demand. Not as many chose Eudora Welty's *One Writer's Beginnings* as I had hoped, but those who did seemed to appreciate this author's wisdom.

> Dear Mrs. Barbieri,
>
> I finally finished the book, *One Writer's Beginnings,* by Eudora Welty. The last section of the book, "Finding a Voice," has some very moving things in it. For instance, Eudora said after father died, she learned about how well he knew what he was doing. She appreciated all the things he had done for her. She also said we learn more about our parents after they die. This reminded me of when my grandfather died, and after everyone dried their wet eyes, they talked about what a great person he was, and how much he had achieved. He worked until he could walk no longer.
>
> Another interesting thing she said about her writing was that she was her own teacher. She told herself, "This doesn't make sense," or "This is good writing." I think it's important, even though it's very hard, to do this. I remembered what you said at the beginning of the year: "There is not only one teacher in this writing room, there are nineteen."

Neeti is teaching herself to be a writer all the time, and she wants to keep learning more about it from Eudora Welty, from her classmates and teacher, and from her own practice. The memoir project served her well.

When everyone had completed a piece, it was time for the long awaited visit to University School. It was a clear January afternoon when we walked over to the school, nervous but eager. We gathered in the library and one by one, the girls read their pieces. Since the boys and girls were not used to working together, response was a bit formal and polite. Later Bill Johnson confessed that the boys were surprised that the girls' pieces were "so much more emotional," while my students wondered why the boys' pieces were so short and to the point. It would be a mistake to generalize, however. I was struck by the tenderness and compassion in many of the boys' pieces, particularly Jay's:

The Red Coat

My dad, second oldest of four, had a grandmother named Nana. Nana always liked Jeff, my dad's older brother, the best. The three of them had many confrontations together. One of them was with a red coat. It gives you a taste of what Nana was like.

Jeff spun around in the room with the red coat on his back, as the family watched with joy. Nana sat in the center and complimented her buy and her wonderful grandson Jeff. Jeff thanked her for the red coat as they kissed and hugged and the night was over.

Sunday nights were like this in the Williams' family for quite awhile, but after some time Jeff outgrew the red coat, and it was my dad's turn to get it. All the hand-me-downs went to my dad. Being my dad's age, he thought the coat would make him the most popular at Sunday night family get-togethers. He was extremely excited.

It was a Sunday night and time for the family to go out. My dad was finally ready to go too, after standing in front of the mirror for what seemed to be an hour. With Kathy, his sister, in her new white dress and Nancy in her stroller, the family headed off.

When they got to Mayfield, my dad's heart was racing. He took occasional glances at Jeff in his navy blazer, and he knew that he had it made.

As they entered the lobby of the country club, everybody smiled, hugged and said hello. Nana stood there with arms open as Jeff gave her a big hug and they shared their weekly compliments.

My dad walked out from the crowd and smiled with the little red coat on. Nana frowned as she stared at the boy. Aunts and uncles, cousins and friends quietly looked to see what the problem was.

"That's Jeff's coat!" Nana scolded.

"Yes, Nana, but Jeff has outgrown it and it's now David's," their mom said with hope.

There was a pause and then, "Well, I'll just have to get Jeff a new one," Nana happily pronounced as she gave Jeff another hug.

My dad bowed his head and walked away. One woman's words can do a lot to one kid's heart.

During the closing weeks of the trimester, I asked my girls to evaluate the memoir project. What did it mean to them?

Maureen had this to say, "I learned that writing about my family makes me closer to them. Now there are no hidden stories that I haven't heard. When my mother or just my family and I look back on memories, we'll rejoice or cry. That is what brings us together," demonstrating that her writing is personally useful and meaningful to her and to those around her.

Hallie was just a little less enthusiastic: "I feel that my memoir improved as I revised it. In my story there were solid facts and I remembered them very clearly. If we hadn't read most of those pieces, then I think the project wouldn't have been as good. But, I think we might have done a little much, and we were on the breaking point of being overly memoired."

From my perspective, I have rarely seen students this engaged. Listening to student writing every day has always been what I love best about teaching, but the writing and the talk about writing and living that emerged and flourished during this project surpassed even my expectations. Certainly narrative—specifically memoir—has a place in the middle school writing curriculum and in the development of girls' voices of care, compassion, and connection; voices that boys need opportunities to develop too.

As a writer, I know firsthand the value of remembering, of hearing and telling my own family stories, and now my students know it too. Our stories open up unchartered realms for us, redefining our families and reshaping our lives. Our stories help us understand who we are and why we are here.

Lorene Cary writes, "What my stories do is tell me why—why the old people looked at us with such unforgiving eyes, why they pushed us away, but wouldn't let go. Without the stories, I'd have nothing to explain the cacophony in my head in the indigo New Hampshire night. . . . I did not ask for the stories, but I was given them to tell, to retell and pass along. I was given them to plait into my story, to use, to give me the strength to take off my skin and stand naked and unafraid in the night, to touch other souls in the night." (1991, p. 237)

10

Things Worth Doing: Forging New Connections

———

But the thing worth doing well done has a shape that satisfies, clean and evident . . .

—Marge Piercy, *"To be of use"*

AT A place like Laurel, steeped in four generations of tradition, proud of its high standards, and determined to guard its reputation for excellence, being a new teacher is hard. Faculty members may be welcoming, but there is a definite sense of expectation in the air, a skepticism, a careful watching and waiting. Besides being new, I had the added dimension of being "different," more process-oriented, more radical than veterans who had been honored by the school community for years. The fact that I did not teach English traditionally, with lots of formal grammar exercises and plenty of classical literature assignments, made me immediately suspect, and left me feeling more than a little apprehensive.

But the wonderful thing about independent school administrators is that they encourage and support independence in teachers. Each fall, I would write professional goals, turn them in to the division head, and implement the English curriculum for my students as I saw fit. I knew several of my colleagues were critical of my methods, but no one questioned my commitment. For two years I shut my door, reading, writing, and talking with the girls, believing they were thriving. Seventh-grade life was stressful, thanks to high academic expectations, increasingly complex social demands, and rigorous extracurricular schedules. For some girls, the biggest challenge was American history where their teacher was known for his stern demeanor and his exacting study requirements.

Held in highest esteem by faculty, parents, and students, Gene Rosaschi is a tough task-master. His map quizzes are legendary for their precision; students believe he knows more than anyone alive about the geography of the world, and they are probably right. He runs his class like a drill sergeant, expecting—and getting—one hundred percent engagement from his students. It's his habit to call each girl by her last name, unusual at Laurel. Anyone late or without a textbook is not admitted to class. And he is proud of his reputation as a "tough grader." New to Laurel, even I was a bit intimidated by his businesslike manner. I suspected that he had little use for my attitudes towards reading and writing, and I tried, those first years, to steer clear of him.

My objective was to help the girls build confidence in themselves as they internalized notions of what it meant to read, write, and think effectively. I wanted them to love reading and writing as much as I did, and love, in some cases, the poems and books that I loved too. But it is fair to say that my students, as human beings, are more important to me than the content of any curriculum; I have always felt that I teach people, not literature or writing. Thus, content in my class was always negotiable.

In her wonderful book, *Care: A Feminine Approach to Ethics and Moral Education*, Nel Noddings argues that the development of an ethic of caring should be a primary goal of education. She describes an effective teacher as "one-caring," an image that feels natural and appropriate to me.

"The one-caring as teacher is not necessarily permissive," Noddings writes. "She does not abstain from leading the student, or persuading (her), or coaxing (her) toward an examination of school subjects. But she recognizes that, in the long run, (she) will learn what (she) pleases. We may force (her) to respond in specified ways, but what (she) will make (her) own and eventually apply effectively is that which (she) finds significant for (her) own life. . . . The special gift of the teacher, then is to receive the student, to look at the subject matter with (her). Her commitment is to (her), the cared-for, and (she) is—through that commitment—set free to pursue (her) legitimate projects." (Noddings, 1984, p. 176–177)

Literacy Beyond English Class

Noddings' model of learning was one I embraced gratefully; it was, in fact, my ideal. But I began to notice that, while they were indeed coming to love words, poems, and books, and while they were beginning to take more risks in their writing, the girls were obviously confused about what literacy meant beyond the walls of our English room. In other school contexts, they felt less in charge and less confident than they felt in my room.

"Good writing," one after another told me, "means one thing in here and another thing in history class." Frustration grew for all of us. "Good writing has to be correct, with perfect spelling," they'd tell me when I urged them to write quickly during writing practice. One day, upon reading her teacher's comments on a recently returned history paper, Danielle came into our classroom lamenting, "I'm no good at syntax. I have to work at syntax. I'm going to make that my goal from now on—syntax." She frowned as she turned the pages. "Mrs. B.," she asked, "what is syntax?" Clearly, something had to give. Their respected history teacher and their radical English teacher were working at cross purposes.

Of course, I had known it all along. The need for connectedness applies in all facets of girls' lives, not just in their relationships, but also in their academic disciplines. Often, their ways of learning involved making associations, understanding how one concept fit into their scheme of personal knowledge. While some boys find it comfortable and logical to look at facts objectively, most girls want to see the big picture early on. (Gilligan et al., 1990) The Carnegie Report on Middle Schools, *Turning Points,* criticizes schools for compartmentalizing learning, making it trivial, thwarting any real understanding or ability to transfer knowledge to other contexts: "Too often, middle grade curricula promote competency in specific subjects but not the ability to reason critically and integrate information from several disciplines . . . Superb opportunities to develop the values and sense of social responsibility important for citizenship exist for young adolescents but are often overlooked." (p. 12)

I knew that, as teachers concerned with this research, we should be talking about our common goals for the girls, addressing our differences, and finding ways to compromise. So why didn't I take the first step in this direction? For one thing, I was in awe. Many alumni of the school insisted Gene was the best teacher they had ever had. Other teachers in the school looked up to him; some even audited his classes! And Laurel had bestowed on him her highest honor—the coveted Hostetler Award for excellence in teaching. I respected his intelligence, his experience, and his convictions. I also believed strongly in my own principles, and I wanted, above all, to avoid a confrontation. It did not occur to me that I might have been deferring to him because he was a man.

I thought of all Gilligan had written about "adult good women," how we encourage self-sacrifice and self-silencing, avoiding conflict at all costs, passing a message on to girls that this is what is expected of them too. (Brown and Gilligan, 1992) Was this what I was doing? Was I modeling something harmful through my own reluctance to enter into a difficult conversation? What exactly was I so afraid of anyway? This teacher and I valued different elements in the girls' learning; I was certain of that.

I found him to be authoritative and rigid in his response to their work. He seemed appalled that I asked the girls to choose their own titles, even romance novels, for the reading component of my course; often in study hall, he'd tell them to do some real work instead of reading such "fluff." The noise coming out of my room baffled and annoyed him. And I suspected that he found my manner of teaching writing to be too laissez-faire. Instead of explaining the theory behind what I did, I avoided talking to him. The students were getting so many mixed signals that anything they might have been learning in my room was in serious jeopardy. How could this be remedied?

Finding Common Ground

The eighth-grade team, led by this same history teacher, had implemented a block schedule for English, history, and science, meeting together regularly to plan themes. When Andrea Archer took over as middle school director, she encouraged me to find common ground, perhaps in the literature, as a way to work more closely with him. I knew from our weekly team meetings and from the girls' descriptions what was going on in history class, and I began to bring in books—poetry, fiction, and nonfiction—that would tie in with their studies. Slowly, I became aware that my knowledge of the literature and my attempts to correlate my course with his met with his tacit approval and appreciation. The girls read regularly, responding in their notebooks and sharing reactions in group conversations in English class.

> *Christine:* When I read "For My People" by Margaret Walker, I could actually see the black people working in the fields and kitchens. The small children imagining things they knew might never come true and wondering why not.
>
> This poem makes you feel the way the slaves and their children must have. How it felt to be controlled by another person who was really just as equally as yourself but couldn't do anything about it without being punished severely.
>
> I feel ashamed for the people who started slavery and excepted it. I despise them all.
>
> But like it says in the last stanza, we can not do anything about what is gone now, but we can about the present and the future. We can change the mistakes that were made.

A month later, the girls were studying the Civil War, and although "war books" were not their favorite genre, I asked them each to read something that addressed the effects of the war, rather than the actual battles.

Sarah saw value in looking at the same historical material from two perspectives when reading Jakes' *North and South.*

Dear Mrs. B,

It was neat to take what I learned in history class and apply it to fictional, but in a sense real, characters. I enjoyed reading about something in *North and South* and then being able to say, "Oh, yea, we talked about that in history class." I also learned a lot from reading that the history text doesn't cover or we haven't read yet.

So intrigued was Sarah with the Civil War era that she chose to read another book dealing with this time period.

Dear Mrs. B.,

I am reading *The Last Silk Dress* by Ann Rinaldi. I get a different view of the Civil War than I got from reading Jakes' *North and South.* The main character is a fourteen year old girl named Susan. I can relate to her and her life. I guess over time parents don't change. Her parents don't want her to grow up and my parents don't want mc to grow up.

It is quite humorous to think of the high-society women giving up their silk dresses to help the "Cause." Like the author, Ann Rinaldi, I would like to believe the story is true.

I like reading historical fiction, because I get a feel for what the feelings were like before, during, and after the Civil War. A feel for the personal side of things. I like the main character Susan. She is rebellious in small ways. Susan loves to read, her mother hates that; Susan's mom considers reading unlady-like. Also Susan isn't allowed out of the house alone, her mom thinks it isn't safe. Susan's solution—she borrows her brother's old clothes and goes out as a boy. This book is good so far, and in a way, it seems tinged with mystery. I guess time will tell.

Of course, there is nothing new about asking students to read historical fiction; teachers do it every day, developing whole theme studies across the curriculum. I had resisted this in the past for two reasons. I saw many themes as trivial and contrived, and I feared that reading literature for its own sake—story, fully developed characters, beautiful language, and metaphor—would be lost in the process. The attempt to guide their choices with a deliberate eye towards what they were doing in another class was new for me. I tried to make sure the girls had a wide range of books in my room, and I provided lists of other titles they might find in the school or public libraries, assuaging my concern about assigning a specific topic. *Gone with the Wind* by Margaret Mitchell was a big favorite; *Across Five Aprils* by Irene Hunt and other YA titles were equally popular.

Danielle:

Dear Mrs. Barbieri,

I'm reading *The Slave Dancer* by Paula Fox. I think this book tells a lot about the Civil War, how slaves were prohibited in England but slaves were profitable so people still sold them. I feel very sorry for Jessie, the boy in this book, especially because he is only thirteen years old. When he was going to his aunt's house, these people grabbed him and put him on a boat.

The part that is really sad is that Jessie may never see his mother again, and his mother doesn't know where he is. This reminds me of a lot of the cases in World War II. Lots of families would be separated when they were hiding or would be picked off the street to be a soldier.

This also reminds me of *My Brother Sam Is Dead* (Collier and Collier). In that book it told how the mother had felt when Sam was gone and I can imagine in this book how awful it must feel to not see his mother for a period of time.

Jessie seems like he has to be friends with the older people on the boat since there's no one his age. His so called friends don't even seem to be that nice. They all are hungry and act like pigs for any available food, beating people if they took more than their share. I would have probably wanted more food, but I probably wouldn't have risked getting beaten for food.

As I read their responses to their Civil War books, I saw clearly that the girls were doing much more than learning history. In coming to know the characters "in a personal way," they were developing compassion and empathy for human beings whose experiences were radically different from their own. They made references to other literature and to their own experiences and observations of life, demonstrating their ability to read intertextually.

In addition to writing to me about their books, the girls also wrote to one another. (Atwell, 1987) Knowing classmate Jane's propensity for romance novels, Sarah tried to entice her into reading *The Last Silk Dress,* demonstrating her awareness of her responsibility to others in her reading community. Because she likes Jane, Sarah hoped to share a positive reading experience with her:

> Dear Jane,
>
> Right now I am reading *The Last Silk Dress* by Ann Rinaldi. I love the main character Susan. Susan is a bit on the rebellious side. Her mother wants her to be a lady, but Susan wants to read, something her mom deems "unladylike." . . . Susan is fourteen and easy to relate to . . . She reminds me of Jo from *Little Women.* (Alcott) Ann Rinaldi has a very good way of showing the personal side of the Civil War. Not only is the story interesting, but it is factual. I think you would love this book because it's a way of romanticizing the beginning of the war.

Tying history and English together seemed to be having a positive effect on the girls in both classes. As teachers, Gene and I discovered we had more in common than we had previously believed. As we talked about the girls' writing, I realized that what the history teacher valued was clarity, specific information, good organization, and adherence to mechanical conventions. He may have been a bit tougher evaluating these elements of their pieces than I was, but he and I agreed on the value of writing in any learning experience. We decided to try to work together.

The first idea came from Claudia Boatright, the head of the history department. Familiar with Gilligan's work, and eager to have the girls understand women's roles in the history of the nation, she suggested that we do a theme on women's suffrage. The history assignment would be to take on the role of a particular woman from the time from 1840 to 1870 and to do research on this woman's life. Roles included a reformer, an Irish immigrant, a textile mill worker, a woman moving west, a tribal Indian, a farmer's wife, a black slave, a frontier wife, a wealthy upperclass wife, and an abolitionist, among others. Would I like to get involved? Thinking immediately of books like *Lyddie* by Katherine Paterson and *Prairie Song* by Pam Conrad and even *O Pioneers* by Willa Cather, I was eager to help. I would gather as many books as I could—fiction and nonfiction—and I would help the girls with their research. Would Gene, I asked, be willing to give them some freedom in the genre of the research reports? Could they, for example write diary entries or fictional stories? After thinking it over, he agreed, as long as certain specified information would be included. We were off on our first true collaboration.

Journals, Research, Discovery

Might journal writing be a natural beginning for the research, I wondered, or would that be a little too "soft" for a history project? Since time is always at a premium, and since there was lots of ground to cover during history class periods, I offered to make the journal writing a part of my class routine for the duration of the project. It would supplant writing practice; rather, the girls would continue to do writing practice, but for now it would be writing practice as their assigned characters.

The girls greeted this idea with disdain. "How can I write as a mill girl when I don't know anything about her?" "I haven't started my research yet, so I can't do this." "This is stupid. I don't know what to write about a farm woman." "I can't. . . ."

While I understood their reluctance to write in strange voices,—after all, these were girls accustomed to knowing the parameters of an assignment and fulfilling them—I believed they knew more than they thought they knew. I suspected that their intuition and their experience (Belenky et al.) would lead them in good directions and that their writing would raise the very questions that would guide their research.

"Use your imaginations," I told them. "Write whatever you think this woman would have been concerned about. Just let yourselves go. Just try."

After some more groaning, they settled in and wrote, most remembering the first rule of writing practice, "Keep your hand moving." Once again, I was amazed at their efforts.

Danielle became a farm woman:

> Today was a better day than yesterday. My husband wasn't in a bad mood when he came home. I had prepared his favorite cornbread with some sugar on it, apple pie, and we ate pork. I remembered that dreadful day when the pig was slaughtered. We had only had one pig at that time, and we didn't have enough food to feed him. My husband decided that we needed the pig to eat, so one day he slaughtered it. He was the pig that we had raised since he was born. The children

had loved him. The day that the pig was killed for meat my husband came home in a bad mood. I have saved the meat for a few weeks because now we have more pigs slaughtered, so the children won't think we are eating their pet. Today, some of my husband's friends had come to eat with us. I wish I would have known ahead of time, so I could have made more food, but we are a poor family.

For Danielle, living on a farm would mean having to kill beloved animals. She writes here of her concern for her children and of her desire to please her husband. Even before doing any reading, she is putting herself in her character's place, speculating on what it must have been like to be a wife and a mother during hard times. As the weeks went on she became more comfortable in her role:

We live in the north. We don't own much land. My children go to a New England school while I stay home and cook and sometimes work on the farm although our farm isn't very big. My husband mainly works on the farm each day while I'm inside tending to things. My husband is very strict, always questioning me and always ordering me what to cook. He guards me every minute, and sometimes when he comes off the farm in a bad mood, maybe because the animals weren't cooperating with him, he always blames it on me. I can't fight back because there's no use, women are practically owned by the men. My husband works all day on the farm and when he comes in, he expects a good dinner.

Christine became a woman moving west:

It's hard traveling across the prairie. The scattered bones along the worn road are left to be gathered by the following travelers. It's merely a grave yard. The sick children lying along the road left to be eaten by wolves makes me gag. It's just an adventure for my brother Tom, but for me a punishment. I think the loss of loved ones is far more important than land. We had plenty where we lived, and we shouldn't be moving.

At every river we have to unload all 2000 pounds of supplies, ford the wagon, then load it on the other side. The Platte River's water is a thick dirty cream that is bearly drinkable, but will have to do. Every day the men in the train go hunting.

Alix Travis, the upper school librarian, helped us compile resources, and I brought in both fiction and nonfiction titles to help students come to know their characters. Their formal reports for history were due in one month's time, to be followed up by a simulated Women's Suffrage meeting where they would demonstrate their knowledge orally. Excitement grew as time went on. Christine read Pam Conrad's *Prairie Song* and a nonfiction book entitled *Women's Diaries of the Westward Journey* by Lillian Schlissel. Fulfilling the ongoing requirement of responding in writing to her nightly reading, she wrote:

Dear Mrs. B.,

Women's Diaries of the Westward Journey by Lillian Schlissel is a very helpful resource for my history report. I like the comparison made to show you the different reasons men and women traveled west and their feelings toward the journey.

I feel, after reading parts of this book, that women played a much larger role in the travel west than the men. When men went hunting, they usually came back with nothing, and the long hours they were away, the women were in charge. All the tasks they did were unbelievable.

The differences of men's and women's outlook toward Indians, were very interesting. I agree with the women and say the Indians were more helpful than harmful.

I'm uncertain after reading whether the hardships they went through were worth just a new plot of land.

Sarah, whose role was to be a mill girl, read Katherine Paterson's *Lyddie,* and in her journal entries showed how the book increased her understanding of her character:

Dear Diary,

It is my first day working at the Mill. I am so tired that I keep on drifting off to sleep. My feet are covered with blisters, and I have worked harder today than I would have on any given day at the farm. I didn't even work as hard during harvest as I did today.

So much has happened since I got here three nights ago. First I went and signed a contract and had to read it. Lucky for me Tommy taught me to read. Our days are controlled by belles. Sometimes I think I hate the belles, but most of the time, I like them, they keep me on schedule.

Today was kind of exciting, and kind of scarey too. I mean, I had to work two looms. A man who was near me, helped me learn how to do the weaving. I was so confused! The spindle flew off and hit one of the girls, she had a big gash in her head and she had to be rushed off to her boarding house where doctor saw her.

Today I met a girl named Hanna. Hanna told me some awful things about her life hear at the mill. I guess in a way she scared me with some of the atrocities that go on. But I'm still glad to be hear. I do miss the farm, though, I miss Mama, Papa, Tommy, and Rosealy, but I needed to come hear. The family needs my support so hear I am. Maybe if Tommy wasn't going to Harvard, and Rosealy wasn't an invalid, I wouldn't be here, but there's no reason to think about the what-if's. I'm here, so I might as well make the best of it. I hope my family is alright and I will pray for them before I fall to bed. The bell has rung, signalling bed-time.

Good-bye,

Katherine

Dear Diary,

I'm so worn out, today I worked for 12 hours. I was on my feet the whole time. I'm beginning to think the petition going around demanding a ten-hour work day is definitely a good thing. I think I'll sign my name, despite the fact that I may be black-listed and fired. I keep on thinking of Oberlin. In Oberlin there is a college which excepts girls; I want to go there; but that is only wishful thinking! My family needs the money.

Sincerely,

Katherine

As we continued to read and write in English class, the girls were learning about the abolitionist movement and the women's suffrage movement in history. Their journal writing began to take on these concerns, as they prepared for the eventual suffrage meeting they would all attend at the conclusion of the project.

Christine began to write to a fictional sister:

Dear Julia,

More than ever I would like to attend the Suffrage Meeting in Akron. I'm planning to complain about our elected officers who seem to be doing nothing about slavery in the South. I'm sick and tired of the crops here. The crops are horrible and our land can only produce potatoes and who can live on that for your life? We are moving West now. We haven't met up with any Indians yet and hope not to for our entire journey. My daughter Lisa Marie is slowly recovering from a mild case of cholera.

The report deadline was fast approaching, and we discussed various options for presenting what the girls had learned. They were also nervous and excited about the prospect of doing a dramatic role-play at the suffrage meeting and deluged me with factual questions. "How would a slave girl get to a suffrage meeting?" "How about me; I'm a German immigrant. How will I get there?" I realized that the girls needed more specific information than I could provide, so I turned to Claudia Boatright for help. Would she be willing, I wondered, to come into my room and field all these questions for us? Happily, we set the date, and the girls brainstormed their questions ahead of time. While all the girls planned well for this guest in our room, Danielle's questions were particularly exhaustive, demonstrating her developing ability to use writing as a means of inquiry. Danielle, along with many of her classmates, was fascinated with the different roles men and women played at this time in history:

1. Did the farmers' wives often go to the general store, or did the men go more?
2. Could a farmer's wife sneak away from her drunk husband while he was sleeping to go to a meeting?
3. Although they grew potatoes, did they also grow other crops?
4. Why would a farmer's wife want to vote?
5. Did New England farmers' wives have accents?
6. Was Maine a good place to have a farm?
7. Did the New England farms run into any weather trouble?
8. Did the farm husbands chat with other farm husbands?
9. How did the women know to get up at 4 o'clock each morning?
10. Did the women ever get some extra cash? If so, how and where would they use it?
11. Were they ever paid by their husbands?
12. About how many acres were on a farm in the north?

13. Would the farmers' wives read a woman's magazine or just a magazine for the men?
14. Would the husband start off nice and gradually get more demanding?
15. Did the wives have to at least buy some utensils from the General Store?
16. Did the wives dislike their life?
17. Did the farmer's family make any money?
18. Did the husbands read?
19. Did the farmer's wives (in the north) care about slavery at all?

History Becomes Personal

What shocked the girls more than anything as they learned more about this time period was the fact that women had no means of avoiding pregnancy. Their guest speaker emphasized the fact that childbearing was the woman's chief role in life and that this affected everything else she did or thought about doing. Danielle wrote the day after the visit:

> I'm a Christian. I go to church every Sunday, and that's my source of gossip. I want the right to vote to own myself and my children. Now my husband owns everything. I get pregnant every two years . . . one of my children died. I've decided a Suffrage Meeting is the place I need to go. I haven't had much time to think about my worries, but when I do, more and more gets on my mind. Today I snuck out while my husband was drunk. He came home drunk with a few guys. He went right to sleep on the floor. He does this often and doesn't wake up until the middle of the night. I walked to the meeting, since it was only a few miles away. When I got there, there were a whole bunch of women, some of them farmers' wives. I thought women should vote because I heard there were town meetings. Actually, I once sat at a meeting while my husband voted.

Danielle began to ponder the question of male superiority, realizing finally that it was unfair to deny women equality, since they did the same hard work the men did:

> At the Suffrage Meeting we talked about women's right to vote. I think it should be very important for women to vote.

My husband votes and I don't. The husbands think they're
superior to the women. They always think that they should
vote and women can't. I think we're just as intelligent as the
men, especially my husband. Besides, I don't know how we
could get more superior than each other when we're both
working on the farm. He though doesn't think women, especially me, should vote.

Some of the girls chose to write traditional papers, organizing
their information into three- or four-page reports, while others
chose to present diaries, simulated newspaper accounts, or letters
to fictional family members. I listened to their emerging drafts in
writing conferences and did not ask them to do any other writing
for English during this project. We talked about their work in
terms of its content and its form, as we always did in writing workshop. The girls were nervous about turning the paper in to their
history teacher for a grade, and I continued to reassure them that
they were doing important and valuable work and that they had
learned a great deal about their characters already. I applauded the
creativity of their projects. Molly burned the edges of her paper to
make it look really old. Emily practiced her German accent for the
suffrage meeting. Danielle compiled a newspaper from her character's hometown and included political and social news as well as
advertisements for hair tonic. Each girl cited at least three sources
at the end of her paper, and their history teacher evaluated the
writing based on accuracy of information and grace of presentation. Christine titled her work *Trail of Opportunity.*

Preface

In the 1850s the Western Territories held great promise for
women. The stories heard in the East characterized these
frontier settlements as cooperative, tolerant, and marvelously
free. (Reiter, 161) It was this settling which would give
women a hand in shaping their country's future. By challenging the people and laws which limited their own activities
and rights as women, they helped to win new freedoms and
greater opportunities for *all* women.

This is a letter written by Agnes Millington to her sister living in Independence, Missouri. Agnes, newly widowed, has
no sheltering relatives in the East, so she has decided to leave
New York and move to Oregon with her sister's family. While
in transit, she shares some of her expectations as well as how
a Woman's Suffrage Meeting has stirred her inner desires for

self-reliance, freedom, and a sense of equality with men, unfelt in her Eastern homeland.

Akron, Ohio
March 27, 1852

Dearest Helen,

I'm accepting your invitation to accompany you and Jake on your journey to Oregon. But I must sadly tell you, I will be coming alone. A month ago, my beloved Charles was tragically killed while tending our dairy cattle in the barn. A bull pinned him against the stall door, crushing his chest. The sorrow was almost too much for me to bear, especially when it closely followed the death of our Baby Elizabeth last fall. My strong faith in God has sustained me, and my dear friends of the Presbyterian Church back home in Oswego, New York, were of immense support. My life suddenly became empty and widowhood made me falsely believe I had no future. You are my only family now, and as we have no relatives in the east, I wish to be near you. For this reason, I left the farm and have sold many of our possessions. With thirty-five dollars of this money, I have secured stagecoach passage out to Independence. (Schlissel, p. 100) But for now I am stopped in Akron, Ohio for the next week due to a transportation delay.

Most interestingly I have met some fellow travelers who have journeyed to this town specifically to attend a Women's Suffrage Meeting. Much of their discussion has me curious about these public gatherings and bold crusaders for women's rights. After my husband's death, I was surprised that I was able to retain my property rights, being there were few laws to protect me. These women have helped me see the law's inequities and that there is definitely a need for women's right to vote.

I remember reading about the first Women's Suffrage Meeting held in Seneca Falls, not far from my home, in 1848. (Rappaport, p. 59) At that time our small community of Oswego listened to the words of the clergymen who denounced these conventions, calling them "unwomanly." (Rappaport, p. 60)

My difficulties since Charles' death have made me realize what a male dominated world we live in. This is why I have chosen to join the crusade here in Akron. I hope to meet other women like myself who share my same interest in promoting women's rights. I already feel a sense of camaraderie with those I have met, filling me with hope, courage, and determination to gain equal suffrage. Charles would turn over in his grave if he knew of my actions here, for you can't forget his displeasure at my "over involvement" with the antislavery organizations.

I am on my own now and questioning what my livelihood will be. With my ten years of schooling and teaching experience, I am considering returning to that field. My friends say that Oregon and other western territories will open doors to women, especially in careers once only open to men. I envision having my own school room in the Willamette Valley filled with the eager faces of settlers' children benefiting from my Christian teachings. I've been inspired by Narcissa Whitman and Eliza Spalding, Christian missionaries. I have been contacted by Catherine Beecher of Cincinnati, Ohio, who has been placed in charge of recruiting and placing women teachers in western towns by the Board of National Popular Education. (Rappaport, p. 131) Like her, I believe that teaching is a Christian calling, my way of doing God's work. With the thousands of wagons on the Oregon Trail, there is a growing need for teachers of the children of these migrants moving west.

As others, I know we are both seeing the West as a cure for personal and economic woes. I have heard of the glories of Oregon and Jake must already know of its marvelously mild weather. Why he can farm the year round with plenty of timber, pure water, abundant fish and game, and rich soil! I estimate it will take five to six months to cross the 2,000 miles, and if we start the journey in April when the mud hardens, we should arrive at our new home before the trail is impassable due to snow and ice. I will help with the $1000 cost of the trip. (Rappaport, p. 118) I also plan to pay for supplies along the way and to financially tide your family over until the land turns a profit. I suspect the long journey from Missouri to Oregon will be grueling, but feel assured the rewards will be worth our hardship.

I will be reaching Independence shortly and will be ready for our westward departure as soon as provisions are gathered. I am bringing very little baggage aside from a small leather trunk which holds some most treasured possessions, the family Bible, Mother's royal blue china tea set, and Grandmother's patchwork quilt. For you and Jake, room has been made for a small parcel of coffee and tea.

I am looking forward to our reunion. Please pray for my safe arrival.

Your loving sister,
Agnes

Gene was pleased with the solid information Christine had packed into her report. He graded the paper 96% and commented: "This is a great job! It shows good research, understanding of your character and it seems to come to life for the reader!"

He was enthusiastic about several other papers and seemed pleased, overall, with the girls' efforts. He criticized other students' papers for their mechanics and lack of chronology in presentation more than I would have, but we agreed that they had reached an unprecedented understanding of the lives of the women they had researched. I was particularly gratified with their ability to use their fiction and their journal writing as means of developing such compassion, and I commended them heartily for the originality of their final reports. We both counted the writing a ringing success, believing it had enhanced their thinking, not only historically but also personally. They were, after all, female people with vested interests in total equality, and this project brought this concern to the forefront of their minds. In looking at the lives of women who had lived before them, they were also exploring their own notions of what it would mean to be grown women themselves.

Three days after the reports were turned in, we held the long-awaited Suffrage Meeting down in the history room. Having raided grandparents' and parents' attics, borrowing whatever they could to look authentic, the "women" arrived in a motley array of costumes. The wealthy Southern wife came in a hoop skirt and ribboned bonnet. One of the mill girls wore black boots and a smock over her long dress. One tribal Native American wore a suede vest. Several carried baby dolls or sewing baskets. After all their research, they had no trouble becoming their characters, and they obviously reveled in the chance, finally, to argue their rights to full suffrage.

One by one they told of abusive husbands and of courts that did not recognize their status. The slave girl rolled her eyes when others complained of their plight; the northern women expressed support for her freedom. Emily, a German immigrant spoke of the hardships of leaving her country and of her dreams for a better life in America. Farm wife Danielle lamented her sense of being trapped and disrespected. One wealthy Northern wife expressed her disdain for the whole meeting, insisting that she had no reason to want to vote, since her husband took perfectly good care of her. Another wife voiced her approval of slavery, an economic necessity in the South. Others argued vigorously with these sentiments.

Witnessing the drama, I felt proud for them. They had worked hard, and they had gained insight. Safe behind the persona of an assigned role, they had no hesitation disagreeing with one another.

The wealthy Southern wife smoothed her skirt, lifted her chin haughtily, and protested the very idea of suffrage.

"Why are you here, if that's how you feel?" asked the Reformer, charged with running the meeting.

"Well, I was just curious," Jane replied. "I have a wonderful life in the South. We treat our slaves very well. They are like members of the family. They have a good life."

"Slavery is a moral outrage," retorted a woman from the North.

Cries of assent arose in the room, and the Reformer banged her gavel for order. Too quickly the double class period we had allotted for the meeting ended, and we were forced to return to twentieth-century life. "We really should do more things like this," someone said. "I wish I had had more of a chance to talk."

We asked the girls to evaluate the whole experience. How had they liked working with two teachers on one theme? What had they learned? What would they suggest we do differently next time?

Danielle was quite candid:

"I've learned a lot from the Suffrage Meeting and the report. I liked working with both teachers because if I didn't have the information you [Mrs. B.] gave me, my report would have probably lacked information. I liked talking with Mrs. Boatright. . . . As a whole, I learned a lot about my character, but I also learned a lot about other people's characters."

Amy confessed her discomfort with having to argue with other women at the meeting:

"I liked the project. I had fun writing it and I liked doing the writing practice. It was fun to get into a mode of thinking: Indians are savages. Voting is wrong. Irish are ignorant. They were so prejudiced!"

"I thought it was awful that your husband could legally beat you! As long as the weapon is not more than one inch in diameter."

"The Suffrage Meeting was fun. It was very hard to stand up against everyone beating me down: 'How can you call yourself a woman?' from Sarah. Trying not to buckle down under pressure was hard, because I was very much in character."

The relative success of this project gave us the impetus to work together again. For years, history students had been required to interview relatives or acquaintances who had served in a war, while English students had been asked to interview grandparents about their lives. Combining these assignments seemed natural, and we were eager to try. In preparing specific guidelines, we sat down and talked to each other and discovered we shared one crucial goal—the development of empathy. Through the study of literature and of history, and especially through listening actively to the experiences of another person, we intended that the girls' understanding of human beings be manifestly increased. Again, as they conducted their interviews, gleaned their notes for relevant information, and wrote narrative and expository papers for both teachers, the girls seemed to thrive on our team approach.

Gene and I will always be very different teachers, he more traditional, I more experimental. He is determined that his students reach for excellence and achieve the highest objective standards possible. While I share some of the same goals, I am more concerned about the girls' self-confidence, their willingness to deviate from the norm, to try something risky when they write and get passionate in the process. He will emphasize content, and I process; but we will both value thinking, learning, and developing empathy. He made me more aware of the careful attention that must be paid to detailed research, and I came to respect his commitment to his students' learning in ways I never would have expected.

It will never be easy for me to face the fact that not everyone agrees with or approves of my classroom practice, but I am convinced that the whole enterprise of teaching and learning will thrive only when we open ourselves to questions, responses, and challenges from others who care about our students as much as we do. It will thrive, too, when we force ourselves to admit that our way is not the only way, that other teachers, even those with a different stance entirely, have much to give.

Nel Noddings writes: "Perhaps we should try more seriously to find out what teachers are doing, and to work cooperatively with them toward perfecting the methods to which they are devoted and in which they reveal their talent . . . surely, we should cease coercing teachers to adopt particular philosophical, psychological, or pedagogical positions and should, instead, talk with each other about the methods we have chosen, the ends we seek, and the pleasure we experience in knowing each other." (1984, p. 197)

Through this year of working with my colleague, I did come to understand his goals, to appreciate his vast store of knowledge, and to revel in the pleasure of knowing him. I realized that true collaboration is essential if we are to continue to offer our students a real range of learning experiences, including experiences in co-operation and compromise. As teachers, we need to discover what unites us and what we can learn from one another. We also need opportunities to reexamine our theories. Gene Rosaschi forced me to rethink much of what I had held sacred in my room, to remember that the girls' needs are cognitive as well as affective, and to reconsider what it might mean to be truly literate in many contexts. I am indebted to him.

When the end of school came, we were sure we'd have many more years of working together ahead of us. He had heard that I planned to take a year off to do some writing, and he shook his head, avoiding my eyes. "I'm really going to miss you," he said.

We had come a long way.

11

Celebrating Possibilities: A Valuable Experiment

———

*Then I go
wandering off,
following all
of my favorite
trails
to all of the places I like.*

*I check how
everything
is doing.*

*I spend the day
admiring
things.*

—Byrd Baylor, *I'm in Charge of Celebrations*

SOMETIMES IT seems as if our whole country is obsessed with the idea of evaluation. Education is failing, we read, let's have better tests! Let's have stricter accountability! Higher standards! But as educators, we know this is not the answer. Students caught in the excitement of risk-taking worry about what external grade their work will ultimately receive from people whom they believe know more than they know. Teachers eager to support ambiguity and tentativeness in young language learners balk at being required to capture stories of courage, imagination, and growth in a single letter or number grade. Like Byrd Baylor, we are more interested in celebrating the surprises that occur day in and day out in the lives of literate young people. Like Mary Oliver, we want always "to be willing/to be dazzled. . . ." ("The Ponds," 1990) by the discoveries our students make in their work and share in the classroom. Like Emily Dickinson, we want always to "dwell in possibility."

Coach or Critic

Judging their work, when what we seek to nurture is an attitude of curiosity, joy, and passion, has never felt right to us. In addition to my fear that my "evaluation" will not help my students improve their work, at the heart of my dilemma is the possibility that it will put our relationships at risk. How will they trust me when I urge them to pursue their own wonderings as they read, write, research, talk, and listen together and individually? How will they be able to believe me when I insist that there is no one "correct" reading of a poem or a story, no one "right" way to revise a piece of writing? How can I be their mentor, coach, and more-experienced colleague one minute and their superior, critic, and judge the next? It seems such a contradiction.

But this is the world we live in. Parents, teachers, administrators, and students themselves recognize the need for criteria for good work. No matter how reassured we are to hear William Stafford's admonition to discouraged writers—"Lower your standards."—we all know that there must always be standards. As people who *love* words and stories and poems, of course, we want to challenge our students and ourselves to stretch, to grow, to produce work that is stunning and vital and compelling in the eyes of the world. Letter grades, traditionalists argue, gratify students who achieve excellence and motivate those who need to work harder. Perhaps.

Peter Elbow acknowledges the problem in his book *Embracing Contraries: Explorations in Learning and Teaching* (1988). "Evaluation is a tar-baby," he says. *"To kick at it is to become stuck fast."* (p. 161) Teachers cannot help but be subjective in our evaluations, according to Elbow, because we have been so involved with our students' composing processes. We ponder absolute criteria for good writing and struggle at the same time to find ways to make judgmental comments truly helpful to students.

The girls expected me to take an evaluative stance towards their writing and looked for judgement in my eyes and in my body language. I, on the other hand, wanted them to tell me what they found exciting, surprising, or moving in their own work. When we read poems or stories together, or when they read their own individual novels, they were quick and astute at citing passages they felt were beautiful, often quoting these in their notebooks. (Atwell, 1987) Why was it so hard for them to bring this same ear to their own work? Before they could begin to evaluate, of course, they had to care about more than a grade.

"The best hope for teaching trustworthy self-evaluation is to give a more accurate and explicit message of evaluation than traditional grades contain," writes Elbow. "Grades can only wither away in importance when they cease to be ambiguous and magical. The present system too often allows the student to feel them as judgements based on hidden criteria, judgements which she *(sic)* cannot understand and has little power over. If she is rewarded she feels she did the right things, but if the reward fails she never knows which step in the rain dance she missed." (1986, p. 168)

We had to demystify the grading process, but I wanted the girls' help in doing it. We worked hard to establish a class list of criteria for effective writing, and kept changing the list as the year went on. "Good vocabulary" was usually one of their early priorities, along with "correct spelling and punctuation," both manifestations of inordinate concern over surface elements of writing.

"Flow" seemed to be a big issue too, but when we tried to determine how our favorite authors, Cynthia Rylant, Katherine Paterson, Bette Greene, and Norma Fox Mazer, created "flow," we discovered inner dialogue, concrete detail, sensory images, and graceful transition paragraphs. These became part of our growing list of criteria. As the year progressed, we added focus, plausibility, use of figurative language, seductive leads, poignant endings, and more. Our standards were high for writing; we were determined to create pieces that would move readers, just the way Cynthia Rylant's work moved us. But as we talked about the literature we loved, we realized that beautiful writing is bigger than any letter grade.

Little by little, as we wrote together every day, the Laurel girls came to understand that they could indeed evaluate themselves, not in terms of an *A* or a *B*, but in more important ways. "This bit is effective because it sounds just like a mother would talk." or "Here I used a good metaphor, the pomegranate." or "I stayed to the main point and made my readers see why I believe that using animals in medical research is wrong." They began to notice that it was the writing that meant something to them personally that was also writing they were proudest of.

At end-of-the-trimester conferences, I would ask them to review all their writing and to identify particular strengths and specific evidence of growth, referring in each case to our class established list of criteria. (Atwell, 1987) They collected samples of their best work in portfolios. (Tierney, et al.) But the fact remained that our school policy demanded a letter grade at the end of each trimester.

Did the girl who wrote fluently and gracefully every single time she uncapped her pen deserve an automatic *A*? Was growth in writing worth an *A* or a *B*? If a girl had decided to work on focus as a trimester goal and had subsequently sharpened her focus in one or more of her pieces, what would that mean on her report card? And what about a student who went beyond her announced goals, surprising herself and me by trying new points of view or a new genre altogether? Shouldn't this be worth at least an *A* at the end of the trimester? And what if she had not worked on focus but had instead gotten so excited by a new idea in her writing that she chose to digress and explore it in depth? How did letter grades support passion, curiosity, and risk-taking?

What about literature? Since we did lots of free choice reading, was stretching oneself by reading a greater variety of texts deserving of a higher grade than last trimester's? And how about class participation? Rachel never turned in written literature responses and rarely completed drafts of writing, but she was often most articulate and insightful in any poem or book discussion. How much should that count on a report card?

There was another issue. As we sat together at evaluation conferences (Atwell, 1987) before telling me what grade they felt they had earned, many girls would jot down the grades they expected in their other classes, figure out what they needed in English to make either honor roll or high honor roll, and announce that this was the grade they deserved. "I think I should have a *B+*," might mean that a girl's other grades were sufficiently high—probably lots of *A*s—to put her on the honor roll, where she needed to be in order to keep peace at home. "What I've done deserves an *A*," often meant that she needed this grade to receive an "honors" designation overall, since not all her other grades were this high and she could count on English to bring up her average. How removed from authentic learning this seemed to me!

But honor roll is a very big deal at Laurel. On the day report cards come out, there are deluges of tears in the middle school corridors. "My mother is going to kill me," is the frequent lament among seventh graders. In light of all this, I had difficulty justifying a low grade for anyone who was making even a minimal effort in my class. Would a *C* or a *D* nudge a student to do more, or would it convince her that she was not a good reader or writer and might just as well stop trying? But, on the other hand, would a high grade for low achievement send a dishonest message? I wanted to challenge my students to push themselves towards greater engagement with literature and to discover new insight into themselves and the world as they wrote. I was absolutely confounded by the system of letter grading.

In recognition of the girls' need for some concrete and regular feedback, I graded their reading responses each week. We established tough, specific criteria for response, and grades reflected each reader's willingness to reflect on her reading in a variety of ways. Students in seventh grade often have trouble being organized, and it was the girls who neglected to turn in their notebooks whose grades suffered, not the ones who shared their thinking. I did not grade individual pieces of writing, but continued instead to confer with students about their goals as writers and their progress in meeting them, all in the context of regular dialogue about specific criteria.

We determined a writing grade which counted for half the English grade each trimester; the other half derived from the weekly literature responses. In spite of the girls' participation in the evaluation, I knew the system was less than adequate, since it still leaned on my own external measurement of their literature responses and still had as its end product a single letter grade. Instead of building greater self-knowledge and the self-confidence so vital to girls, this approach fostered continued dependence on authority, and this haunted me.

In *Womens' Ways of Knowing,* Belenky, Clinchy, Goldberger, and Tarule cite examples of educational systems thwarting girls' learning. Incessant academic pressure may, they say, stunt rather than nourish intellectual development. (p. 207)

"It is not evaluation per se that subverts the aims of instruction but evaluation in the separate (impersonal, objective) mode. Evaluation in the connected mode requires that the standards of evaluation be constructed in collaboration with the students."

Our approach seemed to fit this recommendation; we collaborated on setting criteria; we were, in some sense, connected. My goal, of course, was to help the girls need my opinion less as they internalized high standards and high expectations for themselves. And I still worried about the integrity of my relationship with them. When forced to evaluate students, Nel Noddings says, a teacher "suddenly, grindingly must wrench herself from the relationship and make her student the object of scrutiny." (1984, p. 195) This is how I felt—wrenched! Noddings understands my essential fear. "The point is that the caring teacher does not shrink from evaluating her student's work along all the dimensions proper to the field she is teaching; but she feels no need, and no right, to sum it up with a report to the world. At this point the relationship crumbles; it is altered. In many cases, it is utterly destroyed." (1984, p. 195)

I dreamed of a day when I wouldn't have to reduce all we did as readers and writers to a summary letter grade in our "report to the world," but such a time seemed far off, probably not to occur within my tenure at Laurel. And then Andrea Archer took over as director of our middle school.

Narrative Evaluation

Coming to us from Crossroads, a progressive K-12 college preparatory independent school in Los Angeles, she was concerned from the beginning about the stress level she sensed at Laurel. After about one month, she asked the faculty to think of ways we might alleviate the situation a bit. At a seventh-grade team meeting, she wondered aloud what our school might be like if we were freed from the constraint of trimester grades. "I've always wanted to try that," I blurted. "I'd like to do narratives the way they do in primary. It would be a way to convey much more information about each kid."

At Andrea's previous school this had been the norm. Middle school teachers did not give letter or number grades, and students moved on to the rigorous upper school where grades were given. The transition from narrative reporting to letter grades, according to Andrea, was not a problem at Crossroads. She asked us if we would like to try such an experiment at Laurel, and of course, I eagerly agreed. Gene Rosaschi, the social studies teacher, concerned about the tension the girls were experiencing, was willing to put off grading for one trimester to see if things changed. Since he was known as a traditionalist, a stickler for good grades, we were all surprised and delighted at his offer to experiment.

He and I agreed to write specific comments about each girl's strengths and growth and to make it clear to students and parents exactly how she might do better in each of our classes. I was ecstatic.

At a meeting of seventh-grade parents, Andrea announced our plan. She assured them that we would seek their reactions at every turn. The parents, equally concerned about high anxiety among their daughters, were willing to give our new idea a try.

Several weeks later I asked the girls to write about the experiment in their notebooks. How did this feel to them? Should it continue? Should it be expanded to other subjects? As usual, many were ambivalent.

Marlana shares her qualms about the whole idea and uses her writing to ponder her teachers' motivation for the whole experiment, echoing Noddings' belief that it is the student-teacher relationship that really matters most of all:

> I'm not really sure how I feel about having no grades. I'm not upset. I'm not happy . . . I do think that this makes life easier for people who try really hard and only get *B*'s and *C*'s. I am very curious of why Mr. R. volunteered for this. Maybe he likes us and has a heart too, but he doesn't know how to show it.

Jen M. also thinks about her teachers' behavior:

> Teachers tell students not to worry about the grades just your learning. But then they tell our parents, "Well, she got a '*C*' in

this, etc." They never really get to the point on why he/she is getting these grades.

Plus if teachers just write comments, it won't really hurt the student. If they see their grade is a *D* or *F* or something else below their standards that makes them feel bad.

If we do have no grades, I feel there should be no high honors, honors, etc. That makes a student feel bad if she didn't get that award. Actually I feel there shouldn't be any of those types of awards anyway. It hurts some students to know that one person is smarter than he/she is . . .

Jennifer exhibits a clear desire not to be compared to anyone else as a learner. A strong student herself, in anyone's eyes, she shows empathy for others, knowing how "it hurts" to think someone else is smarter than you are. To her, a grade is often no more than a punishing "label," and she seems happy to be moving away from such a system.

Sara was thrilled:

This year my attitude on learning has changed—* I LOVE IT * * I like waking up in the morning and knowing I have school. I don't complain anymore.

Bernice was one of the most vehement in her objections to the whole idea, showing logical reasoning and a strong work ethic:

Grades. I don't think everybody understands them. Sure, I'm pretty certain people work for the grade—extra hard! So, it pays off. To do your utmost best on an assignment is great! I'd think that would be what every teacher would want. You're reducing stress. Too much though.

Grades show my parents and myself how I'm doing, what I have to improve, how I can help my study habits. Yes, at times it's the grade that counts, but it's paying off because I'm trying a lot harder! I don't see how working harder and more efficiently is bad, even if it is for the grade. Without grades if everyone tried just as hard in schoolwork, the stress level would be the same! Our school is known for its academic achievement. I can go to a public school where there isn't this much stress. But we all will get used to the stress; for example my brother was really stressed out before in middle and high school. But after a while he got used to it and with grades he knew exactly what he had to improve . . . I hope, I truly hope, that grades will always remain. . . . So *please* everyone, try to get grades back.

But in English, Bernice was not to get her way. Our classroom life flourished, in spite of her fears, as we continued the experiment. Freedom from letter grades challenged all of us to be even more specific in our responses to pieces of writing, and the girls became more interested in making it more real, more personal. My comments or questions now seemed less like veiled instruction for revision than honest interest in hearing more. Because I was no longer the ultimate "judge" of good writing, they listened to one another more as they shared emerging drafts. They got excited about their writing, as I had hoped they would. They also trusted their own intuition about what was working well in their pieces.

Evaluation was ongoing and rigorous, as our class list of criteria grew. Eventually, "the writing should mean something to the writer" became number one on the list. Their memoirs, their suffrage reports, their fiction, and much of their poetry became writing that mattered. We began to collect authors' comments about writing and hang them on the wall. Since so many of the girls were skaters, we liked Ralph Waldo Emerson: "Good writing is a kind of skating which carries off the performer where he would not go." (Smith, 1986, p. 132) "Writing orders thought," says Maxine Hong Kingston. "It gives meaning to life. And I create beauty and help change the atmosphere of the world." (Smith, 1986, p. 103) This is what we were shooting for in Room 311.

I asked the girls to select their most effective work along with anything else that demonstrated growth in literacy and to save it all in portfolios. As in other classrooms around the country, sharing portfolios helped us know each other better and brought us closer together as a community. (Graves, Sunstein, 1992) Our experiment was clearly strengthening relationships among us. In the absence of letter grades, true evaluation flourished.

At the end of the trimester, the girls wrote letters to their parents explaining what they had accomplished and what they valued in their own learning. Each letter reflects the idiosyncracies of its writer, and reveals her individual obsessions. Christine, a shy, serious, conscientious writer, had fallen in love with poetry:

Dear Mom and Dad,
     Reading and writing are very important to me and are the basis of my life presently and will be in my future. Without

literacy we would have limited communication with the world around us. That's why I have included magazine covers and newspaper sections in my portfolio.

I prefer poetry over stories because I feel they are more enjoyable to write. You can express your feelings and thoughts in a secretive way. Their meaning can be revealed with just a word or a winding pattern of words that fit together like a puzzle, to support one or a series of thoughts and feelings.

I've learned over the years that in order to write a poem that you and others enjoy, it doesn't have to rhyme. This type of poem inhibits you when you try to write because you can't say what you want if you're merely searching for words that rhyme.

Walt Whitman, whom I recently discovered in a class assignment, is now one of my favorite poets. I haven't read many of his poems, but the ones I have are outstanding. "There Was a Child Went Forth" and "A Noiseless, Patient Spider" are fine examples of his work. Both are very well written and thought through. They relate life with nature. He expresses two thoughts at once.

Linda Pastan has somewhat a similar writing style as Walt Whitman's, as you will notice in her poems, "Egg" and "A New Poet." Two subjects are discussed at once. This is called metaphor. I find her poems interesting, though some of them are difficult to read.

"Dog's Death," which was written by John Updike, is included in my portfolio because it conveys feeling. It is the first poem I have read that upset me, and for that reason, I did not like it initially.

"Mirage" is the first piece of poetry I wrote this year that I felt satisfied with. It flowed easily from start to finish with little effort. Sometimes my more spontaneous creations are better than those I dwell over.

I chose to include the poem "Sisters" by George Vai in my portfolio because it communicates nicely the deep bond that exists between siblings.

A poem by Mary Bolt, my second grade teacher is an important part of my portfolio because I feel she was my first inspiration to get involved in writing poems and the extensive reading of books. One page in my portfolio lists some of the books I've read and enjoyed over a period of time.

Writing my memoir, "Autumn Reminiscence," allowed me to reflect and record a special moment in my life.

My Williamsburg Journal displays a writing effort in diary form. Journal writing is something that I have done over the years in various classes. It's always rewarding to look back at my impressions of experiences.

English this trimester has made me a better listener and I can now read material with greater comprehension. I'm pleased and more confident with my efforts. My personal goal is to become more verbal in this class and to express my ideas and feelings.

Please read my portfolio and respond in writing. I would like to hear your thoughts and impressions about my entries.

Love,
Christine

Dear Christine,

We were delighted to have the opportunity to read the many entries in your portfolio. Through your letter and well written pieces, we can see that you have most definitely grown as a literate person.

What pleases us most is that you have found enjoyment and satisfaction in expressing your thoughts on paper. We see great sensitivity, imagination, and style in both your poetry and story writing.

We share your pride in these writing efforts and hope that you continue to enjoy and pursue writing in the years to come. You possess a very special talent.

Love,
Mom and Dad

Often we avoid making big changes in school policy because we are afraid our students' parents will resist them. "Parents need to receive frequent letter grades," one argument against alternative assessment, may be, in some cases, a paper tiger, an excuse to avoid change. During our year without English grades, my girls' parents were most supportive and grateful. Surely the portfolio and her reflections on it made Christine's strengths as a reader and writer clear. It also put her reading and writing into a personal context that was vital to her and to her parents. Other girls' letters from parents continued to encourage us with the ungraded portfolio approach. (One dad wrote to Andrea Archer in protest, however. "You are grading gym and not English," he lamented. "What do you think you are, Ohio State?" He was, fortunately, in the minority.)

While most of the parental response to dropping grades in English was positive, opinions on continuing the policy in history were mixed. Many students and parents felt that, since the course was so content-laden, and since frequent tests were very much a part of the routine, grades seemed logical and relevant. True to her commitment to listen to the girls and their parents, Andrea approved of the history teacher's decision to return to regular letter grades for the second and third trimesters. My students and I were grateful for her permission—and encouragement—to continue evaluating work in English without grades.

The portfolios were ongoing. New material was added, and at the end of the second trimester, they wrote again to their parents. Wallis's letter demonstrates her growing ability to set her own goals and make plans for her writing.

Dear Mom and Dad,

I'm writing to tell you about my portfolio this trimester. I'm keeping my pictures from last trimester because good memories deserve recognition for more than three months. My two new characters this trimester are Mimi and Dad. Next trimester I'll put a picture of Poppi in. . .

My two pieces are a poem, "Recital," and a story, "Nightvision." "Recital" is a piece about how you can't dwell on the worst, and that you must move on in life. Sometimes one has to think, "I did my best, now I just have to go for it."

"Nightvision" got its name because the mother and daughter realize how much they need to work on their relationship. They see the reality in the dark of the night after the streetlight went off for a moment. This seems important to me.

I have my list of questions for the short stories we've read and the responses to show my beginning question and how I created a response from them. I was in a reading group with Priya and Rachel. It was hard in the reading group because if we disagreed, people would scramble to say what they thought. Then there was the problem of people complaining to me about the other group member. Over all it was nice to discuss our opinions in a small group and we all learned to deal with each other more patiently and nicely.

I think poetry is a way to express feelings and thoughts however you want. When writing poetry you're in control, whether its' writing a thought or simply choosing your own style of grammar. Poetry is untouched by everyone except you.

I think I did a better job finding things to write this trimester, instead of waiting for an idea to find me, but I would like to be able to develop a story from scratch. I think I might write a piece of fiction this trimester to practice being inside a character's mind and acting accordingly in my own story.

I'd like to try and make more time for reading. I'm presently reading a collection of fiction stories by Cynthia Rylant, and I'll be starting *Tancy*, a fiction piece about a freed slave. *Tancy* is a post Civil War book I'm reading for English and history. It's by Belinda Hurmence.

I hope we have more class discussions in the new trimester because I really enjoy them and we haven't had many this trimester.

I'll be bringing home my portfolio tomorrow, and I look forward to showing it to you.

Love,
Wallis

The girls knew that I would read their letters, even though they were addressed to their parents. They wrote to me every single week in their notebooks, anyway, so when it was portfolio time, they focussed on their parents. It saved them the trouble of writing a second letter to me, and they were comfortable with this arrangement. In our portfolio/evaluation conferences, they were free to add comments or to expand on the letter, and of course, I asked lots of questions about the collected work.

Reading Wallis's letter is helpful to me in ways that an exam would never be. I see her initial frustration in working with a small group for literature study; I see that there was some discord I had not been aware of and that the girls solved it themselves, learning to be "patient" and "nice." I wonder if this preoccupation got in the way of real discourse, and I made a mental note to sit in on their next discussion to hear for myself how willing they were to disagree when they examined their stories. I hear Wallis's wish for more whole class discussions, which have indeed lessened in frequency in the weeks of the small group meetings and due to our commitment to finishing final drafts by the end of the trimester. Reading her letter, and the letters from all the girls, helps me understand what they need next from me and from our classroom environment. Invaluable insight for any teacher.

Linda Rief has written,"As teachers/learners we have to believe in the possibilities of our students by trusting them to show us what they know and valuing what they are able to do with that knowledge." (Rief, *Portfolio Portraits*, "Eighth Grade: Finding the Value in Evaluation," p. 47)

What can a *B* or a *C* or even an *A* help anyone see about our students' possibilities? More importantly, what can a single letter grade help a student see about herself? How does it help her believe that we value what she is "able to do with that knowledge?"

So what did we conclude after our grand experiment? The girls, even Bernice, saw real value in what we accomplished. Our year without grades challenged the girls to go beyond their perceptions of anyone's expectations. They read and wrote for their own purposes, and, freed from seeing their efforts reduced to a single letter grade, they pushed themselves in new directions. They were rigorous in their self-assessment and saw more and more "possibilities" in their work. Most importantly, our classroom community took on a new texture, one of greater trust and apprenticeship, and my relationship with them flourished.

Of course, there are lingering questions. Honor roll remained, and each trimester, I had to submit a list of girls whose English achievement was worthy of this distinction. This seemed to contradict everything we were doing, and, guilty as it left me, I had to acquiesce. Some faculty and some students in other classes began to see English as less important as an academic discipline, and this bothered me a bit at first. Then I realized that English in middle school should be *more* than an academic discipline. Becoming excellent readers and writers would certainly enable the girls to learn more in all their other classes, a goal we all shared. But there is another important issue here. Eliot Eisner writes, "The major goals of schooling are not realized by performances on tasks defined in classrooms or within schools. The important effects of schools are located in the kinds of lives that children lead outside school and the kinds of satisfactions they pursue there." (1991)

If my girls' lives are affected in real ways by their reading and writing—and I know they are—then I am willing to endure my colleagues' perplexity, dismay, or condescension. All in all, this was a noble experiment, one that changed me as a teacher and the girls as learners. I would do it again in a heartbeat.

Now, when I remember that year—all our reading, writing, talking—I appreciate the freedom we had. Like Byrd Baylor we learned how to celebrate:

And they came—
dancing
in time to
their own
windy music.

We all started counting.
We all started looking
for more.

—*I'm in Charge of Celebrations*

12

What Matters Most: Loving What We Love

―――

Creation has brought you
great excitement, as I knew it would
as it does in the beginning.
And I am free to do as I please now,
to attend to other things, in confidence
you have no need of me anymore.

—Louis Gluck, *"Retreating from the Light"*

"I'M LOOKING forward to all the end of the year things we have planned in English," Brady writes in her notebook, "especially having the boys from U.S. come over."

Her classmates feel the same way. The U.S. boys have been here before, of course, at dances, joint concerts, or plays, or to share their writing. This time will be different. This time we are going to talk about gender.

Gender Questions

Charlie Obendorf, seventh-grade English teacher, is a big help in our planning. When I invite him to bring the boys over to discuss men's and women's roles in our society, not only does he agree, but he also sends over poems, song lyrics, and an excerpt from Betty Friedan's *The Feminine Mystique*. We are grateful. We read "I'm Gonna Be an Engineer" by Peggy Seeger; "Stand by Your Man" by Tammy Wynette and Billy Sherrill; and "Free to Grow" by Holly Near. As we have before, we talk about women's choices, agreeing that any job a woman wants should be open to her, if she is qualified. If she wants to be a train engineer, like the woman in the song, so be it. If a father chooses to stay at home with his kids, like the man in the poem, this would be great, the girls say. Some feel skeptical: "It would only work if the mother has a very good job." "A lot of men wouldn't do this." "I admire a man who spends time with his kids."

Next we read "The Problem That Has No Name," from Friedan's *The Feminine Mystique*, tracing the early stirrings of the Women's Movement when women began to acknowledge wanting more than husband, family, and a house in the suburbs, and offering the hope for a future when women and men will share roles and responsibilities at home and at work. Some girls nod as they read. Others are surprised that things were so different for women just two generations ago. No one disputes Friedan's vision of womanhood, one that argues for a respect for intelligence as well as love and a sharing of responsibilities with men. But the burning question remains, "What do the boys think?"

To get ready, we brainstorm lists of questions, and these fall into two categories, future expectations and present day experiences. These girls are curious about more than what may or may not happen in ten years.

Questions about the Future

What is expected of men in today's society?

What is expected of women?

Who has the responsibility for earning money for the family?

Should all husbands work? Should all wives work?

Do men have the same respect for women with jobs as they have for women at home?

Do some men have more respect for women who have good jobs away from home?

Should all jobs be open to women? What about combat jobs?

Are men better at some jobs? Are women better at some jobs?

Who should give up a job in the event that one spouse gets a better job in another area? What if one person doesn't want to move?

Should a couple have children, if no one wants to stay home?

Who should be responsible for housework? Child care? Who stays home if a child is sick?

Who should get family leave after a birth?

Why do men get paid more than women in some jobs? Is this fair? What would you do to prevent it?

Why do you think women are sometimes afraid of men?

Questions about Right Now

Who should ask for the first date?

Why does it seem that boys are turned off when they realize that a girl is aggressive?

Do boys think about girls all the time, the way some girls think about boys?

When they see gorgeous girls, do they still want us?

Do they prefer older, younger, or same age girls?

Do boys worry about the way they look all the time?

Do boys buy new boxers before a date, like girls buy new lingerie?

Do boys clean their rooms before they have someone sleep over?

Why do guys drink more than girls?

Do boys really care about a good relationship or do they just care about sex?

Do all guys want sex?

Why do guys talk about their "conquests?"

Why do guys tend to want to physically hurt someone, rather than telling him off?

Why do boys feel they have to be better in sports than other boys?

Why do guys think girls will break if they throw a ball hard?

What do guys really feel inside?

What do boys worry about at night before they fall asleep?

What do guys really want out of life?

I love their questions! These girls are wondering about what women have wondered about for ages—what do men really think, feel, and want? The girls want to understand. Why is it so hard to get to know boys at this level? But while I know the urgency of their curiosity, I suspect they may feel uncomfortable raising some of these issues with the U.S. boys.—"How do boys really feel inside?" might not get any response at all. What should we do, I ask them? After some conversation, the girls decide it might be best to stick with questions about the future, with one exception. Almost everyone is eager to hear what the boys think about asking for a date. We agree that this should stay on the table. We will break into small groups to talk things over when the boys come; and to save time on the day of the meeting, Charlie and I prearrange the groups, trying to keep a balance of personalities.

The sun-filled morning dawns, glistening with possibility. The boys burst into the front foyer, as eager as the girls for the talking to begin. They know their way around Laurel and head right for the dining room. We are here so kids can sit at round tables, six to a group. We shuffle index cards, each containing one question, and give each table three. We ask that every group appoint a note-taker who will report back to the whole meeting at the end of thirty minutes, and the discussions begin. They are a little shy at first, and I notice that, in most cases, it is a girl who opens the conversation. There is a bit of raucous behavior in one corner. Brady rolls her eyes. Things settle down.

Then—disaster. Andrea Archer appears at the door, beckons me over to her. "You're going to have to send them all home," she says. "There's a problem with the water main. We have to close school. We're calling parents and buses now."

No! I want to shout. This can't be happening, not today. My mind races through the calendar for the remainder of the school year, and I know there will be no time to reschedule this discussion. If I send the girls home now, they will never forgive me.

"Can we please just have one period?" I plead. "Their parents won't be here for a while anyway. Can't we please proceed for a little while?" Smiling, she agrees. It's a health issue, I realize. You can't keep school open if there's no running water.

Quietly, I explain to Charlie what is going on. He groans, then laughs. This is life, after all. I tell the kids the problem, and the girls' eyes widen in panic. "Keep talking," I say. "We won't have a double period, but we do have now."

Charlie and I move from table to table, trying to hear what's being said, but we quickly notice that the kids talk more when we move away. Dissention, at one table, centers on the issue of child care, with one boy's thinking that the woman should be in charge and the man should "help." I hear confidence in several female voices, as the girls struggle to make their points. They argue that it should be an equal responsibility—"Both parents decide to have a child, so both parents should take care of it."—and another boy agrees. Just as we learned in the memoir project, the inclination towards a "voice of care" is not limited to girls. Boys may feel less ready to talk about it, but some seem to understand the need to think about a family's needs, for example, when making career decisions.

Author Mem Fox, concerned with stereotypical messages kids get from their literature, believes boys, as well as girls, need to be reassured that they too can do anything. "Why should they live, as most of them do," she wonders, "with the idea that it is, in the main, their crippling responsibility to provide for a family when they become grown-up boys? Don't boys need liberating too?" (1993, p. 153) I wonder about this as I wander from table to table.

When we move to the whole group discussion, Charlie asks about job opportunities, child care, and any other issues that have come up, and one by one, students stand and present the smaller groups' views. Girls speak representing two of the six groups, making me wonder how table reporters have been chosen. Too soon, our time is up. Groans, giggles, and murmurs of "Thanks for coming" ring through the halls.

Later at home, I write in my journal: "I love those boys—so earnest, so serious . . . surprised me with their traditional values in some cases, but not all. They think that boys should pay for dates, and lots of the girls argued that. If a boy has to pay, where is the equality, they wonder? That seems a contradiction to most, but not all, of them. They mention different cultures—Indian, Pakistani, Arabic—where men are considered boss. How different will it be for these kids?

Boys wish girls would call them and ask them out more often, but this is not happening. They don't really mind aggressive girls, they say. Is this true? Women should have any jobs they want. Child care and housework should be shared. Moving should be determined by who has the higher paycheck. Women are morally superior (e.g. when it comes to having sex before marriage, boys are eager, girls more reluctant) but men are better at making decisions. Women are more emotional, men physically stronger—girls say not always true. Aren't men sometimes emotional too? Aren't women strong? Brady says that women are braver but really means more vulnerable—mentions rape. All in all, an excellent beginning. Proud that the girls hold their own. In most cases, the girls spoke first . . . the boys may have been being polite."

Teaching Girls, Renewing Ideals

Reading this journal entry, I am dismayed that it is so easy—irresistible even—for me to focus my attention on the boys. Is it because they have been our guests, unfamiliar at Laurel, to the girls and to me? Or is it because, no matter how conscious I am of the girls' need to speak out, I am inextricably drawn to these boys, curious about what they think and feel? The boys are aggressive and articulate, for the most part, untroubled by the self-doubt or indecisiveness I have seen so often in my girls, and I find myself wondering what it would be like to study their voices of justice and care. Then I remind myself that boys have been studied much more often and much more thoroughly than have girls. In the professional literature I read, it is usually boys who are the subjects of extensive case studies. We need, I believe, to focus on females too, and not only in comparison to males. Because the girls are sometimes less assertive, we must work harder to draw them out, to challenge their assumptions, and to support their emerging points of view.

The next day in writing practice, Brady says:

I thought the discussion with US went very well, and I hope people learned from others and compromised on their disagreements. Unfortunately T was in our group and we didn't have many agreements on the questions because he wouldn't change his mind at all. Although we did make our points and I think he felt a little intimidated by us because he couldn't come up with any better ideas.

I think we should follow up on these discussions because it teaches us to listen to others and refer to what they say. It also teaches us to speak our opinions in a group we are not familiar with, and hopefully the boys will change their minds on their past impressions. It taught us to know their points of view. I like working with boys because once you say something that is powerful or affects them, they sort of watch out, and you feel more comfortable. Other people in our class might have different opinions on working with boys because they feel uncomfortable around them and think the boys will make fun of them. They have got to learn to block those rude remarks out and just tell themselves that the boys are immature and will eventually grow up so that you can have a normal conversation with them.

Hopefully we learned from each other and can take our knowledge elsewhere.

One of the criticisms of single-sex education is that it denies girls the opportunity to interact with boys, and that this is unnatural, given the fact that we live in a two gender world. How will girls ever learn to communicate, cooperate, and compete with boys, if they are not together in school? I worry about this myself, from time to time, but whenever the boys visited from U.S., most of the girls managed to speak their minds fairly clearly. Some shyness is probably inevitable at this age, since there is always a social agenda. But our women's rights discussion assured me that many of these girls can be assertive. They would all like to do more of this kind of thing, and I lament the fact that the year is ending. Brady talks about "compromise" as she reflects on the day, confirming Deborah Tannen's and Carol Gilligan's notion that girls working in groups are more concerned with connection than with status. However, what she has really enjoyed is saying "something powerful" and influencing the boys' thinking. It seems clear that she has not backed down in the face of disagreement. She and many of her classmates have been able to say what they know.

And one part of what they know is that dependence is not a weakness, autonomy not necessarily a goal. Indeed, we are all interdependent on one another for so much. Compromise in the face of dissention seems logical and right to them. "They should have found a way to talk it over instead of getting violent. . . ." they said when they read about war. But they are not girls who see themselves circumscribed by society's expectations. They understand that their choices will be difficult, but they know that they have choices to make.

Some critics have argued that Carol Gilligan's theories may tend to reinforce stereotypes of women, that by focusing on women's inclination towards care and nurturance, she may encourage women to be less aggressive in their quest for equality. Many of the seventh graders strike me as both caring and aggressive; they care about other people, and they want to succeed in the world. It is my impression that they shy away from conflict when they think it may put their relationships in jeopardy; they probably need to see women acknowledging anger and managing it effectively more often than they do now. What matters most, however, is that these girls know how important, valuable, and necessary their own insights are. All these "sounds from the heart" will always be vital, as the girls go into the world and establish families and communities and nations.

Noted author Naomi Wolf criticizes Gilligan, Tannen, Belenky and others for what she calls an attitude of "difference" feminism. She supports much of their theory, but believes that there may be more to consider. "I am cautioning against a picture of femininity that blanks out the female will to power and that can keep women from using worldly might," she writes. (1993, p. 273) In Wolf's research, she finds that women, like men, have a healthy, aggressive desire to compete, succeed, and achieve, even if it is at the expense of their connections to others. "The women I spoke to confirmed my own memory: In contrast to theories of different feminists— that girls never need to separate and claim autonomy the way boys do; that they embrace egalitarianism and eschew hierarchy; and that they cannot disengage their own identities from the feelings of those around them—it seemed clear to me that healthy girls fantasize separation, recognition, achievement, mastery, and conflict too—in lush detail." (1993, p. 262, 263)

Wolf cautions that supporting women in their inclination to avoid disrupting connections may block their other natural drive to take what they need from life. In advocating "power" feminism she suggests that girls "challenge the impulse to shy away from acknowledging the power or admitting to the leadership skills that we possess . . . welcome dissent and differences of opinion among women; foster debate. . . ." (1994, p. 317, 318)

Her book *Fire with Fire* intrigues me, and reading her words, I remember Sarah, Wallis, Kim, Jennifer, Bernice, and others showing me "girlhood will to power and fantasies of grandeur." Gilligan calls these girls "resistors," as they struggle against detachment and disconnection and fight to hold onto their own knowledge and to forge relationships where they feel understood and accepted. But do they also seek the kind of "power" Wolf describes? At what price? I want to consider her ideas seriously to see how they too might influence my classroom.

I have also been thinking about the literature curriculum. Lois Stover, Cynthia Ann Bowman (1992), and others have studied the effects reading certain books or certain types of books may have on adolescents' emerging perspectives on gender roles. I want my girls to read books that show both men and women as people who can focus on care, and not only justice, as a moral imperative. I want them to see characters exercising a range of options in their lives—showing compassion for others, competing and achieving in the arts, sports, medicine, law, engineering, business, or any other field, struggling with issues of fairness and equality, making themselves heard and respected, working out differences together. While I will always squelch censorship and promote choice in my classroom, I want to think more carefully about the books that fill our shelves, and plan my recommendations and whole class selections more sensitively.

I am grateful for the beautiful new book *Weaving in the Women* by Liz Whaley and Liz Dodge, (1993). Their ideas are exciting, provocative, and long overdue. Any work I do in classrooms in the coming years will be strongly affected by what they have shared.

The year at Laurel, however, closes now, and I wonder where these girls will go from here. Eighth grade. Upper school. College. Work. I hope they will keep reading, and find in their books respite, faith, and courage. I hope they will keep writing, learning about themselves and what matters in their lives. I hope what they know will stay with them.

I have a poster of an illustration from Margaret Wise Brown's lovely classic *The Runaway Bunny* hanging in my hall at home. It reads, "If you become a bird and fly away from me," said his mother, "I will be the tree that you come home to."

Some people scoff and accuse the mother in the story of wanting to smother her children or keep them tied to her forever. But it gives me great solace to know that, no matter how far my children may go in pursuit of their own dreams, they do, eventually, come home to me. But it's not the same with our students, is it? Oh, we may get letters from time to time, or even the occasional visit, but essentially, when they leave our classrooms, they leave our lives. Feeling as I do about them, this wrenches. I do not want our time together to end. Ever. I tell them that what matters most to me is that they will be readers and writers all their lives. . . . And this is true, but only partly. The other thing that matters is that we have been in relationship, real relationship, and it is excruciating for me to step back from that.

It is what teachers plan and strive for, but the end of the year is hard, nonetheless. Surely, we think, there will never be another class like this one. Surely, they cannot have learned one half what I have learned from being with them. Reading Emily's notebook for the last time, I hear a voice full of care, an awareness that we are all connected, that things cannot go on the way they are, that the future is what matters. Hers is just one voice I have heard this year, and I will not forget her:

> I wish that everyone could be friends and love each other. That there could be peace, harmony, and friendship in whatever we do or where we go. Things would be so fun and certainly there would be no stress. All things would be for sharing, and there would be shelter over everyone's heads and food on everyone's table. I also wish for world peace for the animals and forests. Where will we go if we cut down all the trees? What will we eat if we ruthlessly kill all the animals? We need to stop a minute and think, can this wish really come true? My answer is *yes*. If all people big and small were kind and sharing to everything and everyone, there would be peace and harmony once again. People are human, we all make mistakes, so why criticize anything? None of us is perfect and flawless, why make things bad and unacceptable? We do it because we don't know any other way. All we know is to stand up for yourself and fight for survival yourself. We can't ignore the needs anymore. We have to start giving and help others out as best we can. Things have to be better for our kids and grandchildren.

Epilogue: Vigilance Renewed

———

Like trees we have our common roots.
But our growth is very different.

—Nancy Wood, *Many Winters: Prose & Poetry of the Pueblos*

YEARS AGO a friend gave me a tee-shirt that reads, "Bloom Where You Are Planted." Little did we know how prophetic those words would be. Leaving Cleveland was only a little less traumatic than leaving New Hampshire, but leaving Laurel was another story. Leaving Laurel broke my heart.

South Carolina is a long way from Ohio, not only in miles, and when my husband's work required his increasing presence there, we realized another move was necessary. Once again, life meant change. Once again, we packed our bags, and began house-hunting. Once again, I became the new teacher, this time of eighth graders, in yet another new school.

Chaotic Coeducation

The first weeks were tough. I missed the comfortable informality of Laurel, the sense of intimacy we'd had there, the camaraderie. Things were different here. Here there were those Southern accents, drawn out and sugary sweet. I became "Ma'am" for the first time in my life, but it was impossible to know when the friendly greetings were sincere and when affected. Here there were bells ringing all the time, people racing through the halls boisterously, a good deal of shouting. And here there were boys.

As I tried to talk to my new students about what I hoped we could do together, the boys rolled their eyes in disgust. "I thought you were really weird," one boy confessed in his notebook. It was difficult—impossible—to get them to listen, even for a few minutes. They were intent on using class time to flex muscles, make contacts, score points with one another. When I told them we'd be doing lots of writing and that they would be choosing their own topics as well as their own books, I heard grumbling, under-the-breath comments, and sneers. How could we start, if this was their attitude? They rearranged their desks to hold private conversations, seemingly oblivious to the fact that they were in class, that this was a place for work. Many boys ignored me, no matter what I said or did. They seemed to be daring me to challenge their rituals, and I was at a loss as to how to win them over.

"You'll have to get used to us," one told me proudly. "We drive all the teachers crazy."

"We're the worst class in the school," another said, grinning.

"You should have seen what we did to our last year's English teacher!"

Before I realized what was happening, the boys became the center of my attention, the center of everyone's attention. I tried asking offenders to leave the room, but there were so many that this seemed futile. I didn't want an empty classroom; I wanted a literacy community. I tried calling parents at home, and although they were supportive, most assured me laughingly that this was just "a rowdy class."

One boy, a class leader, would make mock-serious faces in response to whatever I said, pretending to be very impressed. He would nod slowly, widening his eyes, and mimic my every gesture. The class went wild. Another boy just made crazy contortions with his face and body to get similar attention from the group. Another shared joke after joke, each one a new sexual innuendo. And yet another banged his fist on his desk whenever I even mentioned the word "homework." I was not at Laurel any more.

Walking through the crowded hall to get to our room one afternoon, I felt a hard smack across my back. Frightened, I saw stars, lost my breath and my balance, and stumbled. Where was I? What was going on? "Hey, Mrs. B.," came a deep voice. I turned to see one of my students grinning at me. Was this a friendly gesture, or was he venting his hostility towards me? Either way, it hurt! And, of course, the class found it hilarious.

I called my friend Sharon Miller, who had left Laurel a few years earlier and was now teaching in a co-ed school in Pittsburgh. Had it been a difficult transition for her too, I wondered. "Yes," she laughed. "For the first two years, I thought it was me against them." That's exactly how I felt—me against them. Sharon's advice was that I "just hang in there." Things would, she promised me, work themselves out eventually.

But there were other problems. Eager to make the room theirs, not mine, I asked students to create something—poster, diorama, scrapbook—to show us who they were as readers. Who were their favorite authors? I asked them. What books did they love? Did they know any quotes by writers? What did reading mean to them?

Jennie brought what she called "an object lesson," a big wooden box filled with artifacts of her literacy. Books from her early childhood, quotes from professional writers as well as from her parents, letters from friends, a diary, a doll from a foreign country—"Reading takes you all over the world."—and a collection of her own poetry. I was speechless! Then I noticed the boys on the other side of the room snickering, hands at their faces, and whispering to each other. Jennie was new to our school; she didn't know yet that being excited about learning was not cool.

Most students did posters covered with magazine pictures. The girls read about (or looked at) fashion, while the boys preferred motorcycles, guns, or hunting. Very few students had favorite authors or best-loved books. Okay, I thought, we're going to have a great year of discovery here.

We began writing together. I tried to ignore the disruptive behavior—coming in late was common, as was running back and forth to lockers, talking all through class, using suggestive language to embarrass girls, making obscene noises, throwing spitballs, passing notes—and forge ahead with what I hoped would eventually pull them in. They thought writing practice was "stupid." Many claimed to hate reading. They seemed to dig their heels in hard.

I read aloud Byrd Baylor's *The Other Way to Listen* and we went outdoors with notebooks to see what we could observe. Two older boys, evidently free that period, were having a catch.

"We're supposed to listen," Heath told them, grinning.

"You'd hear more if you smoked a few joints," the upperclassman called. Delighted at his irreverence, my kids collapsed in laughter. This was recess, they decided, not English class.

I urged them to separate, to find a spot where they could really concentrate. "This is stupid." "I'm getting bugs all over my legs." "How long does this have to be?" "What happens if I don't hear anything?" Four or five boys climbed trees and settled in strong branches. Fine, I thought, maybe this will hook them. "Crash," rang out from the brush. "Mrs. B?" came a laughing voice, "I dropped my notebook." Relieved he hadn't fallen himself, I handed it back to him. Later, he did fall, or hurl himself, from his branch, causing even more chaos among the group.

Unexpected Gifts

Weeks went by, and a strange thing began to happen. I read to them every day, and slowly, the class quieted down. They also liked reading poems aloud and sharing their reactions to Gary Soto's short stories which we were reading together. We identified

elements of effective writing wherever we found it, and we began
to feel more like a class. The boys, crazy and aggressive as they
were, made me laugh. As I got to know them, I appreciated their
quick wits, their curiosity, and their big hearts. And the boys who
had been the worst troublemakers at first were the ones who now
had the most to contribute in class. What energy they had! What
vigor!

"This is a cool poem," John would say.

"It's deep," added Workman.

"Can I read?" asked Heath again.

When we discussed a story, hands would fly furiously in
the air. One boy, newly arrived from Germany, would point at me
and snap his fingers when he wanted me to call on him. This left
me nonplussed, until I realized it was part of his school culture
at home. When I asked him to stop, he complied at once. Others
didn't wave or raise hands at all; their ideas simply burst forth
spontaneously. This is fine, I thought, we are coming together.
They are engaged.

Once in the hall, I heard one of my boys say, "It's a pretty cool
class." I walked on air for hours.

It was difficult at first for many of them to find ideas for writing, and we spent lots of time talking about family stories, special
interests, and memories. They wrote every day in their notebooks,
and I knew they would eventually find their way. Soon we were
hearing about father-son fishing expeditions, motorcycle acci-
dents, pet ducks, trips to the emergency room. Achim, the German
student, wrote a letter to his English teacher back home, and later
a moving account of the day he had left Germany. Another boy
wrote about the death of his brother and its effect on his father.
McLean wrote about his sorrow at leaving his childhood home to
move to a new house in town, and, remembering my own house
back in New Hampshire, I shared his anguish. Their stories were as
diverse and as surprising as any I had heard before. This was going
to be, after all, a good year.

As I prepared to write comments at the end of our first six
weeks, I was startled to discover that it was the boys who were
clearer in my mind. I knew who had a snake up in his bedroom
and who had stood face to face with a turkey in the woods at
dawn. I knew whose sister was off at college and whose brother
was dating a girl in my eleventh grade class. I knew whose parents
owned a restaurant, whose mother was a disaster on the ski

slopes, and whose dad was a basketball coach. When I thought of the girls, I was not as sure. The girls seemed bunched together in my mind, a cute, quiet group. Oh, there were a few flirts, a few who didn't turn in any work, but for the most part the girls were "nice." Jennie's work stood out, of course, along with Marie's and a few others'. But I didn't know them as people, the way I knew the boys.

"To participate in class," writes Deborah Tannen, "you have to put yourself forward and claim center stage. Boys are more comfortable doing that, and they are more likely to state their opinions as fact. Girls are more likely to sound tentative, even when they are sure of themselves." (NCTE's *Council Chronicle*, February, 1992)

This was certainly true in my class. Many boys would not hesitate to disagree with me or with one another, vehemently and loudly. Few girls dared to challenge a boy's ideas, even when they disagreed. Echoes of "I don't know" were alive and well among these South Carolina girls.

My teaching journal was filled with accounts of early behavior problems and more recent incidents of boys' participation in class. How had this happened? After all I had learned at Laurel about the specific needs of girls, how had I let this happen? Things, I realized, had to change quickly. I knew that the girls' voices were being stifled in my classroom, and this was intolerable to me. As much as the boys intrigued me, as a teacher and as a researcher, I felt that it was the girls who needed much more from me than I was giving. Confident that many teacher-researchers had already written volumes on the needs and development of boys, I determined to pursue my own concern for girls' behavioral differences, literacy issues, and unique patterns of learning.

Of course, girls who sit quietly in class have plenty to say, but often they have to be persuaded to say it. I began to make a conscious effort to elicit my girls' ideas. What do you think? Talk more about that. . . .

They liked writing conferences, but these were problematic because, as I tried to talk to one person at a time, the boys would seize the opportunity for fun. We had lots of brush fires during those early writing workshops, and it seemed that our progress was less than steady. I did get to know the girls better in the conferences, but it was at the price of a higher level of turmoil in the room. Girls were much less willing to read their drafts or their finished pieces to the group. Coming from English classrooms where grammar was the heart and soul of the curriculum, they were not used to this approach to learning writing, and it scared them.

In class discussions of literature, if I called on girls too much, or if a particularly enthusiastic young man did not get the floor the minute he wanted it, we would have chaos. Myra and David Sadker, professors at American University, have researched girls' experiences in coed classrooms and have discovered problems. "Each time the teacher passes over a girl to elicit the ideas and opinions of boys," they write, "that girl is conditioned to be silent and to defer." (1994, p. 13) This was the last thing I wanted! I knew better.

In a panic, I wondered what Nancie Atwell would do. The notions that, if you involve the kids in making decisions, if you give them plenty of time, choice, and response, if you share your own passion for literacy, things will go well, seemed not to apply here. I told the class how worried I was that the girls didn't have enough opportunities to speak out, but the girls themselves protested. "It's okay, Mrs. B." said Mo. "We talk plenty." But the "talk" she meant consisted of flirting, giggling, and gossiping. They were social beings first, last, and in between, and their main concern was obviously winning the boys' admiration. I worried about their literacy, their self-awareness, and their confidence. Mo's words were no comfort to me.

Because it wasn't okay. I needed to keep the boys talking, or risk losing them entirely, but I also needed to get closer to the girls to discover what they knew and what they needed. I had to win their trust, and every day lost made that feel less likely. The situation worsened. If I wanted any meaningful growth to occur this year, the girls would have to become more involved.

The Sadkers' findings, though shocking, reflected what I was experiencing. ". . . girls' good behavior frees the teacher to work with the more difficult-to-manage boys. The result is that girls receive less time, less help, and fewer challenges. Reinforced for passivity, their independence and self-esteem suffer." As girls lose ground in school, boys learn that grabbing attention in whatever manner they like pays off.

I knew the research, and I believed it was important. I remembered my work at Laurel, all the talks the girls and I had had together. And I felt defeated here. These Southern girls, I knew, were not having the kind of experiences in my room that they needed in order to make strides as thinkers. But, no matter how hard I tried to bring them in, the boys ran the show. And then a miracle.

Single-Sex Classrooms

Since the eighth grade was in two sections, while one section was having English, the other would be in social studies. I asked the social studies teacher if we might split the class according to gender, creating one boys' section and one girls'. She had done this in the past, she said, and it had been great. Of course we could do it again. At first the kids protested:

"If my parents wanted me to go to an all girls' school, they would have sent me to one!"

"No, you can't do this to us!"

"I hate this; it's not fair!"

We proceeded in spite of their attempts at revolt. For the next twenty-four weeks we met in single-sex classes, and gradually, the complaining stopped. The girls' section was bigger than the boys, which meant that we had to create a small extra girls' group to meet during what had been a free period. This turned out to be a bonus, as it gave us the chance for some lengthy writing conferences and extended conversations. We became a community within a community.

As far as I was concerned, all the classes thrived. Oh, the boys felt even freer to be gross—how many odd noises can come out of one body anyway?—but they also seemed more serious about their reading. We did small group literature studies and the boys discovered Gary Paulsen and S. E. Hinton and Robert Lipsyte. Several young men who had been quiet and shy earlier emerged as funny, bright, sensitive thinkers. Freed from the tension of competing with their more aggressive friends for the girls' attention, they relaxed and focused more on reading and writing. Again, I found myself telling colleagues about the progress the *boys* were making under the new arrangement, in spite of the fact that we had made the switch for the girls' benefit.

But the girls were changing under this new system, and their resistance to it faded quickly. Painfully aware of the jeopardy they were in at this point in their lives, I felt reassured that at least now the girls had a fair shot at being heard. "Mrs. B," Jessica said, "we are talking more than ever!"

Slowly our conversations became more candid. We read lots of poetry, and shared lines and images that moved us. For the first time the phrase, "My favorite poet" became familiar in the room. We looked at female characters in short stories by Cynthia Rylant, Anne Tyler, and Nadine Gordimer, freed from the male lament, "I don't want to read about girls!" Rylant, Katherine Paterson, Bette Greene, Norma Fox Mazer, Lois Duncan, and Cynthia Voigt made the rounds, as girls shared their enthusiasm for newly discovered authors. *One Child* by Torey Hayden was in constant demand, and when Marie read *The Bluest Eye* by Toni Morrison and *Like Water for Chocolate* by Laura Esquival, others searched out their own copies.

We spent much more time sharing writing as a group, and the girls' work seemed to me more thoughtful; they took risks now—points of view, internal conflict, attention to sensory detail—that had not been possible earlier. New voices rang out in the room— "Can I share my piece today?"—and I realized we were making progress at last.

Kristin and Marie collaborated on a story about prejudice entitled "Against the Grain," meeting together in my office during class, experimenting with dialect, and proudly sharing emerging drafts in conference. Other attempts at collaboration were less successful, but I reveled in the knowledge that the girls were trying new genre, new processes, and new topics. They were turning into writers for the first time. Vanessa wrote about a friend in Germany who had become ill, and many of us felt our eyes sting as we listened to her read it aloud. Kate, resistant from the beginning to the very idea of writing, discovered an affinity for poetry and created a metaphor for new learning:

First Dive

I bend down,
scared thinking,
if I proceed I will drown.
My mind a jumble of thoughts,
I bend and propel
myself off the edge.
I just know
I will belly-flop.

I enter the water,
and then I swim
only from instinct.
I reach the ladder
and climb up.
Then I realize,
I have done it.

Marie wrote to the head of the school asking for more up-to-date computer programs. Jenny B. sent a letter to the school newspaper arguing that cheerleading should be credited as a required sport, just as field hockey and soccer were. And Belle submitted an argument against enforced study halls. The girls were growing in confidence before my eyes, willing and eager all of a sudden to risk having and sharing opinions. I rejoiced in their open-heartedness.

Once in a while they would sigh wistfully, claiming they wanted the boys back, but because their work was thriving, I suspected it wasn't true. They came into the room each day with new vigor, as eager as I was to talk and talk and talk. Willing as they were to take risks with writing and with responses to literature, they became, inevitably, curious about evaluation. "How are we going to have an exam on the kind of stuff we do in here?" Marie asked.

At this school, three hour semester exams were traditional and required, but, after my experiences at Laurel and my conviction that self-evaluation is vital for students, I wanted to have them do portfolios. What did they think of the idea, I wondered? "We hate exams," they groaned. "But how would the portfolios work?" I explained the notion of demonstrating literacy in and beyond the classroom and shared with them my own portfolio. Intrigued with the idea, they urged me to find a way to implement it.

In December I wrote a petition to the department head and the division director, explaining why we felt portfolios were more relevant to our curriculum, and one of the boys did the same. "It's hard to sit still in an exam for two or three hours," he argued. "We can show what we know in portfolios. They are more like a year long exam." Over some protests from other faculty members, we were given the administration's blessing to go ahead with our plan. We were off and running.

In all classes, we experimented with fiction, memoir, and poetry—reading, writing, and identifying effective elements in each genre. Of course, we left plenty of room for student-selected writing, and their favorite genre quickly became "free choice!" Many—most—grew excited about writing in just the ways I had hoped, reminding me of Mem Fox's belief that when writers "ache with caring," there is no end to what is possible. Once in a while we would regroup as a coed class to share finished pieces, the pride on each face brilliantly evident. Nervousness did not disappear, of course, but a new confidence had definitely taken root.

We met in the library to read our poems aloud to the whole group or to see films together. The students were not losing touch, and most recognized real benefits in our new division. We made poetry posters and hung them in the classroom. Near the end of the year we held a poetry performance for seventh graders and interested faculty members. Sally's poems explore contradictary emotions, reminding us that such fluctuations are par for the course for adolescents:

Hope

A rainbow after a storm,
A light in the darkness,
A blanket in the cold,
or a breeze in the heat.

Will there be any cereal left in the box,
or orange juice in the carton,
toothpaste in the tube,
or ink in the pen?

Is there any honey left in the hive,
or pollen for the bees,
sun for the sunflower,
or water for plants to grow?

Will that prayer be answered,
that was made looking up to heaven,
offered from the heart,
with eyes full of hope?

Sorrow

An old bare tree,
A sunless grey sky,
A flower brown and wilted,
A crow in the garden.

A quivering lip,
Red swollen eyes,
Heads buried in hands,
Rising, streaming with tears.

Listening to Sally and her classmates, it was hard for me to remember the early days when we struggled to find ways to care
about writing. Sally shared herself with poise and grace, eager that
her audience understand her point and know what it is that she
wonders about these days. Other girls attested to the importance
of what we were doing: "I love working on poetry, especially
showing emotion," Marie commented in her notebook. "I think it
helps so much to write poetry because when you write you understand better." Indeed.

In May we published a poetry anthology which included two
poems from every student in the class. Seven eighth graders also
had work chosen by upper school editors for the school literary
magazine, further tribute to their growth as writers.

The students' portfolios shone with all they had done through
the incredible year—dozens of books read, newly discovered love
of poetry, drafts of writing leading to polished pieces to save forever—and the students' pride was unmistakable. Although one
purpose of using portfolios to evaluate growth is to respect each
student's uniqueness, it was also clear to me that, in this class,
the girls' group made more significant gains in both reading and
writing. In their notebooks, I saw candid, creative, complex responses to literature, and I saw increasing attention being given to
women's rights, women's challenges, and women's relationships.

Dear Mrs. Barbieri,

I'm reading *The Joy Luck Club* by Amy Tan, and I really like
how she uses metaphor to get her points across. Like, in the
chapter I just read the mother tells the girl that she was born
without wood. How she bends too much to listen to other
people without following her mother. I like how Rose Hsu
Jordan says that there is a person who opens the doors into a
dream world and how she was afraid to go in b/c she always
had nightmares.

This book shows the differences between the relationships
of the mothers and daughters but also the sameness, how all
the daughters think that the mothers are always looking
down on them but how the mothers are only trying to protect
their daughters from the dangers that the mothers perceive

around them. But yet even though it seems like all the mothers and daughters do is fight in the beginning, you begin to see the sacred loving bond that they all have between each of them and that is what makes this book very special.

Amy is also very descriptive especially when it comes to telling about the crabs. It gives me an empty feeling inside. I also like how she goes back into their past to show us a little bit about what their lives were like back in China. It reminds me of how I sometimes have to stop and remember.

Dear Jenny,

Good Night Mr. Tom by Michelle Magorian is getting really good. One of Willie's friends, Carrie, is trying to take an examination that before only boys took. She kind of makes me think of how my mom might have been in those days. She wants everybody to be equal. She kind of reminds me of how Mrs. Barbieri (all respect intended, Mrs. B.) might have been in those days, always standing up for girls and women to get fair treatment . . .

Dear Mrs. Barbieri,

I finished *The Drowning of Stephan Jones* by Bette Greene. My favorite part was the end . . . I felt sad for Carla because the attorney saw everything differently and could explain her actions as a punishment against Andy for dancing and hanging out with other girls. I really felt sorry for her because she was the one who wanted justice and tried so hard to get it. The question about how many boyfriends Carla had was probably pretty embarrassing for her, but I think it would be more embarrassing to get caught lying to the court . . . Anyway this case also had one good side to it and that is that Carla and her mother are now closer than ever and are not just mother-and-daughter but best friends. I think it was good that Debby and her mom were in the courtroom too every time. I bet this gave Carla a more comforting feeling than being all by herself . . .

Like the Laurel girls, my new students were passionate in their admiration for Nikki Giovanni, filling their portfolios with her work. "Woman," "nikki-rosa," and "You Are There," hung proudly in our classroom, and I bought new copies of *Cotton Candy on a Rainy Day*, since so many girls asked to take it home. My new students were becoming real connoisseurs, finding poets on their

own, and delighting in sharing their discoveries. In Jennifer's portfolio she included a poem we had not read in class, one she found
on her own and continues to treasure. Her attached notecard
reads:

> "Endurance" by Fran Portley is one of my favorite poems be-
> cause I like the way the poet tells me how women have had
> to endure hard times. She really shows how women have
> relied on each other, and that their suffering goes back a long
> time. . . ."

Reunion

During the last six weeks of school, at the students' request, we re-
combined the groups. We were back where we had started—boys
and girls together. "We need to hear the boys' ideas now," the girls
told me. Confident that much good learning had already gone on,
and willing to take a risk to accommodate their wishes, I agreed.
Some girls reverted to their previous shy ways, as did a few boys.
But, in spite of this, I saw an honest effort on most of their parts to
listen to one another more earnestly. Although some lamented the
regrouping, most wanted to be together as school came to an end.
Flirting became the order of the day once again, as did discreet
note passing, and other subtle socializing.

But the girls were more eager to share their writing, and the
boys did not balk at giving them equal time. We finished Lois Lowry's novel, *The Giver*, felt unnerved by its implications, and constructed several possible interpretations of its ending. I was glad to
hear that the girls were as excited about it as the boys, arguing per-
suasively for their points of view.

In her final portfolio self-evaluation, Marie writes:

> . . . . The past year has been such a new experience for me
> that I would not trade it for anything. I am a totally new born
> person in my writing and reading. I remember the first six
> weeks with Mrs. Barbieri. We were all like total airheads
> compared to what we are now. It is almost indescribable what
> we have become. We not only have become more literate but
> we have also learned what it *means* to be literate. I will never
> forget the fun we had discussing poetry or having some thou-
> sand writing conferences. . . .

Many girls seemed more assertive now, more willing to challenge boys' opinions. On a hot May afternoon, the boys were arguing about the best way to conduct an interview of a family member. Several tried making a farce of the whole assignment, although one or two were earnest in their attempts to role-play the situation. I had hoped to give the kids lots of leeway here, trusting their ability to work well together, but the class threatened to disintegrate, and I pondered whether I should intervene. Suddenly a new voice—

"Can I say something?" Nina interrupted, "I have a really good idea." Stunned, the boys turned to her and listened.

I thought back to Laurel—to Brady and Sara and Wallis and Rachel and Danielle and Marlana and Bernice, all my girls—and felt them cheering Nina on. What had seemed impossible in September was now comfortable, natural, and right. Our class separation—another noble experiment—had yielded valuable growth.

Do I think that coed classrooms make learning impossible for girls? Perhaps not. However, I do believe, after my experiences in three schools, that we who teach girls must be ever vigilant to their willingness, even their preference, to avoid conflict, discord, or risk, and that such vigilance is certainly more possible in single-sex classrooms. Boys, it seems to me, will find ways to get what they need from the system; it's the girls who are in the greatest danger of slipping away from us, quietly, unobtrusively, politely slipping away.

We must be proactive in finding out who they really are, what they really need, and how we can lead them to it. Drawing girls out, valuing their tentative ideas, and supporting their speculations will continue to be my highest priority in classrooms. Their "I don't know's" are all too common, whether they are alone or with boys, but we must not let such insecurity go unassuaged. The girls are not, in Mo's word, "okay," just because they are cooperative; indeed their very cooperation is often a symptom of the danger they are in academically, psychologically, and socially.

If we truly "don't know," it becomes incumbent upon us to wonder, to search, and finally to discover. But often, as I learned at Laurel and at my new school, these girls *do* know; they need their knowing validated. Nina speaks for all girls—those who are underground, those whose voices have been trained to polite docility, and those who in their hearts resist society's expectations—when she says with such vigor, "I have a really good idea."

Appendix A

Some of the Poetry My Students and I Love

———

Adoff, Arnold. 1982. *All the Colors of the Race*. New York: Lothrop, Lee and Shepard.

———. 1973. *Black is Brown is Tan*. New York: Harper Collins.

———. 1989. *Chocolate Dreams*. New York: Lothrop, Lee and Shepard.

———. 1979. *Eats*. New York: Lothrop, Lee and Shepard.

———. 1988. *Flamboyan*. New York: Harcourt Brace.

———. 1988. *Greens*. New York: Lothrop, Lee and Shepard.

Adoff, Arnold, ed. 1970. *I Am the Darker Brother: An Anthology of Poems by Negro Americans*. New York: Macmillan.

Adoff, Arnold, ed. 1973. *Poetry of Black America*. New York: Harper Collins.

———. 1986. *Sports Pages*. New York: Harper Collins.

Agard, John, comp. 1990. *Life Doesn't Frighten Me at All*. New York: Henry Holt and Company.

Baylor, Byrd. 1992. *Guess Who My Favorite Person Is?* New York: Macmillan.

———. 1980. *If You Are a Hunter of Fossils*. New York: Macmillan.

———. 1986. *I'm in Charge of Celebrations*. New York: Charles Scribner's Sons, Macmillan Publishing Co.

———. 1978. *The Other Way to Listen*. New York: Charles Scribner's Sons, Macmillan Publishing Co.

Berry, James. 1991. *When I Dance*. New York: Harcourt Brace.

Bierhorst, John, ed. 1987. *In the Trail of the Wind: American Indian Poems and Ritual Orations*. New York: Farrar, Straus, Giroux.

Clifton, Lucille.

———. 1991. *Quilting: Poems 1987–1990*. Rochester, NY: BOA Edns.

cummings, e. e. 1940. *poems 1923–1954*. New York: Harcourt Brace.

———. 1989. *hist whist*. New York: Crown Books for Young Readers.

Daniel, Mark, comp. 1991. *A Child's Treasury of Seaside Verse*. New York: Dial Books for Young Readers.

Dickinson, Emily. 1978. *I'm Nobody, Who Are You*. New York: Stemmer House.

———. 1982. *The Collected Poems of Emily Dickinson*. New York: Outlet Book Company.

Dunning, Stephen, Edward Lueders, and Hugh Smith. 1966. *Reflections on a Gift of Watermelon Pickle and Other Modern Verse*. Glenview, IL: Scott Foresman.

Esbensen, Barbara Juster. 1987. *Words with Wrinkled Knees*. New York: Harper Collins.

———. 1984. *Cold Stars & Fireflies: Poems for the Four Seasons*. New York: Harper Collins.

Fletcher, Ralph. 1991. *Water Planet*. Paramus, NJ: Arrowhead Books.

———. 1994. *I Am Wings*. New York: Bradbury Press, Macmillan.

Frost, Robert. 1979. *The Poetry of Robert Frost*. New York: Henry Holt and Company.

———. 1990. *Birches*. New York: Henry Holt and Company.

———. 1990. *Christmas Trees*. New York: Henry Holt and Company.

Giovanni, Nikki. 1980. *Cotton Candy on a Rainy Day*. New York: Quill.

———. 1993. *ego-tripping and other poems for young people*. New York: L. Hill Books.

———. 1971. *Spin a Soft Black Song*. New York: Farrar, Straus and Giroux.

Gordon, Ruth, comp. 1987. *Under All the Silences: Shades of Love*. New York: Harper Collins.

Greenfield, Eloise. 1978. *Honey I Love and other poems*. New York: Harper & Row.

———. 1988. *Nathaniel's Talking*. New York: Black Butterfly Children's Books.

———. 1991. *Night on Neighborhood Street*. New York: Dial Books.

Greenfield, Eloise and Tom Feelings. 1985. *Daydreamers*. New York: Dial.

Harrison, Michael, ed. 1989. *Splinters: A Book of Very Short Poems*. Oxford University Press.

Hughes, Langston. 1962. *The Dream Keeper and Other Poems*. New York: Knopf.

Janeczko, Paul, collector, 1985. *Pocket Poems: Selected for a Journey*. New York: Bradbury Press, Macmillan.

———. 1989. *Strings: A Gathering of Family Poems*. New York: Bradbury Press, Macmillan.

———. comp. 1987. *Going Over to Your Place: Poems for Each Other*. New York: Bradbury Press, Macmillan.

———. comp. 1991. *Poetspeak: In their work, about their work*. New York: Collier Books, Macmillan.

———. comp. 1986. *Dont forget to fly: a cycle of modern poems*. New York: Bradbury Press, Macmillan.

———. comp. 1990. *The Place My Words Are Looking For*. New York: Bradbury Press, Macmillan.

———. comp. 1987. *This Delicious Day: 65 Poems*. New York: Orchard.

———. comp. 1988. *The Music of What Happens: Poems That Tell Stories*. New York: Orchard.

———. 1991. *Preposterous: Poems of Youth*. New York: Orchard.

———. comp. 1993. *Looking for Your Name: A Collection of Contemporary Poems*. New York: Orchard.

Kennedy, X. J. and Kennedy, Dorothy. 1982. *Knock at a Star: A Child's Introduction to Poetry*. Boston: Little, Brown and Company.

———. 1991. *The Kite That Braved Old Orchard Beach*. New York: Macmillan.

Koch, Kenneth and Kate Farrell, eds. 1985. *Talking to the Sun: An Illustrated Anthology of Poems for Young People.* New York: Henry Holt.

Larrick, Nancy, selector, 1982. *Piping Down the Valleys Wild: A Collection of Poetry for Children.* New York: Dell.

Little, Leslie Jones. 1988. *Children of Long Ago.* New York: Macmillan.

Livingston, Myra Cohn. 1989. *Remembering and Other Poems.* New York: MacMillan.

———. 1988. *There Was a Place and Other Poems.* New York: Macmillan.

Martz, Sandra K., ed. 1991. *When I Am Old I Shall Wear Purple.* New York: Papier Mache Press.

Mazer, Norma Fox and Marjorie Lewis, eds. 1989. *Waltzing on Water: Poetry by Women.* New York: Bantam Doubleday Dell.

Merriam, Eve. 1986. *Fresh Paint: New Poems.* New York: Macmillan.

———. 1986. *A Sky Full of Poems.* New York: Dell.

———. 1984. *Jamboree: Rhymes for All Ages.* New York: Dell.

———. 1985. *Blackberry Ink.* New York: Morrow Junior Books.

Norman, Howard A., trans., comp. 1982. *The Wishing Bone Cycle: Narrative Poems of the Swampy Cree Indians.* Ross Erikson.

Nye, Naomi Nyhab. 1992. *This Same Sky: A Collection of Poems from Around the World.* New York: Four Winds Press.

Rylant, Cynthia. 1990. *Soda Jerk: Poems.* New York: Orchard Books.

———. 1984. *Waiting to Waltz: A Childhood.* New York: Bradbury Press.

———. 1982. *When I Was Young in the Mountains.* New York: Bradbury Press.

Sandburg, Carl. 1970. *Sandburg Treasury: Prose and Poetry for Young People.* New York: Harcourt Brace.

Soto, Gary. 1990. *A Fire in My Hands.* New York: Scholastic Inc.

———. 1990. *Who Will Know Us?* New York: Chronicle Books.

Stevenson, Robert Louis. 1985. *A Child's Garden of Verses.* New York: Children's Classics, Random House.

Sullivan, Charles, ed. 1993. *American Beauties.* New York: Harry N. Abrams, Inc.

———, ed. 1989. *Imaginary Gardens: American Poetry and Art for Young People.* New York: Harry N. Abrams.

Thoreau, Henry David. 1992. *The Poet's Delay.* Boston/New York: MFA, Boston, Rizzoli International Publication.

Viorst, Judith. 1981. *If I Were in Charge of the World.* NY: Macmillan.

Whitman, Walt. 1988. *Voyages: Poems.* New York: Harcourt Brace Jovanovich.

———. 1975. *Walt Whitman: The Complete Poems.* New York: Penguin.

Willard, Nancy. 1981. *William Blake's Inn: Poems for Experienced and Innocent Travelers.* New York: Harcourt Brace.

Wood, Nancy. 1974. *Many Winters: Prose and Poetry of the Pueblos*. New York: Doubleday.

Adult Poetry I Like to Share with Students

Angelou, Mary. 1986. *Poems*. New York: Bantam.

Brooks, Gwendolyn. 1981. *to disembark*. Chicago, IL: Third World Press.

Heaney, Seamus. 1990. *Seamus Heaney: Selected Poems 1969–1987*. New York: Farrar, Straus & Giroux.

Kinnell, Galway. 1982. *Collected Poems of Galway Kinnell*. Boston, MA: Houghton Mifflin.

McBride, Mekeel. 1988. *Red Letter Days*. Pittsburgh, PA: Carnegie Mellon.

Oliver, Mary. 1983. *American Primitive*. Atlantic Monthly Press.

———. 1990. *House of Light*. Boston, MA: Beacon Press.

———. 1992. *New and Selected Poems*. Boston, MA: Beacon Press.

Pastan, Linda. 1985. *A Fraction of Darkness*. New York: W. W. Norton & Company.

———. 1982. *PM/AM: New and Selected Poems*. New York: W. W. Norton & Company.

———. 1988. *Imperfect Paradise*. New York: W. W. Norton & Company.

———. 1991. *Heroes in Disguise*. New York: W. W. Norton & Company.

Piercy, Marge. 1990. *Circles on the Water: Selected Poems of Marge Piercy*. New York: Alfred A. Knopf.

Rich, Adrienne. 1973. *Diving Into the Wreck: Poems 1971–1972*. New York: Norton.

Wilbur, Richard. 1963. *Poems of Richard Wilbur*. New York: Harcourt Brace.

Yeats, William Butler. 1983. *The Collected Works of W. B. Yeats, Vol. I*. New York: Macmillan.

Books I Use to Teach Poetry

Ciardi, John. 1975. *How Does A Poem Mean?* Boston, MA: Houghton Mifflin.

Drake, Barbara. 1983. *Writing Poetry*. New York: Harcourt Brace.

Grossman, Florence. 1982. *Getting from Here to There: Writing and Reading Poetry*. Portsmouth, NH: Boynton/Cook, Heinemann.

Heard, Georgia. 1989. *For the Good of the Earth and Sun*. Portsmouth, NH: Heinemann.

Appendix B

Memoirs of Writers
We Love

———

Angelou, Maya. 1969. *I Know Why the Caged Bird Sings*. New York: Bantam.

———. 1987. *All God's Children Need Traveling Shoes*. New York: Random House.

Baker, Russell. 1982. *Growing Up*. New York: New American Library.

———. 1991. *The Good Times*. New York: NAL Dutton.

Cahill, Susan, ed. 1993. *Growing Up Female: Stories by American Women from the American Mosaic*. New York: Penguin Books.

Cisneros, Sandra. 1986. *The House on Mango Street*. Houston, TX: Arte Publico.

Cleary, Beverly. 1988. *The Girl from Yamhill*. New York: Morrow.

Dahl, Roald. 1988. *Boy: Tales of Childhood*. New York: Penguin Books.

———. 1988. *Going Solo*. Viking Penguin.

Dillard, Annie. 1987. *An American Childhood*. New York: Harper & Row.

———. 1990. *The Writing Life*. New York: Harper Collins.

Duncan, Lois. 1982. *Chapters: My Growth as A Writer*. New York: Little.

Fox, Mem. 1992. *Dear Mem Fox, I've Read All Your Books, Even the Pathetic Ones*. New York: Harcourt, Brace, Jovanovich.

Fritz, Jean. 1982. *Homesick: My Own Story*. New York: G. P. Putman's Sons.

Hall, Donald. 1961. *String Too Short To Be Saved*. New York: Viking.

Greenfield, Eloise, and Lessie J. Little. 1979. *Childtimes: A Three Generation Memoir*. New York: Harper Collins.

Hughes, Langston. 1974. *I Wonder as I Wander*. New York: Hippocrene.

Little, Jean. 1987. *Little by Little: A Writer's Education*. New York: Viking.

MacNeil, Robert. 1989. *Wordstruck*. New York: Harper.

Meltzer, Milton. 1991. *Starting from Home: A Writer's Beginnings*. New York: Puffin.

Paterson, Katherine. 1981. *Gates of Excellence: On Reading and Writing Books for Children*. New York: Elsevier/Nelson Books.

———. 1990. *The Spying Heart*. New York: Dutton.

Rawlings, Marjorie Kinnan. 1971. *Cross Creek*. New York: Macmillan.

Rylant, Cynthia. 1989. *But I'll Be Back Again: An Album*. New York: Orchard Books.

———. 1984. *Waiting to Waltz: A Childhood*. Scarsdale, NY: Bradbury Press.

———. 1982. *When I Was Young in the Mountains*. New York: Dutton.

Soto, Gary, ed. 1988. *California Childhood: Recollections and Stories of the Golden State*.

Updike, John. 1989. *Self-Consciousness: Memoirs*. New York: Alfred A. Knopf.

Walker, Alice. 1989. *Living By the Word: Selected Writings 1973–1987*. New York: Harcourt Brace.

Welty, Eudora. 1982. *Collected Stories of Eudora Welty.* New York: Harcourt Brace.

———. 1983. *One Writer's Beginnings.* New York: Warner Books.

———. 1990. *The Eye of the Story: Selected Essays and Reviews.* New York: Random House.

White, E. B. 1983. *One Man's Meat.* New York: Harper Collins.

Wolff, Tobias. 1989. *This Boy's Life: A Memoir.* New York: Atlantic Monthly.

Wright, Annie, ed. 1986. *The Delicacy and Strength of Lace Letters between L. M. Silko and James Wright.* St. Paul, MN: Graywolf.

Yolen, Jane. 1987. *Owl Moon.* New York: Putnam.

Zinsser, William. 1987. *Inventing the Truth: The Art and Craft of Memoir.* Boston, MA: Houghton Mifflin Company.

Appendix C

Memoir Resources

The following books were helpful to us in our exploration of memoir. Some helped me prepare mini-lessons, some I read aloud to the girls, and others were available for students to borrow.

Anthony, Carolyn. 1991. *Family Portraits: Rembrances by Twenty Distinguished Writers*. New York: Viking Penguin.

Capote, Truman. 1989. *A Christmas Memory*. New York: Knopf.

———. 1987. *I Remember Grandpa*. Atlanta, GA: Peachtree Publishers.

Cary, Lorene. 1991. *Black Ice*. New York: Alfred A. Knopf.

Carter, Forrest. 1986. *The Education of Little Tree*. Albuquerque, NM: University of New Mexico Press.

Coles, Robert. 1989. *The Call of Stories: Teaching and the Moral Imagination*. Boston, MA: Houghton Mifflin Company.

Cormier, Robert. 1991. *I Have Words to Spend: Reflections of a Small Town Editor*. New York: Delacourt Press.

Cooney, Barbara. 1990. *Hattie and the Wild Waves*. New York: Viking Children's Books.

———. 1982. *Miss Rumphius*. New York: Penguin Books.

Farber, Norma. 1979. *How Does It Feel To Be Old?* New York: E. P. Dutton.

Geras, Adele. 1990. *My Grandmother's Stories: A Collection of Jewish Folk Tales*. New York: Knopf.

Giovanni, Nikki, ed. 1994. *Grand Mothers: Poems, Reminiscences, and Short Stories about the Keepers of Our Traditions*. New York: Henry Holt and Company.

Gould, June. 1991. *The Writer in All of Us: Improving Your Writing Through Childhood Memories*. New York: Penguin Books, Ltd.

Hamilton, Virginia. 1993. *The People Could Fly*. New York: Knopf.

Houston, Gloria. 1988. *The Year of the Perfect Christmas Tree: An Appalachian Story*. New York: Dial.

———. 1992. *My Great Aunt Arizona*. New York: Collins.

Janeczko, Paul, ed. 1984. *Strings: A Gathering of Family Poems*. New York: Macmillan.

Kingston, Maxine Hong. 1977. *The Woman Warrior, Memoirs of a Girlhood Among Ghosts*. New York: Vintage.

McLerran, Alice. 1991. *Roxaboxen*. New York: Lothrop, Lee & Shephard Books.

Proulx, Annie E. 1993. *Heart Songs and Others Stories*. New York: Macmillan.

Ringhold, Faith. 1991. *Tar Beach*. New York: Crown Publishers, Inc.

Rodriguez, Richard. 1982. *Hunger of Memory: The Education of Richard Rodriguez*. New York: Bantam Books.

Silko, Leslie Marmon. 1989. *Story Teller*. Berkeley, CA: Arcade Publishers,
   Inc.
———. 1986. *Ceremony*. New York: Viking Penguin.
Simon, Kate. 1983. *Bronx Primitive*. New York: Harper and Row.
Sternburg, Janet, ed. 1980. *The Writer on Her Work*. New York: W. W. Nor-
   ton and Company.

Appendix D

Female Protagonists in My Seventh Graders' Reading Choices

Laurel School, Shaker Heights, Ohio 1991–92

"The texts we select and the questions we ask to legitimize those texts determine whose story in a society is worth telling and whose voices are worth hearing."

—Laura Apol Obbink, *English Journal*, Nov. 1992

Angelou, Maya	*I Know Why the Caged Bird Sings*
Angell, Judie	*Don't Rent My Room*
	Leave the Cooking to Me
Anonymous	*Go Ask Alice*
Atwood, Margaret	*The Handmaid's Tale*
	The Cat's Eye
Avi	*The True Confessions of Charlotte Doyle*
Betancourt, Jeanne	*More Than Meets the Eye*
Blume, Judy	*Just As Long As We're Together*
	Deenie
	Tiger Eyes
Calvert, Pat	*When Morning Comes*
Cather, Willa	*My Antonia*
	O Pioneers
Clapp, Patricia	*The Tamarack Tree*
Cole, Brock	*The Goats*
Conrad, Pam	*Prairie Songs*
Crew, Linda	*Children of the River*
Daly, Maureen	*Acts of Love*
Danziger, Paula	*The Cat Ate My Gymsuit*
	Can You Sue Your Parents for Malpractice
	The Divorce Express
Derby, Pat	*Goodbye, Emily, Hello*
Dillard, Annie	*An American Childhood*
	The Writing Life
Duford, Deborah & Stout, Harry S.	*An Enemy Among Them*
Duncan, Lois	*Stranger With My Face*
	Don't Look Behind You
	Chapters: My Growth as A Writer
Fox, Paula	*The Moonlight Man*
Frank, Anne	*The Diary of A Young Girl*
Furlong, Monica	*Wise Child*
	Juniper
Greene, Bette	*The Drowning of Stephan Jones*
	Summer of My German Soldier
Guy, Rosa	*The Friends*
Hahn, Mary Downing	*December Stillness*
Hamilton, Morse	*Effie's House*
Hamilton, Virginia	*Cousins*
	A White Romance

Hano, Renee Roth   *Touch Wood*
Hayden, Torey   *One Child; Somebody Else's Kids; Just Another Kid; The Sunflower Forest*

Herlihy, Dirlie   *Ludie's Song*
Hoffman, Alice   *At Risk; Seventh Heaven*
Hooper, Nancy J.   *The Truth or Dare Trap*
Hurmence, Belinda   *Tancy*
Irwin, Hadley   *What About Grandma?*
Johnson, Norma   *The Potter's Wheel*
Keehn, Sally   *I Am Regina*
Kincaid, Jamaica   *Lucy*
Kuchler-Silberman, Lena   *My Hundred Children*
Lasky, Katherine   *Pageant; Night Journey*
Lowry, Lois   *Number the Stars; Rabble Starkey; Anastasia at This Address*

Lunn, Janet   *Root Cellar*
MacLachan, Patricia   *The Facts and Fictions of Minna Pratt*
Markandaya, Kamala   *Nectar in a Sieve*
Mazer, Norma Fox   *After the Rain; Silver; A Figure of Speech; Mrs. Fish, Ape and Me, the Dump Queen, Babyface*

Mickle, Shelley   *The Queen of October*
Morrison, Toni   *Sula*
                                    The Bluest Eye

Motas, Carol   *Lisa's War*
Naylor, Gloria   *Women of Brewster Place*
Oneal, Zibby   *In Summer Light*
                                    The Language of Goldfish

Orgel, Doris   *The Devil in Vienna*
Paterson, Katherine   *Lyddie; Jacob Have I Loved*
Rinaldi, Ann   *The Last Silk Dress; Wolf By Ear*
Rylant, Cynthia   *A Couple of Kooks*
                                    But I'll Be Back Again: An Album

Sebestyen, Ouida   *The Girl in the Box; Words by Heart*
Smith, Betty   *A Tree Grows in Brooklyn*
Snyder, Zilpha Keatley   *Libby on Wednesday*
Staples, Suzanne Fisher   *Shabanu: Daughter of the Wind*
Sullivan, Faith   *The Cape Ann*
Taylor, Mildred   *Roll of Thunder, Hear My Cry*
                                    Let the Circle Be Unbroken
                                    The Road to Memphis

Thesman, Jean	*The Rain Catchers*
Townsend, Sue	*The Secret Diaries of Adrian Mole, Aged 13 3/4*
Voigt, Cynthia	*Homecoming; Dicey's Song; Come A Stranger*
Walker, Alice	*The Color Purple*
Walsh, Jill Paton	*Fireweed*
Welty, Eudora	*One Writer's Beginnings*
Weyn, Suzanne	*The Makeover Campaign*

Appendix E

Laurel School Seventh Graders' Suggested Reading List

———

THESE BOOKS were named as top choices by seventh grade girls during my four years with them.

Alcott, Louisa May. *Little Women; Little Men; Jo's Boys*
Angelou, Maya. *I Know Why the Caged Bird Sings*
Anonymous. *Go Ask Alice*
Atwood, Margaret. *The Handmaid's Tale*
Avi. *The True Confessions of Charlotte Doyle*
Bess, Clayton. *Story for A Black Night*
Blume, Judy. *Just As Long as We're Together; Tiger Eyes*
Bunting, Eve. *Sharing Susan; Jumping the Nail*
Burns, Olive. *Cold Sassy Tree*
Carter, Forrest. *The Education of Little Tree*
Cather, Willa. *My Antonia; O Pioneers!*
Clapp, Patricia. *The Tamarack Tree*
Cole, Brock. *The Goats*
Collier, James and Christopher. *My Brother Sam is Dead*
Conrad, Pam. *Prairie Songs*
Cormier, Robert. *Take Me Where the Good Times Are; Fade; We All Fall Down; Eight Plus One*
Dahl, Roald. *Matilda; Boy; Solo*
Daly, Maureen. *Acts of Love; Seventeenth Summer*
Duford, Deborah and Harry S. *An Enemy Among Them*
Dillard, Annie. *An American Childhood*
Duncan, Lois. *Don't Look Behind You; Stranger With My Face; Chapters: My Growth as A Writer*
Els, Betty Vander. *The Bombers' Moon*
Flagg, Fannie. *Fried Green Tomatoes at the Whistle Stop Cafe; Daisy Fay Harper and The Miracle Man*
Fox, Paula. *Moonlight Man; The Slave Dancer*
Frank, Anne. *The Diary of A Young Girl*
Glassman, Judy. *The Morning Glory War*
Godden, Rummer. *An Episode of Sparrows*
Gordon, Sheila. *The Middle of Somewhere*
Greene, Bette. *The Drowning of Stephan Jones; Summer of My German Soldier*
Green, Bob. *Be True to Your School*
Guy, Rosa. *The Friends*
Hahn, Mary Downing. *December Stillness*
Hamilton, Virginia. *Cousins; M. C. Higgins, the Great; A White Romance*
Hano, Renee Roth. *Touch Wood*

Hayden, Torey. *One Child; Somebody Else's Kids; Murphy's Boy; Just Another Kid; The Sunflower Forest; Ghost Girl*

Highwater, Jamake. *Legend Days*

Hinton, S. E. *The Outsiders; Tex; That Was Then, This Is Now*

Hoffman, Alice. *At Risk*

Hunt, Irene. *Across Five Aprils*

Hunter, Mollie. *The Sound of Chariots; Cat, Herself; Hold on to Love*

Hurmence, Belinda. *Tancy*

Jakes, John. *North and South*

Johnston, Norma. *The Potter's Wheel; The Delphic Choice; The Dragon's Eye*

Kerr, M. E. *Gentlehands*

King, Stephen. *The Skeleton Crew; Misery*

Knowles, John. *A Separate Peace*

Kuchler-Silberman, Lena. *My Hundred Children*

Lasky, Kathryn. *Pageant; Night Journey*

Lee, Harper. *To Kill A Mockingbird*

LeGuin, Ursula. *The Wizard of Earthsea; The Tombs of Atuan; The Farthest Shore*

l'Engle, Madeleine. *Meet the Austins; A Wrinkle in Time; The Summer of the Great-Grandmother*

Lester, Julius. *To Be A Slave; The Long Journey Home*

Lipsyte, Robert. *One Fat Summer*

Lowry, Lois. *Anastasia at Your Service; Anastasia at This Address; Autumn Street; Number the Stars; Rabble Starkey*

Lunn, Janet. *Root Cellar*

MacLachlan, Patricia. *The Facts and Fictions of Minna Pratt*

Magorian, Michelle. *Back Home; Good Night, Mr. Tom*

Markandaya, Kamala. *Nectar in a Sieve*

Mazer, Norma Fox. *After the Rain; Silver; A Figure of Speech; Mrs. Fish, Ape and Me, the Dump Queen*

McDaniel, Lurlene. *When Happily Ever After Ends; Too Young to Die; Somewhere Between Life and Death; Time to Let Go; Now I Lay Me Down to Sleep*

Mitchell, Margaret. *Gone With the Wind*

Morrison, Toni. *Sula*

Motas, Carol. *Lisa's War*

Myers, Walter Dean. *Won't Know Til I Get There*

Naylor, Gloria. *Women of Brewster Place*

Nolan, Christopher. *Under the Eye of the Clock*

Oneal, Zibby. *In Summer Light; The Language of Goldfish*

Orgel, Doris. *The Devil in Vienna*

Parks, Gordon. *The Learning Tree*

Paterson, Katherine. *Lyddie; Jacob Have I Loved; Bridge to Terabithia; Rebels of the Heavenly Kingdom; The Master Puppeteer*

Paulsen, Gary. *The Winter Room; Woodsong*

Peck, Robert Newton. *A Day No Pigs Would Die*

Pike, Christopher. *Remember Me; See You Later; Fall Into Darkness; Die Softly; Chain Letter 2; The Ancient Evil; Witch; Whisper of Death; Bury Me Deep; Last Act; Spellbound*

Potok, Chaim. *The Chosen*

Raskin, Ellen. *The Westing Game*

Rawlings, Marjorie Kinnan. *The Yearling*

Rawls, Wilson. *Where the Red Fern Grows*

Reeder, Carolyn. *Shades of Gray*

Rinaldi, Ann. *The Last Silk Dress; Time Enough for Drums; Wolf by Ear; The Good Side of My Heart*

Rochman, Hazel (compiler). *Somehow Tenderness Survives: Stories of Southern Africa*

Rylant, Cynthia. *But I'll Be Back Again; A Couple of Kooks*

Salinger, J. D. *The Catcher in the Rye*

Sebestyen, Ouida. *The Girl in the Box; Words by Heart*

Sleator, William. *Fingers*

Smith, Betty. *A Tree Grows in Brooklyn*

Soto, Gary. *A Summer Life*

Spinelli, Jerry. *Maniac Magee*

Sweeney, Joyce. *The Dream Collector*

Taylor, Mildred. *Roll of Thunder, Hear My Cry; Let the Circle Be Unbroken; The Road to Memphis*

Townsend, Sue. *The Secret Diaries of Adrian Mole, Aged 13 3/4*

Tyler, Anne. *Celestial Navigation; The Accidental Tourist; Searching for Caleb; Dinner at the Homesick Restaurant*

Voigt, Cynthia. *The Vandemark Mummy; Homecoming; Dicey's Song; The Runner; A Solitary Blue; Tree by Leaf; Come A Stranger*

Walker, Alice. *The Color Purple*

Walsh, Jill Paton. *Fireweed*

Wiesel, Elie. *Night*

Yep, Laurence. *Dragonwings; Tongues of Jade; The Rainbow People; Child of the Owl*

Yolen, Jane. *The Devil's Arithmetic*

Zindel, Paul. *The Pigman; The Pigman's Legacy*

Works Cited

Alcott, Louisa May. 1981. *Little Women.* New York: Putnam.

———. 1991. *Under the Lilacs.* New York: Puffin.

American Association of University Women. 1990. *Shortchanging Girls, Shortchanging America: Full Data Report.* Washington, D.C.: American Association of University Women.

Angelou, Maya. 1983. *I Know Why the Caged Bird Sings.* New York: Bantam

Atwell, Nancie. 1987. *In the Middle: Writing, Reading, and Learning with Adolescents.* Portsmouth, NH: Boynton/Cook Publishers, A Division of Heinemann Educational Books.

Atwell, Nancie. 1991. *Side by Side: Essays on Teaching to Learn.* Portsmouth, NH: Heinemann Educational Books.

Baker, Russell. 1983. *Growing Up.* New York: NAL Dutton, a division of Penguin.

Baylor, Byrd. 1986. *I'm in Charge of Celebrations.* New York: Charles Scribner's Sons, Macmillan Publishing Company.

——— and Parnall, Peter. 1978. *The Other Way to Listen.* New York: Charles Scribner's Sons, Macmillan Publishing Company.

Belenky, Mary Field, Blythe McVicker Clinchy, Nancy Rule Goldberger, and Jill Mattuck Tarule. 1986. *Women's Ways of Knowing: the Development of Self, Voice, and Mind.* New York, NY: Basic Books, Inc., Publishers.

Berry, James. 1991. "When I Dance." In *When I Dance.* New York: Harcourt Brace.

Brown, Lyn Mikel, and Gilligan, Carol. 1992. *Meeting at the Crossroads: Women's Psychology and Girls' Development.* Cambridge, MA: Harvard University Press.

Brown, Margaret Wise. 1942. *The Runaway Bunny.* NY: Harper & Row

Brown, Rexford G. 1993. *Schools of Thought: How the Politics of Literacy Shape Thinking in Schools.* San Francisco, CA: Jossey-Bass Inc., Publishers.

Burnett, Frances. 1990. *The Little Princess.* New York: Dell.

Calkins, Lucy McCormick. 1986. *The Art of Teaching Writing.* Portsmouth, NH: Heinemann.

Calkins, Lucy McCormick and Shelley Harwayne. 1991. *Living Between the Lines.* Portsmouth, NH: Heinemann Educational Books.

Capote, Truman. 1966. *A Christmas Memory.* New York: Random House.

————. 1987. *I Remember Grandpa.* Atlanta, GA: Peachtree Publishers.

Carroll, Lewis. 1992. *Alice in Wonderland.* New York: Dell.

Carter, Forrest. 1986. *The Education of Little Tree.* Albuquerque, NM: University of New Mexico Press.

Cary, Lorene. 1991. *Black Ice.* New York: Alfred A. Knopf.

Cather, Willa. 1973. *My Antonia.* Boston, MA: Houghton Mifflin.

————. 1994. *O Pioneers.* NY: Viking Penguin

Clifton, Lucille. 1991. *Quilting: Poems 1987–1990.* Rochester, NY: BOA Edns.

Cochran, Jo Whitehorse. 1990. "From My Grandmother." In *Dancing on the Rim of the World.* Tucson, AZ: The University of Arizona Press.

Coles, Robert. 1989. *The Call of Stories: Teaching and the Moral Imagination.* Boston, MA: Houghton Mifflin Company.

Collier, James and Christopher Collier. 1984. *My Brother Sam is Dead.* New York: Macmillan Children's Group.

Conrad, Pam. 1987. *Prairie Songs.* New York: Harper Collins.

Conroy, Pat. 1987. *The Prince of Tides.* New York: Bantam.

Cormier, Robert. 1991. *Eight Plus One.* New York: Dell.

————. 1993. *We All Fall Down.* New York: Dell.

Davis, Jenny. 1993. *Checking on the Moon.* New York: Dell.

Daly, Maureen. 1985. *Seventeenth Summer.* Fort Wayne, IN: PB.

De Castillejo, Irene Claremont. 1990. *Knowing Woman, A Feminine Psychology.* Boston, MA: Shambhala.

Dickinson, Emily. 1961. "I Dwell in Possibility." In *Final Harvest: Emily Dickinson's Poems,* selections and introduction by Thomas H. Johnson. Boston, MA: Little, Brown & Company.

————. 1961. "I'll tell you how the sun rose . . ." In *Final Harvest: Emily Dickinson's Poems,* selections and introduction by Thomas H. Johnson. Boston, MA: Little, Brown, & Company.

————. 1961. "Morns are meeker than they were . . ." in *Final Harvest: Emily Dickinson's Poems,* selections and introduction by Thomas H. Johnson. Boston, MA: Little, Brown, & Company.

Dillard, Annie. 1987. *An American Childhood.* New York, NY: Harper & Row Publishers.

————. 1987b. "To Fashion A Text." In *Inventing the Truth: The Art and Craft of Memoir,* ed. by William Zinsser. Boston, MA: Houghton Mifflin.

Dostoyevsky, Fyodor. 1970. *The Brothers Karamazov.* New York: Bantam Books.

Drake, Barbara. 1983. *Writing Poetry.* New York: Harcourt Brace.

Eisner, Elliot W. 1991. "What Really Counts in Schools." In *Educational Leadership, Journal of the Association for Supervision and Curriculum Development (ASCD),* February, V 48 (5).

Elbow, Peter. 1986. *Embracing Contraries: Explorations in Learning and Teaching.* New York: Oxford University Press.

Esquival, Laura. 1992. *Like Water for Chocolate.* New York: Doubleday.

Fox, Mem. 1993. *Radical Reflections: Passionate Opinions on Teaching, Learning, and Living.* New York: Harcourt Brace & Company.

Fox, Paula. 1991. *The Slave Dancer.* New York: Dell.

Friedan, Betty. 1983. *The Feminine Mystique.* New York: Bantam, Doubleday, Dell.

Geras, Adele. 1990. *My Grandmother's Stories: A Collection of Jewish Folktales.* New York: Knopf Books for Young Readers.

Gilbreth, Frank B., and Ernestine G. Carey. 1984. *Cheaper by the Dozen.* New York: Bantam.

Gilligan, Carol, Nona P. Lyons, and Trudy J. Hanmer. eds. 1990. *Making Connections: The Relational Worlds of Adolescent Girls at Emma Willard School.* Cambridge, MA: Harvard University Press.

Gilligan, Carol, Janie Victoria Ward, and Jill McLean Taylor. eds. 1988. *Mapping the Moral Domain: A Contribution of Women's Thinking to Psychological Theory and Education.* Cambridge, MA: Harvard University Press.

Gilligan, Carol. 1982. *In A Different Voice.* Cambridge, MA: Harvard University Press.

Giovanni, Nikki. 1978. "Woman." In *Cotton Candy on A Rainy Day.* New York: Quill/William Morrow and Company, Inc.

———. 1978. "You Are There." In *Cotton Candy on A Rainy Day.* New York: Quill/William Morrow and Company, Inc.

———. 1978. "A Poem of Friendship." In *Cotton Candy on A Rainy Day.* New York: Quill/William Morrow and Company, Inc.

———. 1993. "nikki-rosa." In *ego-tripping and other poems for young people.* New York: L. Hill Books.

Gluck, Louise. 1992. "Retreating Light." In *The Wild Iris.* Hopewell, NJ: The Ecco Press.

Goldberg, Natalie. 1986. *Writing Down the Bones: Freeing the Writer Within.* Boston, MA: Shambhala.

Gould, June. 1991. *The Writer in All of Us: Improving Your Writing through Childhood Memories.* New York: Penguin Books Ltd.

Grahame, Kenneth. 1980. *The Wind in the Willows.* New York: Henry Holt and Company.

Graves, Donald, Jane Hansen, and Thomas Newkirk. eds. 1985. *Breaking Ground: Teachers Relate Reading and Writing in the Elementary School.* Portsmouth, NH: Heinemann.

Graves, Donald. 1989. *Experiment with Fiction.* Portsmouth, NH: Heinemann.

Graves, Donald H., and Bonnie S. Sunstein, eds. 1992. *Portfolio Portraits.* Portsmouth, NH: Heinemann.

Greene, Bette. 1991. *The Drowning of Stephan Jones.* New York: Bantam Books.

———. 1973. *Summer of My German Soldier.* New York: Dial Books for Young Readers.

Greenfield, Eloise. 1978. *Honey, I Love.* New York: The Trumpet Club, Harper Collins.

Grossman, Florence. 1982. *Getting from Here to There: Writing and Reading Poetry.* Portsmouth, NH: Boynton/Cook Publishers Inc.

Harwayne, Shelley. 1992. *Lasting Impressions.* Portsmouth, NH: Heinemann.

Hayden, Torey. 1981. *One Child.* New York: Avon.

———. 1982. *Somebody Else's Kids.* New York: Avon.

Heard, Georgia. 1989. *For the Good of the Earth and Sun.* Portsmouth, NH: Heinemann.

Hearne, Betsy. 1991. "Listening." In *Polaroid and Other Poems of View.* New York: Margaret K. McElderry Books, Macmillan Publishing Company.

Houston, Gloria. 1988. *The Year of the Perfect Christmas Tree: An Appalachian Story.* New York: Dial Books.

Howe, James. 1987. *I Wish I Were A Butterfly.* New York: A Voyager Book, Harcourt Brace.

Hughes, Richard. 1990. In *Writers on Writing* selected and compiled by Jon Winokur. Philadelphia, PA: Running Press.

Hunt, Irene. 1987. *Across Five Aprils.* New York: Berkley Publishing Group.

Hurmence, Belinda. 1984. *Tancy.* New York: Clarion Books.

Jakes, John. 1982. *North and South.* New York: Harcourt Brace.

Janeczko, Paul. 1984. *Strings: A Gathering of Family Poems.* New York: Bradbury Press, a division of Macmillan, Inc.

Joseph, Rosemary. 1984. "Baking Day." In *Strings: A Gathering of Family Poems,* comp. by Paul Janeczko. New York: Bradbury Press, a division of Macmillan, Inc.

Kassem, Lou. 1987. *Middle School Blues.* New York: Avon.

Kinnell, Galway. 1982. "St. Francis and the Sow." In *Galway Kinnell: Selected Poems.* Boston, MA: Houghton Mifflin Company.

Kilmer, Joyce. 1914. "The House with Nobody In It." In *Trees and Other Poems by Joyce Kilmer.* Garden City, NY: Doubleday & Company.

Kunitz, Stanley. 1983. "End of Summer." In *Poetspeak: In their work, about their work,* comp. by Paul B. Janeczko. Scarsdale, NY: Bradbury Press.

Lee, Harper. 1993. *To Kill a Mockingbird.* New York: Warner Books.

Livingston, Myra Cohn. 1990. *Climb into the Bell Tower.* New York: Harper & Row

Lowry, Lois. 1993. *The Giver.* Boston, MA: Houghton Mifflin.

Magorian, Michelle. 1981. *Goodnight, Mr. Tom.* New York: Harper Collins.

McCracken, Nancy Mellin and Bruce C. Appleby, eds. 1992. *Gender Issues in the Teaching of English.* Portsmouth, NH: Boynton Cook/Heinemann.

Mazer, Norma Fox. 1987. *After the Rain.* New York: Morrow Junior Books.

Merriam, Eve. 1987. *Growing Up Female in America.* Boston, MA: Beacon Press.

———. 1986. "New Love." In *Fresh Paint: New Poems.* New York: Macmillan.

———. 1986b. "Metaphor." In *A Sky Full of Poems.* New York: Dell.

———. 1984. "I Am Looking for a Book." In *Jamboree: Rhymes for All Ages.* New York: Dell.

———. 1986. "Reply to the Question: How Can You Become a Poet?" In *Don't Forget to Fly: A Cycle of Modern Poems,* selected by Paul B. Janeczko. New York: Bradbury Press, Macmillan.

———. 1966. "How to Eat a Poem." In *Reflections on a Gift of Watermelon Pickle and Other Modern Verse,* compiled by Stephen Dunning, Edward Lueders, and Hugh Smith. New York: Scholastic Book Services.

Mitchell, Margaret. 1975. *Gone with the Wind.* New York: Macmillan.

Moffic, Evan. 1992. "Law Versus Morality." In *Merlyn's Pen: The National Magazine of Student Writing.* December/January, 1992.

Moore, Marianne. 1986. "Poetry." In *Don't Forget to Fly: A Cycle of Modern Poems,* selected by Paul B. Janeczko. New York: Bradbury Press, Macmillan.

Mumma, Barbara J. 1989. *Winner's Waltz.* New York: Fawcett.

Murray, Donald M. 1985. *A Writer Teaches Writing,* second edition

———. 1990. *Shoptalk: Learning to Write with Writers.* Portsmouth, NH: Boynton/Cook, Heinemann.

———. 1982. *Learning By Teaching.* Montclair, NJ: Boynton/Cook.

Newkirk, Thomas. 1984. "Looking for Trouble: A Way to Unmask Our Readings." In *College English 46.* Urbana, IL: National Council of Teachers of English.

———. ed. 1990. *To Compose: Teaching Writing in High School and College,* 2d ed. Portsmouth, NH: Heinemann.

Noddings, Nel. 1984. *Caring: A Feminine Approach to Ethics and Moral Education.* Berkeley and Los Angeles, CA: University of California Press.

Norman, Howard A. translator, compiler. 1982. *The Wishing Bone Cycle: Narrative Poems of the Swampy Cree Indians.* Ross-Erikson.

Nye, Naomi Shihab, ed. 1992. *This Same Sky: A Collection of Poems from Around the World.* New York: Four Winds Press.

———. Commentary on "The Rider." In *The Place My Words are Looking For*, collected by Paul Janeczko.

Oliver, Mary. 1990 "The Summer Day." In *House of Light*. Boston, MA: Beacon Press.

———. 1990. "The Gift." In *House of Light*. Boston, MA: Beacon Press.

———. 1990. "The Ponds." In *House of Light*. Boston, MA: Beacon Press.

———. 1990. "Writing Poems." In *House of Light*. Boston, MA: Beacon Press.

———. 1994. *A Poetry Handbook*. New York: Harcourt Brace.

Pastan, Linda. 1991. "The Bookstall." In *Heroes in Disguise*. New York: W. W. Norton & Company, Inc.

———. 1991. "A New Poet." In *Heroes in Disguise*. New York: W. W. Norton & Company, Inc.

———. 1985. "Prosody 101." In *A Fraction of Darkness*. New York: W. W. Norton & Company, Inc.

———. 1982. "Egg." In *PM/AM*. New York: W. W. Norton & Company, Inc.

———. 1983. "September." In *Poetspeak. In their work, about their work:* A Selection by Paul B. Janeczko. Scarsdale, NY: Bradbury Press.

Paterson, Katherine. 1990. "The Heart in Hiding" in William Zinsser's *Worlds of Childhood: The Art and Craft of Writing for Children*. Boston, MA: Houghton Mifflin.

———. 1981. *Gates of Excellence: On Reading and Writing Books for Children*. New York: Elsevier/Nelson Books.

———. 1992. *Lyddie*. New York: Puffin.

———. 1989. *The Spying Heart: More Thoughts on Reading and Writing Books for Children*. New York: Lodestar Books, E. P. Dutton.

Paulsen, Gary. 1990. *Woodsong*. New York: Puffin Books.

———. 1993. *Nightjohn*. New York: Delacourt Press.

Pearlman, Mickey, and Katherine Usher Henderson. 1990. *A Voice of One's Own: Conversations with America's Writing Women*. Boston, MA and New York: Houghton Mifflin Company.

Peck, Robert Newton. 1972. *A Day No Pigs Would Die*. New York: Knopf.

Piercy, Marge. 1990. "To Be of Use." In *Circles on the Water*. New York: Alfred A. Knopf, Inc.

———. 1990. "What's That Smell in the Kitchen?" In *Circles on the Water*. New York: Alfred A. Knopf, Inc.

Ransom, Candice. 1990. *Going on Twelve*. New York: Scholastic.

Rappaport, Doreen. 1990. *American Women: Their Lives in Their Words*. New York: Thomas Y. Crowell Company.

Rawls, Wilson. 1974. *Where the Red Fern Grows: A Story of Two Dogs and A Boy*. New York: Bantam.

Reeder, Carolyn. 1989. *Shades of Gray.* New York: Macmillan Children's Group.

Rief, Linda. 1985. "Why Can't We Live Like the Monarch Butterfly." In *Breaking Ground: Teachers Relate Reading and Writing in the Elementary School,* ed. by Donald Graves, Jane Hansen, and Thomas Newkirk. Portsmouth, NH: Heinemann.

————. 1992. "Eighth Grade: Finding the Value in Evaluation." In *Portfolio Portraits,* ed. by Donald Graves and Bonnie Sunstein. Portsmouth, NH: Heinemann.

————. 1992b. *Seeking Diversity: Language Arts with Adolescents.* Portsmouth, NH: Heinemann.

Rinaldi, Ann. 1990. *The Good Side of My Heart.* New York: Scholastic Inc.

————. 1989. *Time Enough for Drums.* New York: Troll Associates.

————. 1990b. *The Last Silk Dress.* New York: Bantam.

————. 1993. *Wolf by the Ears.* New York: Scholastic Inc.

Rochman, Hazel, ed. 1988. *Somehow Tenderness Survives: Stories of South Africa.* New York: Harper Collins.

Rosenblatt, Louise. 1983. *Literature as Exploration,* 4th ed. New York: MLA.

Rylant, Cynthia. 1982. *When I Was Young in the Mountains.* New York: E. P. Dutton, a division of NAL Penguin, Inc.

————. 1984. *Waiting to Waltz: A Childhood.* New York: Macmillan Children's Group.

————. 1989. *But I'll Be Back Again: An Album.* New York: Orchard Books, a division of Franklin Watts.

————. 1990. *A Couple of Kooks and Other Stories about Love.* New York: Orchard Books/Watts.

————. 1990b. *Soda Jerk.* New York: Orchard Books/Watts.

————. 1993. *The Relatives Came.* New York: Macmillan Children's Group.

Sadker, Myra & Sadher, David. 1994. *Failing at Fairness: How America's Schools Cheat Girls.* New York: Charles Scribner's Sons.

Scheele, Roy. 1984. "A Kitchen Memory." In *Strings: A Gathering of Family Poems,* selected by Paul B. Janeczko. New York: Bradbury Press.

Schlissel, Lillian. 1982. *Women's Diaries of the Westward Journey.* New York: Schocken Books.

Schoenfein, Liza. 1982. In *Getting from Here to There: Writing and Reading Poetry* by Florence Grossman. Montclair, NJ: Boynton/Cook Publishers, Inc.

Sewell, Anna. 1945. *Black Beauty.* New York: Putnam Publishing Group.

Sidney, Margaret. 1990. *The Five Little Peppers and How They Grew.* New York: Puffin.

Silko, Leslie Marmon. 1977. *Ceremony.* New York: Penguin Books Ltd.

Skalrew, Myra. 1984. "Poem of the Mother." In *Strings: A Gathering of Family Poems,* selected by Paul B. Janeczko. New York: Bradbury Press.

Smith, Betty. 1943. *A Tree Grows in Brooklyn.* New York: Harper Perennial, a division of Harper Collins.

Smith, Lucinda Irwin. 1989. *Women Who Write: From the Past and the Present to the Future.* Englewood Cliffs, NJ: Jullian Messner, Simon & Schuster, Inc.

Soto, Gary. 1990. *Baseball in April and Other Stories.* New York: Harcourt Brace.

Spyri, Johanna. 1983. *Heidi.* New York: Puffin Books.

Stafford, William. 1990. "A Course in Creative Writing." In *You Must Revise Your Life.* Ann Arbor, MI: University of Michigan Press.

———. 1990. "A Way of Writing." In *To Compose: Teaching Writing in High School and College,* edited by Thomas Newkirk. Portsmouth, NH: Heinemann.

Stevenson, Robert Louis. 1985. *A Child's Garden of Verses.* New Jersey: Crown Publishers, Children's Classics, Outlet Books, a Random House Company.

Tannen, Deborah. 1990. *You Just Don't Understand: Women and Men in Conversation.* New York: Ballantine Books.

———. 1992. NCTE *Council Chronicle.* National Council Teachers of English, February.

Tierney, Robert et al. 1991. *Portfolio Assessment in Reading & Writing Classrooms.* Norwood, MA: Christopher Gordon Publishers.

Twain, Mark. 1959. *The Adventures of Huckleberry Finn.* New York: Signet Classic, Penguin.

Updike, John. 1983. "Dog's Death." In *Poetspeak: In their work, about their work,* a selection by Paul B. Janeczko. Scarsdale, NY: Bradbury Press.

Viorst, Judith. 1981. *If I Were in Charge of the World.* New York: Macmillan.

Walker, Alice. 1982. *The Color Purple.* New York: Harcourt, Brace, Jovanovich.

———. 1991. "Reassurance." In *Her Blue Body Everything We Know.* New York: Harcourt, Brace, Jovanovich.

———. 1991b. "What the Finger Writes." In *Her Blue Body Everything We Know.* New York: Harcourt, Brace, Jovanovich.

Walker, Margaret. 1973. "For My People." In *Poetry of Black America,* edited by Arnold Adoff. New York: Harper Collins.

Welty, Eudora. 1983. *One Writer's Beginnings.* New York: Warner Books.

White, E. B. 1974. *Charlotte's Web.* New York: Harper Collins Children's Books.

Whitman, Walt. 1975. "There Was A Child Went Forth." In *Walt Whitman: The Complete Poems.* New York: Penguin Books.

———. 1975. "A Noiseless Patient Spider." In *Walt Whitman: The Complete Poems*. New York: Penguin Books.

Wilde, Jack. 1993. *A Door Opens: Writing in Fifth Grade*. Portsmouth, NH: Heinemann.

Winokur, Jon. 1986. *W.O.W. Writers on Writing*. Philadelphia, PA: Running Press Book Publishers.

Wood, Nancy. 1974. *Many Winters: Prose and Poetry of the Pueblos*. New York: Doubleday.

Zinsser, William. 1990. *Worlds of Childhood: The Art and Craft of Writing for Children*. Boston, MA: Houghton Mifflin Company.

———. 1987. *Inventing the Truth: The Art and Craft of Memoir*. Boston, MA: Houghton Mifflin Company.

Index